New features:
① Lists and discusses relevant
    diagnostic tests in 6 learning
    and behavior areas
② Reviews widely used materials
and recently published remedial
programs
③ Introduces and incorporates
activities for secondary level
students throughout the book

Teaching Children with
Learning Problems

Teaching Children with Learning Problems

second edition

Gerald Wallace
University of Virginia

James M. Kauffman
University of Virginia

Charles E. Merrill Publishing Company
A Bell & Howell Company
Columbus   Toronto   London   Sydney

Published by
Charles E. Merrill Publishing Company
A Bell & Howell Company
Columbus, Ohio 43216

This book was set in Helvetica and Avant Garde.
The production editor was Frances Margolin.
The cover was prepared by Will Chenoweth.
Photographs by James M. Kauffman.

International Standard Book Number: 0-675-08425-3

Library of Congress Catalog Card Number: 77-84134

1 2 3 4 5 6 7 8   83 82 81 80 79 78

Printed in the United States of America

PREFACE

This book is a guide to remediating learning problems, intended for special and regular classroom teachers in training or in service. Our experience in schools and universities indicates that most classroom teachers can become proficient in the remediation of learning problems when they have appropriate instruction and guidance.

Since the publication of the first edition of this book, remediation of learning problems in the regular classroom has received increased emphasis. Public Law 94-142, the **Education for All Handicapped Children Act** of 1975, mandates the movement toward teaching all types of handicapped children in the mainstream of public education. Consequently, we have tried to make this second edition more useable by regular classroom teachers by adding two new features: (1) informal diagnostic questions accompanying each set of teaching suggestions and (2) brief descriptions of teaching programs for each curriculum area. In addition, we have made other changes that we feel make the book more useful for all teachers. We have rearranged the order of some chapters, starred the teaching suggestions most appropriate for older children, and reorganized and updated the material throughout the book to reflect progress in the field.

Part One of this volume provides a practical approach to remediation. Learning problems are defined in terms of specific behavioral deficits rather than in terms of nonfunctional categories or traditional special education labels. Principles of behavior management and academic remediation are described in understandable language and illustrated with examples drawn from the classroom. Teaching competencies that apply across curriculum areas are also presented. Early detection and good teaching are discussed as primary facets of prevention of learning problems. The material presented in Part One serves as a foundation for the development of Part Two.

Part Two operationalizes the principles presented in Part One. The chapters in this section contain specific assessment techniques and teaching activities for social-emotional problems, spoken language, reading, written language, arithmetic, and visual-motor skills. The beginning teacher will find many proven teaching suggestions, and the more experienced teacher will be able to adapt the suggested activities to the unique requirements of particularly difficult problems. A list of additional readings at the end of each chapter provides a guide to further study.

We appreciate the continued support and assistance of many individuals in completing this book. Teachers and students who used the first edition provided a number of ideas for teaching activities discussed in this edition. We are grateful for the help provided by Patty Burke and Anne Graves in completing the index. Anne LaChance, Sharron Hall, and Linda Wilberger were also highly proficient in typing the manuscript. We are especially appreciative for the patience displayed by Missy Kauffman and T. J. Wallace, whose photographs are on the cover, and by the other children whose photographs open each chapter. Finally, our wives provided encouragement throughout the preparation of the manuscript.

Gerald Wallace
James M. Kauffman

October, 1977

CONTENTS

to Marti and Myrna

Teaching Children with
Learning Problems

part one

A Practical Approach to Remediation

Most children in our schools do not experience major learning problems. Their behavior is generally acceptable to their teachers, and their academic achievement is within the expected range for their abilities. A significant proportion of school children do, however, exhibit social-emotional problems or academic difficulties. Children with learning problems are becoming easier to recognize as the forces of educational technology and humanistic values shape American schools.

Educational efforts to meet the needs of children with school learning problems have not been successful to date. The preparation of special teachers and the establishment of special classes have not resulted in adequate educational opportunities for all children. Nor have personnel designated as "resource," "crisis," "prescriptive," or "consultant" teachers resolved the problem of remedial education. It is becoming increasingly clear that if the educational needs of **all children** are to be met, **all teachers** must become skillful in the instruction of children with learning problems.

All teachers experience the pleasure of teaching children who learn quickly and easily . The frustration and anxiety associated with children who learn slowly and with great difficulty are also felt by all teachers. But, as we have observed, frustration, anxiety, depression, and anger can be replaced by an extra measure of joy and satisfaction for both the teacher and the child when learning problems are successfully remediated. Unfortunately, teachers often unknowingly fail to help children with learning problems because they lack technical skill. Consequently, our emphasis is on the knowledge and application of sound learning principles and instructional strategies. A working knowledge of the principles presented in Part One of this text will increase the probability that the teacher will develop the technical skill necessary to remediate learning problems successfully.

Humanistic education highlights the development of awareness and sensitivity of the teacher to his own needs and the needs of individual children. Self-awareness, self-actualization, and sensitivity to others as persons are prerequisites for good teaching, but they must be accompanied by technical knowedge and skill or the children will not be helped. Self-realization, awareness, and human concern for his patients as persons can enhance but cannot replace the physician's technical knowledge and skill in the practice of medicine. Likewise, sensitivity and humanistic goals can supplement but cannot supplant the understanding and application of learning principles in teach ing. Technical mastery allows the practitioner to give form and substance to humanistic values.

Part One provides a foundation for the development of specific teaching techniques. Chapter 1 is an overview of·characteristics, etiologies, and educational services for children with learning problems. Chapter 2 introduces basic principles of classroom management from a behavior-modification point of view. Chapter 3 presents principles of remediating academic deficits which apply to all curriculum areas. Chapter 4 is an outline of competencies which the teacher may use to evaluate his instructional activities in any curriculum area. Chapter 5 points the way to prevention of learning problems through good teaching and early detection.

1
Dimensions of
Learning Problems

1

Dimensions of Learning Problems

One goal of American public education is equal educational opportunity for every child. Although this goal may be attainable, it has remained elusive for decades. The concept of instructional methods matched to the learning characteristics of each child is familiar to teachers, but individualized instruction has not been the hallmark of this nation's schools. It has taken court decisions, federal legislation, mobilization of parents, and new methods in special education to bring the dream of maximum learning for all children closer to reality.

The pragmatic spirit of America is reflected in traditional educational policies and procedures designed to meet the needs of most children. But for a significant number of children, education designed for the "average" child leads to confusion, academic failure, feelings of inadequacy, disparagement by teachers and peers, and finally, despair or disgust for school. These children, commonly identified as having school learning problems, have been designated by a wide variety of labels, all of them pejorative: *emotionally disturbed, educationally inadequate, brain damaged, educationally handicapped, culturally disadvantaged, learning disabled, educable mentally retarded, slow learning, perceptually handicapped, behavior disordered, maladjusted, hyperactive,* and many more.

Public Law 94-142, the Education for All Handicapped Children Act of 1975, demands a change in the way American schools respond to children whose needs are not met by the typical educational methods. The law demands that **every** child be provided an education that is **appropriate for his needs.** Furthermore, an **individual educational plan** must be written for each child, and the appropriate education must be provided **at public expense.** These provisions of PL 94-142 represent a dramatic change in federal policy regarding the education of exceptional children (see Hallahan & Kauffman, 1978). Although the Act provides funds for children falling into the usual special education categories—learning disabled, emotionally disturbed, mentally retarded, and so on—it is no longer possible for any school district to obtain federal funds without serving the educational needs of *all* its children, regardless of their diagnostic labels.

Our concern in this book is not with labels by which children can be called but with the specific learning difficulties preventing their success in school. We assume that it makes very little difference how a child is labeled or defined for administrative purposes, but that precise definition of his learning problem is the first essential step in remediation. Specifically, it is what the child *does* and *does not do* in response to an educational program that is our focus.

Children defy meaningful classification—the learning problems they experience do not. The history of systems of classification shows that attempting to fit people into neat psychological and educational categories is futile (see Hobbs, 1975). On the other hand, precise definition of the individual's learning difficulties and strengths, which points toward specific treatment procedures, pays enormous dividends in successful remediation. Since they are essential to acceptable performance, the dimensions of learning necessary for school progress provide the most logical framework for defining learning problems. We will describe two major dimensions of learning: social-emotional and academic.

SOCIAL-EMOTIONAL LEARNING

When a child enters school, his progress depends not only on learning academic responses but also on building a repertoire of adequate emotional and social behavior. He must adopt behavior patterns that indicate self-acceptance as well as self-realization. The child most likely to succeed at school is one who is both productive and happy. His behavior reflects confidence, organization, initiative, persistence, self-control, and pride in accomplishment. The successful child relates well to others. Among his peers, he is usually outgoing, friendly, popular, and able to take a leadership role. His relationship to adults and authority figures is characterized by confidence, respect, and cooperation.

Children who have difficulty in learning social and emotional responses which would contribute to success at school show a wide variety of maladaptive behaviors. Those behaviors most likely to attract the attention of the teacher include talking out of turn, moving about the room without permission, hitting other children, throwing a tantrum, and crying. Such inappropriate behavior in schoolchildren can be understood within a three-dimensional framework which includes conduct problems, inadequacy–immaturity, and personality problems (Quay, 1972). Conduct problems include overt aggression, hostility, defiance, boisterousness, hyperactivity, destructiveness, tantrums, and other behaviors associated with striking out at one's environment. The inadequacy–immaturity dimension includes inattention, sluggishness, lack of interest, laziness, daydreaming, and dislike for school. Personality problems are typified by hypersensitivity, self-consciousness, feelings of inferiority, lack of self-confidence, fearfulness, and anxiety.

Individual children often show deficits in social-emotional learning along more than one dimension of problem behavior. For instance, a child's conduct problem does not preclude his exhibiting personality problems. Clarence and Dorothy, described in the following cases, both show social-emotional learning deficits.

Clarence

Clarence is a 12-year-old sixth grader. He is small for his age, and could easily pass for a 9-year-old. He is almost constantly in conflict with his teachers and classmates at school or with adults and other children in the neighborhood where he lives. He bullies younger and smaller children, picks fights with older and larger children, and taunts adults. He has been suspended from school several times, and several times has been apprehended by the police for illegal acts. Academically, he is doing just enough to get by — no teacher wants Clarence in class a second year.

Clarence's mother has a long history of psychiatric problems. She and Clarence's father were divorced, after years of fighting and bickering, when Clarence was 6. Clarence's father, an attorney, remarried when Clarence was 10. In the years between the divorce and remarriage of his father, Clarence lived part of the time with his father and part of the time with his mother. His father finally gained permanent custody of Clarence and his older sister on the grounds that their mother was mentally ill and unable to provide appropriate care for the children. Clarence's stepmother is a withdrawn person who spends little time with her own son (who is Clarence's age) or with her stepchildren. Because his father works long hours and his stepmother ignores him as much as possible, Clarence is unsupervised most of the time when he is not at school. He spends most of his time after school and on weekends roaming the neighborhood, picking fights, destroying property, and needling adults (for example, by walking through flowerbeds, breaking shrubs, riding his minibike — which has no muffler — recklessly back and forth on the street, or throwing trash on lawns). His father, when he is at home, irritates his neighbors by working in his garden with a tractor late at night, racing his motorcycle engine, repairing old cars in his backyard, or screaming at Clarence. If adults in the neighborhood confront Clarence's father about his own conduct or Clarence's, they are threatened with a law suit or told pompously that they have no legal basis for complaint. Clarence's father provides a model of defiant behavior, protects his son from the consequences of his misbehavior, and encourages him to disregard the rights and feelings of others. Yet Clarence is often reprimanded severely by his father for disobedience or failure to perform some chore around the house.

The situation at school has become critical. Clarence brags constantly about his illegal activities, real or imagined (e.g., growing marihuana in his basement, stealing from the neighborhood grocery store), baits teachers, and disrupts other children's work and play. The usual punishment procedures have not worked, and Clarence's father refuses to cooperate with the school in trying to control his behavior. A school psychologist administered a battery of tests and found that, while Clarence has about average intelligence, his achievement in most areas is lagging by 2 years. The psychologist's opinion is that Clarence is emotionally disturbed and should have psychotherapy. The school principal and the psychologist agree that Clarence should be in a special class for disturbed children. Unfortunately, Clarence's father does not want him to see a "shrink," and there is no special class for disturbed children in the school district.

Dorothy

From her first day at school, Dorothy has been a loner. Not only does she maintain social isolation from her peers, but she also maintains a very distant relationship with teachers. She is now in the middle of her second year in school, and she has never been observed to talk to another child. She will reply to teachers only if they are very persistent in demanding a verbal response in a one-to-one situation; then her responses consist of as few words as possible. Academically, Dorothy does about average written work. She will not respond orally in class.

Dorothy is an only child. Her parents are hard-working but poor. They were married at the age of 16, and Dorothy was born during the first year of their marriage. Neither of the parents finished high school. Dorothy's father works as a service station attendant; her mother as a waitress. Her parents find it difficult to believe that Dorothy has a problem in social development, as they report that she talks to them without hesitation. They live in a small house in the country several miles from the nearest neighbor, and they seldom visit anyone with children Dorothy's age.

It is obvious that Dorothy is not mentally retarded; her language skills and written work do not fit a pattern of serious intellectual deficiency. Her teachers are concerned about her lack of social interaction, but they do not describe her as emotionally disturbed. She plays contentedly by herself and does not engage in any hostile or bizarre behavior. Other children have stopped initiating social contact with her, since when they have approached her she has consistently ignored them or walked away. Her teachers have attempted to get her involved in games, projects, and other classroom activities which require social interaction, but they have been unsuccessful. Since she does not appear to be unhappy and causes no disturbance in the classroom, her teachers are taking a "wait and see" attitude toward her social deficits. They believe that with time and patience she will eventually "come out of her shell."

ACADEMIC LEARNING

There are few tasks within our schools which bring greater pressure to bear upon a child than academic achievement (Heilman, 1977). From the first day in school, most children are made aware that the key to success is effective academic performance. No one knows this more than the child with academic difficulties. The frustration and agony of school failure are all too readily apparent in the child who encounters difficulties in learning to read, write, or calculate.

For some children, school problems are limited to specific skill deficiencies in particular academic tasks. Large numbers of other children, however, have severe problems in more than one area. Problems almost invariably overlap among all school-related tasks, including listening, thinking, talking, reading, writing, spelling, and arithmetic.

Children who experience learning problems frequently are considered a homogeneous group. Many of their specific difficulties are obscured, however, by the blanket classification of "academic learning problems." Not all children are hampered by identical deficiencies. In addition to extending across academic tasks, learning problems are complicated by varying degrees of difficulty, by the age of the child, and by the child's attitude toward his disabilities. As the following cases illustrate, children with "academic difficulties" may have very different characteristics.

Bucky

Bucky was an active, healthy 5-1/2-year-old boy referred to a clinic for testing by his kindergarten teacher. While Bucky was not considered a classroom management problem, his teacher reported that he has had great difficulty with almost all kindergarten activities. Bucky has had severe problems in completing many cutting, coloring, and pasting activities because of very poor fine-motor coordination. He also has been somewhat accident prone and has repeatedly fallen and collided with other children and various objects during play. Nevertheless, Bucky has had no peer relationship problems in the classroom.

Bucky's parents have reported that at home he is defiant and often presents a management problem. During observation periods in the classroom, Bucky appeared to be an outgoing, active student who persisted in activities even when he appeared to encounter some difficulty with the task. His speech development seemed slightly immature, with some indications of "baby talk." Language was not considered very fluent.

Bucky had great difficulty in differentiating geometric shapes, in playing games such as **Simon Says,** and in simply buttoning his coat. He could not count to 10 without skipping a number, and he only recently began to show any interest in learning how to print his name. The teacher also reported that when Bucky was faced with an item of some difficulty, he tended to respond without giving much thought to his reply.

Subsequent to his evaluation at the psychoeducational clinic, Bucky was enrolled in a special early intervention class for children with learning handicaps.

Linda

Ten-year-old Linda was referred for help because of severe academic difficulties. In addition, Linda's teacher reported that she was also quite manipulative in gaining attention from peers and adults by relying primarily on very babyish behavior. Linda has had some difficulty in maintaining friendships over an extended period of time.

Although Linda was functioning in the bright-normal range of intelligence, her actual reading achievement was reported to be below the first year level. She was still experiencing some difficulty in differentiating various letters and in sequentially reciting the alphabet from memory. Linda's oral reading was usually marked by excessive substitutions, omissions, unknown words, and word-by-word reading. Her sight vocabulary was limited to approximately 75 words. No consistent word analysis skills could be observed.

During an informal language inventory, Linda had difficulties in both receptive and expressive language skills. She had severe problems in following directions and responding to a listening comprehension subtest. She also experienced some difficulty in producing rhyming words from stimulus words presented to her. Although Linda seemed to enjoy writing short, simple stories, her written language skills were considered to be poorly developed.

Linda's parents and teachers were asked to investigate alternative educational placements for her, since the school district in which she was enrolled merely offered twice-a-week room help for children with learning problems. In the meanwhile, Linda continued to attend school in her fifth grade classroom.

WHY SCHOOL LEARNING PROBLEMS DEVELOP

Children experience learning problems for many complex reasons. There is seldom, if ever, a single cause of difficulty. Some causal factors, such as genetics, operate over a long period of time and reach far into the individual's history to create a **predisposition** for learning problems. Other factors, such as a traumatic event or inadequate teaching, are more immediate in their effect and serve to **precipitate** a learning difficulty. Most learning problems stem from the interaction of several predisposing and precipitating factors (Hallahan & Kauffman, 1976, 1978; Kauffman, 1977; Wallace & McLoughlin, 1975).

Even if an exhaustive catalog of specific causes of learning problems could be compiled, the list would be instructive only if each cause implied a specific remedy and the remedy were available to the reader. At present, few specific remedies are implied by known or suspected etiologies of learning difficulties, and fewer still are useable by teachers (see Kauffman & Hallahan, 1974). Nevertheless, it is useful for educators to be aware of the possible major causes of school learning problems, so that proper referral can be made when remediation by other professionals is appropriate.

Biophysical Factors

A child's genetic endowment and physical status obviously have a profound effect on his behavior (see Cravioto & DeLicardie, 1975; Koupernik, MacKeith, & Francis-Williams, 1975; Scarr-Salapatek, 1975). Birth trauma, oxygen deprivation, infectious disease, drug intoxication, malnutrition, and congenital defects are only a few of the biological events which may influence a child's ability to learn. Attempts to pinpoint specific biological correlates of individual learning problems, however, have not often been successful. Certainly the teacher must be aware of possible biophysical factors contributing to the development of a school learning problem and should refer the child to appropriate medical personnel for evaluation. But most medical diagnoses clearly have few implications for remediation by the teacher, who is not able to give genetic counseling, prescribe drugs, perform surgery, or administer other forms of medical treatment.

Sociocultural Factors

The social and cultural contexts in which the child lives undeniably shape his learning also. Family relationships, social class, the expectations of educational systems, and membership in subcultural groups are known to be determining variables in the child's development (see Martin, 1975; Robins, West, & Herjaniz, 1975; Sameroff & Chandler, 1975). There is little doubt that deteriorating family units, poverty, racial discrimination, manipulation by the media, rigid school policies, cultural fetishes and taboos, and other social and cultural factors influence the child's behavior in school.

Although the teacher should be concerned with the social and cultural conditions which contribute to children's learning problems, he cannot make sociocultural intervention the focus of his professional activity. As Engelmann (1969) has pointed out, teachers are primarily responsible for making children competent academically, not for making social policy.

Psychodevelopmental Factors

It has often been suggested that learning problems arise from an underlying psychological disturbance or developmental delay (Berkowitz & Rothman, 1960; Bettelheim, 1970; Freud, 1965). Undoubtedly, anxiety about growing up, separation from one's parents, establishing one's own identity, experiencing traumatic events, learning to express one's emotions appropriately, building trusting relationships, and many other developmental tasks and psychological processes are related to school learning. There is no reason to doubt that normal psychological development smooths the way for learning or that removal of emotional problems makes the remediation of learning difficulties easier. As in the case of biophysical factors, however, psychological diagnoses seldom point to specific remediation. Furthermore, when specific remediation is possible, the teacher is not able to provide appropriate treatment—he is not trained as a psychotherapist.

Educational Factors

It is axiomatic that learning problems may occur because of inadequate or inappropriate instruction. The child may not learn because the teacher fails to teach. The specific deficits in teaching that account for the child's failure to learn *can* be found. When they are found, it is the teacher's responsibility to correct them, for he is trained to control the instructional variables that govern learning. Thus, the teacher must take responsibility for the learning of *all* children. This does not mean that when the teacher has failed to teach a child, despite his best efforts, he has failed as a person or as a professional. It *does* mean that the teacher will be primarily concerned with educational reasons for children's learning problems and that he will continue to examine and improve his techniques of teaching rather than blame the child or some etiological factor over which he has no control (Engelmann, 1969). Kauffman (1977) has suggested several specific ways in which teachers can contribute to the growth of learning and behavior disorders in children: by being insensitive to a child's individuality, by holding inappropriate expectations for a child, by being inconsistent in management and discipline, by offering instruction in skills that are of no value to the child, and by arranging inappropriate contingencies of reinforcement for behavior.

PROVISIONS FOR SCHOOL LEARNING PROBLEMS

Educational provisions for children with learning difficulties in school have traditionally been assigned to educators who operate outside the realm of the regular classroom. These supportive personnel, teaching in special classes or resource rooms, have had the major responsibility for ameliorating school learning problems. In terms of actual numbers, however, remedial specialists have had little effect in reducing the prevalence of academic difficulties among school-age children. The task has been too overwhelming for specialists alone to handle. Under these circumstances, the concentration of effort outside the regular classroom has proven to be a monumental and unrealistic task.

Nevertheless, only in the past few years has it been widely suggested that working within the regular classroom and allowing classroom teachers the opportunity to remediate learning difficulties may provide a possible alternative for remediation (McKenzie, Egner, Knight, Perelman, Schneider, & Garvin, 1970). In a short time, this approach has proven to be feasible and effective in remediating school learning problems. At the same time, special education arrangements have come to be considered more appropriate for the child with *severe* learning problems. Two prevalent special education arrangements are described below.

Resource Room

In this arrangement, children are enrolled with their peers in a regular classroom. Depending upon the nature of their difficulty, they are seen by a specially trained teacher for various lengths of time to work on specific problems. Some children may be seen individually by the resource teacher for 15 to 45 minutes daily, while others may be seen twice weekly in small groups. The extensiveness of contact with the resource teacher will largely depend upon the severity of the child's difficulty. Normally, the resource teacher is housed in a classroom especially equipped with materials and educational equipment particularly suited to the children's needs.

The resource room has been used successfully both with academically handicapped and behaviorally disordered children. However, the limited number of children who can be seen by one resource teacher is a disadvantage of this arrangement. In addition, because resource teachers must often serve two or more schools, their time for communication with regular classroom teachers may be confined to brief conversations in the hallway or the lunchroom. Some school districts have attempted to overcome some of these problems by varying the role of the resource teacher. One such plan involves using the resource teacher as a curriculum specialist or instructional consultant to the classroom teacher (Blessing, 1969). This approach makes more efficient use of the resource teacher's talents and provides direct help to classroom teachers. The plan also offers additional advantages over the traditional resource room model: it keeps the child with his peers and upgrades the instructional skills of the regular classroom teacher.

Special Classes

One of the oldest special education arrangements is the self-contained special class for specific types of handicapped children. In terms of actual numbers, classes for the mentally retarded have been most common (Simon & Grant, 1968), but the number of special classes for the learning disabled and behaviorally disordered has increased substantially in the past few years (Kirk, 1972). Children enrolled in special classes usually spend the entire day in the class with other similarly handicapped children. Since the maximum enrollment per class is usually dictated by state law, the special class often contains fewer students than does the regular classroom.

Most critics of special classes argue that their segregated nature detrimentally affects the overall development of children (see Hallahan & Kauffman, 1978). Isolation from normal peers and poor academic achievement are often cited as disadvantages of special class placement (Goldstein, Moss, & Jordan, 1965; Stanton & Cassidy, 1964.) On the other hand, the superior social and emotional adjustment achieved by special class pupils frequently provides an argument for their use (Jordan & DeCharms, 1959; Kern & Pfaeffle, 1962). However, legal questions have actually threatened the existence of many special classes (Cruickshank, 1972; Ross, DeYoung, & Cohen, 1971).

Regular Class Remediation

The current trend in American education toward more personalized instruction has provided a means for handling school learning problems in the regular classroom. Teachers and administrators alike have become more aware of individual differences among children. With this increased awareness, particular attention has been given to means for meeting individual differences. Teachers' aides, team teaching, departmentalization, and lay volunteers have provided classroom teachers with both the time and resources needed to meet the instructional goals for children with individual learning needs. The teacher with 30 students, for example, now often has the opportunity to work alone with a single child while another individual works with the larger group.

The wide availability of personalized instructional tools, such as programmed materials and individual study carrels, also makes it possible to remediate learning problems in the regular class. All these changes have helped to make it possible for teachers to teach *all* children within the class. Nothing, however, has been of more help than the recognition by many educators of the necessity of planning for individual instructional needs. This alone has served as an impetus for working with all types of school learning problems within the confines of the regular classroom.

A PRESCRIPTION FOR CHANGE

The principles of behavior management, academic remediation, teacher competencies, and prevention discussed in the next four chapters are intended to provide *all* teachers with a practical guide for remediating school learning problems. Although the role of regular classroom teachers is becoming one of the most crucial components of the remediation process (MacMillan & Becker, 1977), special education teachers can also profit from carefully reexamining their teaching procedures and techniques. The principles and teaching techniques that follow may be used in any type of administrative arrangement. Successful remediation of school learning problems is not dependent upon types of classes, appropriate labels, or detailed etiological studies. **The competent teacher is the key to effective remediation.**

2
Principles of Behavior Management

Principles of Behavior Management

Every teacher is faced with the task of classroom management of problem behavior. Children who have school learning problems often increase the difficulty of this task. It is unlikely that teachers will be successful in remediating academic deficits if they are not skillful in the management of classroom behavior. Consequently, it is essential for them to know many practical and effective techniques for managing specific behavior problems.

Behavior modification is a term that is relatively new. However, the most basic ideas in behavior modification are very old. Indeed, the origins of behavior modification can be traced at least as far back as the very beginning of special education, to the early 1800s when Itard instructed Victor, the Wild Boy of Aveyron (Lane, 1976). What is new about contemporary behavior modification is the use of precise measurement techniques and research designs; what is old is the deliberate use of positive and negative consequences to change children's behavior. Today, there is a tremendous backlog of experience and research indicating that a behavior modification approach to classroom management is highly effective for nearly every type of child, normal as well as handicapped (see Leitenberg, 1976; Lovitt, 1977; O'Leary & O'Leary, 1972; Risley & Baer, 1973; Sherman & Bushell, 1975).

We have chosen a behavior modification approach to behavior management not just because it is the oldest and most thoroughly researched approach, but also because it keeps the focus clearly on teaching and learning. We see the child's acquisition of appropriate classroom behavior as a learning problem for which the teacher is responsible. This point of view makes it possible for the teacher to integrate classroom-management techniques with the teaching of academic skills.

Alternative approaches to the management of problem behavior emphasize intrapsychic conflict, biophysical defects, and interpersonal relationships as the causes of inappropriate behavior. These approaches tend to stress intervention as the primary responsibility of the psychotherapist, the physician, or special school personnel. Although these approaches have undoubtedly made contributions to the education of children with learning problems, they do not enhance the role of the teacher as the primary agent of positive behavior change in the classroom. Consequently, we have chosen to stress a behavioral approach to classroom management which: (a) has been shown by extensive research and practice to be effective, (b) emphasizes the teaching–learning process, and (c) is understandable and practical for the classroom teacher.

DEFINITION OF BEHAVIOR MODIFICATION

Within the past decade, behavioral scientists have developed many techniques for changing behavior. These techniques were derived primarily from laboratory studies of behavior by B. F. Skinner and his associates (e.g., Skinner, 1953), and from the clinical practice of psychologists (see Leitenberg, 1976). The array of techniques developed in the laboratory, clinic, and class-room is often referred to as *behavior modification*. **Behavior modification refers to any systematic arrangement of environmental events which produces a specific change in observable behavior.** This definition emphasizes *systematic* procedures and *observable* behavioral change which can be attributed to *specific* teaching techniques. Behavior-management techniques which are used haphazardly or which produce unobservable changes in children are not included in our definition.

The aspects of behavior management with which we are most concerned are represented schematically in Table 2-1. We are concerned not only with what the child does, but also with events that occur immediately before and after his actions. The events that are antecedents and consequences of the child's responses can be controlled in order to modify his behavior. Therefore, our discussion will be organized around three major topics:

1. Behavior and its measurement;
2. The controlling function of consequences;
3. The controlling function of antecedent events.

BEHAVIOR AND ITS MEASUREMENT

Definition and measurement are foundation stones of any applied science, including "applied behavior analysis," the applied behavioral science usually referred to as behavior modification. Scientific principles—for example, principles of learning—operate whether or not measurement techniques are employed. A child's behavior may be improved by arranging appropriate consequences to follow his behavior, even though his behavior was never defined or measured very precisely. But if someone wants to know when, how much, and why the child's behavior changed, then precise definition and measurement are absolutely indispensable. Definition and measurement are important concerns in this book, and particularly in this chapter, because we are discussing children who do not behave the way their teachers and parents want them to behave; the adults who are responsible for them perceive them as having trouble or making trouble in the classroom. Under these circumstances, it is important to find out when, how much, and why their behavior changes—not to find out by measuring their responses would be, in our opinion, close to educational malpractice. Our point is simply this: Sound educational practice *demands* the objective, reliable definition and measurement of behavior in those cases in which children's behavior is so disturbing that adults are seriously concerned. To deal effectively and competently with children who have learning problems, regardless of whether their problems are in academic or in social-emotional learning, a teacher must go beyond subjective impressions and employ the techniques of applied behavioral science.

Table 2-1

The Essential Elements of a Behavior Management Strategy

program →	stimulus →	behavior →	arrangement →	consequence
The system which programs the presentation of the cue or task; the daily sequence of activities	*Antecedent event:* What happens just before the child's behavior; the cue or task presented to the child; the setting in which the behavior is likely to occur	*Action:* What the child does that can be observed, counted and repeated; a response	The system which arranges the consequence of the child's behavior; the contingency of reinforcement	*Subsequent event:* What happens just afterward; what the child's activity produces; a reinforcing or punishing event
Example: During daily arithmetic period 9:00–9:30	Teacher gives child 10 arithmetic problems to work	Child writes answers to 10 problems	When all answers are written correctly	Child may engage in quiet activity of his choice for remainder of arithmetic period
Example: During weekly P.E. instruction 1:00–1:15	When asked by teacher, to do jumping jacks with class	Child runs crying from P.E. area	Each time child runs crying from P.E. area	Teacher leaves class, runs after child, and returns him to the classroom
Example: Whenever during school day	Child is given seatwork	Child leaves desk and walks around room	Occasionally while child is walking around room during seatwork	Teacher or peer reminds child to sit down and do his work

We are indebted to Ogden R. Lindsley, "Direct Measurement and Prosthesis of Retarded Behavior," *Journal of Education,* 1964, *147,* 62–81, for suggesting the basic elements of this schematic.

Defining Behavior

In applied behavioral science, the individual's behavior must be defined so that it can be measured reliably. The behavior must be *observable* and must be defined objectively enough that independent observers will agree about its occurrence or nonoccurrence. For example, "out-of-seat" and "talking out" are observable behaviors that, with practice, observers can count reliably. Likewise, hitting another child, kicking the wastebasket, showing the "naughty finger," throwing books on the floor, smiling, saying "thank you," completing arithmetic problems correctly, and writing words correctly are observable behaviors. Poor self-concept, anger, hyperactivity, and feelings of humiliation, however, are not directly observable behaviors. Rather, they are *interpretations* of behaviors which will vary considerably from one observer to another. Behavior modification starts with a definition of the problem that is objective enough to allow direct measurement of the problem behavior. If the definition does not allow direct measurement, then it simply is not adequate for purposes of behavior modification. Behavior modification proponents often refer to the process of defining the problem behavior as "pinpointing." Pinpointing is a way of saying, "This is exactly what the child *does* (or does not do) that is a problem, and it is this behavior that we will measure to find out whether or not the problem is getting better or worse."

There are at least three more important points to remember about defining behavior. **First,** children with learning problems often exhibit many problem behaviors, and it is tempting to try to modify all of them at once. However, it is important to choose only the one or two most critical problems and work on those first. Trying to change all the child's faults at once is unrealistic and is almost always an invitation to failure. On the other hand, tackling just the one or two most troubling behaviors first is realistic. Often if the most worrisome behavior is successfully modified, some of the other problems take care of themselves in the process. **Second,** it is just as important to consider what behavior you want to *increase* as it is what behavior you want to *decrease*. Unfortunately, perhaps, when teachers think of behavior modification they typically think first of the undesirable behaviors they want to stop. But behavior modification principles are just as applicable to helping children learn approriate behavior as to helping children stop their inappropriate behavior. A good practice to follow is to ask, "How would I like this child to behave?" and try to frame the answer in positive rather than negative terms (e.g., "Stay in his seat during reading" rather than "Not get out of his seat during reading"). **Third,** it is true that important aspects of teaching and learning do not lend themselves to precise behavioral definition. There are, indeed, affective variables—subjective feelings and emotional states—that go along with the educational process. You do not need to deny these subjective realities to use behavior modification. However, the focus of behavior modification is on observable behavior; and it is important not to confuse objective definitions with subjective impressions.

Measuring Behavior

Direct measurement means that the behavior itself, not a sample of supposedly related performances, will be measured. For example, if you are interested in aggression, then you should measure specific aggressive behaviors (e.g., hitting other children) in the classroom rather than relying on the child's responses to a projective test or an interview (from which you might hypothesize something about the child's aggressive feelings or tendencies). If you are interested in reading, then you should measure the child's rate of correct reading using instructional materials rather than relying on scores from a standardized achievement test (see Lovitt, 1970, 1977).

Behavior modification ordinarily involves direct and *daily* measurement of behavior. Eaton and Lovitt (1972; see also Lovitt, 1977) have shown that measuring behavior daily (or at least very frequently) is superior to the strategy of testing the child with traditional achievement tests—superior in terms of making decisions about instruction and management, communicating information about the child's progress to parents and other teachers, and evaluating the child's learning. Daily measurement provides a more accurate, reliable picture of the child's capacity to perform and a more sensitive indicator of the effects of teaching and management techniques.

When behavior is measured directly and daily, it is usually most efficient and understandable to display the results in the form of a line graph. The graph will indicate quickly the level, variability, and trend in the child's behavior and, in addition, what change, if any, has occurred when a teaching or management strategy is initiated.

Ordinarily, the behavioral data are plotted for many days spanning several distinct phases. Usually, a **baseline** phase preceeds any attempt to change the behavior. The baseline phase indicates just how much a problem the behavior really is (remember that subjective judgments can often be misleading) and also provides an objective basis for judging the effects of the teaching or management technique (often called an **intervention**). If the teaching procedure is effective, there will be a dramatic change in the behavior graph when the procedure is instituted. If there is no marked change in the graph of the behavior when the teaching or intervention procedure is introduced, another procedure should be attempted. The **follow-up** phase provides an objective indication of the permanence of any behavioral change observed during intervention. When a behavior is taught, the teacher usually hopes that it will be maintained without the continued use of the teaching procedure. Measurement of the behavior after intervention indicates whether or not further teaching is necessary.

The baseline condition is usually continued for a minimum of 5 to 10 days before intervention is begun, although it is sometimes necessary to continue the baseline period for a longer time to allow the behavior to stabilize. When the behavior has stabilized, the *trend* of the data plotted on the graph will approximate a horizontal line.

Behavior is generally recorded during the intervention phase until the desired effect is achieved. Although a dramatic change in the behavior should be expected during the intervention phase, it may take several days for the change to become obvious. If the expected change has not been achieved after 10 days, a second teaching procedure should be tried.

Follow-up may be continued as long as necessary to indicate whether the behavioral change is being maintained. Generally, it is advisable to continue follow-up for at least as long as the baseline period.

There are exceptions to the general pattern of recording behavior during the phases discussed here. At times a child's behavior is so disturbing to the teacher or other children that baseline recording is omitted and an intervention procedure is introduced immediately. Occasionally a teacher is so gratified by the behavioral change achieved during intervention that he is reluctant to quit using the teaching technique during follow-up. Too, there are sometimes research considerations. Behavior modification or single-subject research designs typically require careful attention to the nature and sequence of phases, but these research considerations are beyond the scope of our discussion here (see Hersen & Barlow, 1976, and Kazdin, 1975, for discussion of research designs).

Sammy

An example of how a teacher might use direct daily measurement and other behavior modification techniques is provided by the case of Sammy (described by Kaufhold & Kauffman in Worell & Nelson, 1974). Sammy was a third grader who had frequent crying spells each day. The teacher's usual response was to ask Sammy why he was crying and to try to comfort him. One of his spells of crying could last anywhere from 5 minutes to 2 hours, and during these spells the class was disrupted. In fact, other children were beginning to taunt him; and his crying was getting so loud it could be heard in other classrooms. The teacher recorded each crying spell by making a tally mark on a sheet of paper she kept handy for that purpose. She plotted the number of crying spells on a graph each day. As shown in Figure 2 – 1, Sammy had an average of about 17 crying spells per day during baseline (before the teacher tried any intervention technique). Beginning on the eleventh day, the teacher tried to ignore all crying. It was obvious after 5 days that ignoring was not going to work. On the 16th day, the teacher began a new approach. A class discussion was held in which everyone (including Sammy) agreed that as long as Sammy was not crying everyone would call him by his "grown-up" (and preferred) name, "Sam"; if he cried he would be ignored by everyone; if he did not cry for three days, everyone in the class would get a special treat; Sammy would record his crying by making the tally marks on the teacher's recording sheet. Figure 2 – 1 shows the results. A special treat was earned on the third day of no crying. Sam seldom cried again, and his improved behavior continued even though no more treats were given. During the follow-up phase his improved behavior was maintained by occasional praise from the teacher and the self-recording technique.

In the case of Sammy, the teacher recorded the behavior throughout the school day. Recording all day is sometimes not practical, or even possible. Often the teacher can take a *sample* (or samples) of behavior sometime during the day. For example, the behavior might be recorded during the first hour of each day, only during the noon recess, for 30 minutes during math class, or during two 15-minute periods, one in the morning and the other in the after-noon. As a rule, the behavior should be recorded at the time and/or in the setting in which it is the greatest problem. The length of the sample and the time of day it is taken should be consistent from day to day, and the sample should be long enough to give an accurate picture of how often the behavior occurs (i.e., in most cases the more often the behavior happens, the shorter the sample can be).

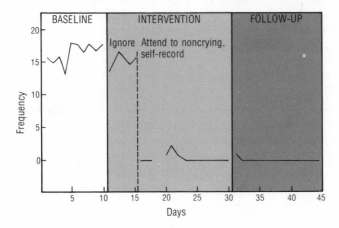

Figure 2-1
Sammy: crying

Source: From J. Worell & C. M. Nelson, *Managing instructional problems: A case study workbook.* New York: McGraw-Hill, 1974, 189.

Instead of recording the *frequency* of a behavior (as in the case of Sammy), it is sometimes more helpful to record the *duration* of a behavior, the *rate* of a behavior, the *percent of opportunities* that a behavior occurs, the *percent of intervals* in which a behavior occurs, or *percent of children present who are doing a certain behavior.* Duration recording usually requires a stopwatch which is run only when the child is exhibiting the defined behavior. Thumbsuck-ing is an example of a behavior for which duration recording might be most appropriate. Skiba, Pettigrew, and Alden (1971) had observers record the cumulative number of seconds (using stopwatches) three third-grade girls had their thumbs on their lips or in their mouths during 50-minute classes. Their graph (Figure 2-2) shows that when the teacher paid attention to the girls for nonthumbsucking behaviors and ignored thumbsucking during 16 lessons, the amount of time they spent sucking their thumbs went down. Skiba et al. went back to baseline conditions and then reinstated the intervention because they wanted to demonstrate the cause–effect relationship between the teacher's attention and thumbsucking.

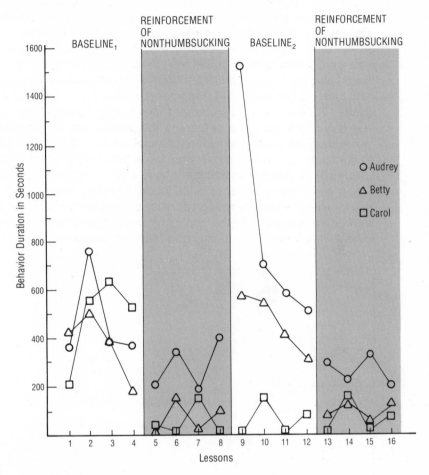

Figure 2-2

Thumbsucking duration (in seconds) for each subject during each of the 16 lessons.

Source: Adapted from "A behavioral approach to the control of thumbsucking in the classroom" by E. A. Skiba, L. E. Pettigrew, & S. A. Alden, *Journal of Applied Behavior Analysis,* 1971, *4,* 123.

The rate of a behavior refers to its frequency per unit of time (usually time in minutes). For example, if a child performs a particular behavior (e.g., talking out) 15 times in 30 minutes, then the rate of his talking-out behavior is 15/30 or .5 per minute. To record behavioral rates, you must not only count the frequency of the behavior but also keep track of the amount of time elapsed while the behavior was recorded. Any behavior can be expressed in terms of its rate, but classroom teachers are most likely to be interested in rates of academic responses. How fast a child reads (words read correctly per minute) or does arithmetic computations (problems correct per minute) may be crucial features of academic performance. Van Houten, Morrison, Jarvis, and McDonald (1974), for example, recorded the rate (words per minute) of fifth-grade children's writing during 10-minute sessions each day. During baseline sessions, the children were merely given a topic and told to write a composition on that topic. After 10 minutes they were told to stop (but they were not told they were being timed). During intervention, they were told they would be timed using a stopwatch and were given feedback on their previous day's rate (and told to try to exceed it). Figure 2–3 shows the results (averaged for all children in the class) for two classes (Section A and Section B) of fifth graders. The delay of three days in starting the intervention for Section B was a research strategy used to reduce the probability that the increase could be attributed to something other than the intervention. Results for individual children (A.M. and S.G. in Section 1; M. A. and B. V. in Section B) are shown in Figure 2–4. Clearly, timing and feedback increased these children's rates of writing when they were writing compositions on assigned topics. Other data showed improvement in the quality of compositions and improved attitude toward writing during the timing and feedback intervention.

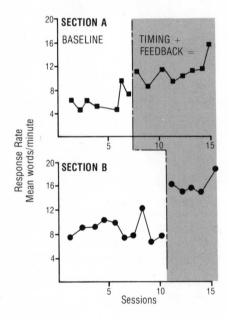

Figure 2-3
The mean response rate in words per minute for both grade-five classes in each daily session. The broken vertical lines represent the introduction of the experimental condition.

Source: From "The effects of explicit timing and feedback on compositional response rate in elementary school children," by R. Van Houten, E. Morrison, R. Jarvis, & M. McDonald, *Journal of Applied Behavior Analysis,* 1974, *7,* 552.

In some cases, a behavior can occur only under specific conditions where it is called for; the number of responses possible is controlled directly by the teacher's behavior (e.g., the number of questions that can be answered correctly is controlled directly by how many questions the teacher asks) or by the written assignment (e.g., the number of arithmetic problems that can be completed correctly is determined by the number of problems given in the assignment). In these cases it is best to record the percent of the possible responses that were attempted or the percent correct (see Lahey, McNees, & Brown, 1973).

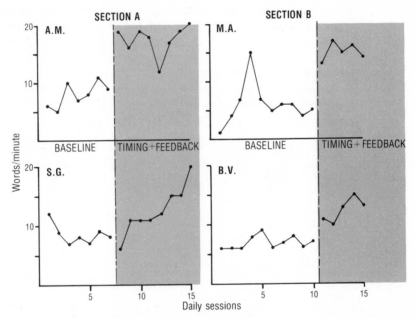

Figure 2-4

The response rate in words per minute of four individual children from both grade-five classes in each daily session. The two graphs at the top of the figure (Subjects A.M. and M. A.) show results of two subjects who were highly responsive and graphs at the bottom (Subjects S.G. and B.G.) show the results of two subjects who were not very responsive.

Source: From "The effects of explicit timing and feedback on compositional response rate in elementary school children," by R. Van Houten, E. Morrison, R. Jarvis, & M. McDonald, *Journal of Applied Behavior Analysis,* 1974, 7, 553.

Sometimes the child's behavior is not observed continuously during the sample. The observer may watch the child for a brief interval (e.g., 10 seconds) and then record whether or not the behavior occurred during that interval. Alternatively, a teacher might glance at a child every 5 minutes and record whether or not the child is engaged in the behavior at that moment. After a reasonable period of time you can determine the percentage of observation intervals during which the behavior occurred. An example is provided by the work of Knapczyk & Livingston (1974). Figure 2–5 shows a record of two children's "on-task" behavior (orientation toward the teacher or instructional materials) during baseline phases and during training phases, when the children were reminded by the teacher to raise their hands and ask questions if they had difficulty with the reading assignment. When prompted to ask questions, both children were on-task a greater percentage of the time (and also improved in reading comprehension). The children were observed for four 10-second intervals each minute (allowing 5 seconds to record data after each observation interval). The vertical axes of the graphs represent, therefore, the percentage of the intervals during which the child was observed to be on-task for the entire 10 seconds.

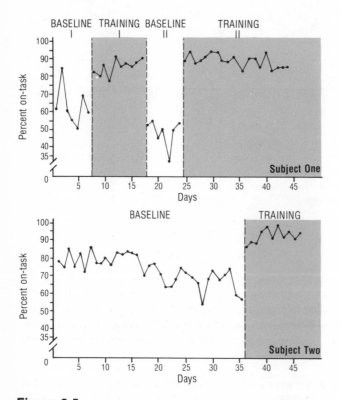

Figure 2-5
Percentage of on-task behavior observed during the 50-minute reading period.

Source: From "The effects of prompting question-asking upon on-task behavior and reading comprehension," by D. R. Knapczyk & G. Livingston, *Journal of Applied Behavior Analysis*, 1974, 7, 119.

There are circumstances involving the management of an entire class in which it is most helpful to record the percentage of individuals engaged in a particular response. For example, the teacher might be interested in increasing the percentage of children in the class who have returned to the room before the end of a recess period (see Hall, Cristler, Cranston, & Tucker, 1970).

There are several effective and efficient ways of making daily observations of behavior. The particular method of observing and recording must be tailored to the situation. It is essential to record the behavior immediately after it occurs so that accuracy is maintained. It is also highly desirable to occasionally have a second observer (e.g., teacher aide, another teacher, or a responsible student) record the behavior simultaneously. The record of behavior may be assumed to be highly reliable when there is nearly perfect agreement between the two observers. (For further discussion of techniques and problems in behavioral measurement see Cooper, 1975; Gelfand & Hartmann, 1975; Hersen & Barlow, 1976; Kauffman, 1975; Kazdin, 1975).

As we have stated previously, it is essential that behavior be recorded at the time of its occurrence. If teachers or other observers rely on their memory of how often the behavior occurred, even for a short period of time, it is unlikely that the record will be accurate. A number of memory aids can be purchased at a low cost or improvised from classroom supplies. Many teachers have found inexpensive golf counters (the wrist type is particularly convenient) and grocery counters ideal for recording behavior. It is also convenient to tally each occurrence of the behavior by making a mark on a strip of masking tape worn on your wrist or on a slip of paper. An inexpensive kitchen timer can be used to cue observations at regular intervals. When work completion and work accuracy are recorded, it is necessary to compute percentage completed or percentage correct after each work period.

In addition to recording the behavior immediately after it occurs, the teacher should enter daily observations on a record form. This provides for the orderly accumulation of data before it is plotted on the graph. A useful record form for nearly any behavior is shown in Table 2–2. For any given behavior, you should use only those parts of the form appropriate for your recording technique.

It is not always necessary for the teachers to record behavior themselves. In many cases the child, a peer, or a teacher's aide can do the recording (see Hall, Fox, Willard, Goldsmith, Emerson, Owen, Davis, & Porcia, 1971). Care must be taken to maintain reliability of the record and avoid unethical or unprofessional practices. The problem of reliability can be minimized by careful training and occasional checks of the recorder's performance. Ethical and professional questions are likely to be raised only when a peer is asked to record the child's behavior. Those questions nearly always can be avoided by informing both the child and the peer of the purpose of the record.

Recording techniques may themselves be used as a technique for the modification of behavior. Not infrequently, the child's knowledge that his behavior is being recorded changes his behavior to a significant degree. Consequently, it is often appropriate to keep the recording hidden from the child during the baseline phase.

CONTROLLING FUNCTION OF CONSEQUENCES

All behaviors are followed by environmental events. Many of these subsequent events may have a profound effect on the person's future behavior.

TABLE 2-2
Record Form for Accumulating Behavioral Data

Behavior recorded: _____ Name of child: _____

day	date	behavior recorded from:	tot. time behavior recorded	# of behaviors observed	rate per min.	duration in min. and sec.	behavior recorded each ___ min for ___ intervals	# of times behavior observed	% of intervals behavior observed	% of work completed	% of work correct	comments
1.		___ to ___										
2.		___ to ___										
3.		___ to ___										
4.		___ to ___										
5.		___ to ___										
6.		___ to ___										
7.		___ to ___										
8.		___ to ___										
9.		___ to ___										
10.		___ to ___										

(Continue in this manner)

Behavioral scientists have clearly shown that much of our behavior is controlled to a great degree by its immediate *consequences*. For example, when a child touches a hot iron he immediately experiences a painful consequence which decreases the likelihood that he will touch a hot iron in the future. If a child is immediately recognized by the teacher when he raises his hand, the likelihood that he will raise his hand in the future is increased.

A **reinforcer** *is an event which controls behavior.* Consequences or reinforcers may be positive (things a person will try to get or retain) or negative (things a person will try to avoid or escape). Reinforcers may be used to increase (reinforce) or decrease (punish) a behavior. A reinforcer may be either presented or withdrawn to influence the strength of behavior. Thus, there are four distinct methods of influencing a behavior by presenting or withdrawing positive or negative reinforcers, as shown in Table 2–3. *The process of reinforcement always results in an increase or strengthening of behavior. Punishment always results in a decrease or weakening of behavior.* Note that negative reinforcement should not be confused with punishment. *Negative reinforcement,* withdrawing something unpleasant after a behavior, has the effect of *increasing or accelerating* the behavior it follows. *Punishment,* withdrawing something pleasant or presenting something unpleasant after a behavior, has the opposite effect of *decreasing* or *decelerating* the behavior it follows.

A nearly infinite number of environmental events occur subsequent to any behavior, not all of which have a controlling function. In many cases it is difficult to identify precisely the events which *do* control behavior. In the classroom, positive reinforcers for maladaptive behavior often go unidentified because someone makes an inappropriate assumption about the reinforcers. *Reinforcers are defined by their effects on the behaviors they follow, not on the basis of how one thinks they should function.* Although it is possible to generalize regarding the classification of events, the reinforcing property of a subsequent event may vary for a *specific* individual or group under certain circumstances. Teachers often assume that their reprimands and "desist" signals (e.g., "sit down," "don't interrupt when someone else is talking," "I don't want to have to tell you again," finger-snapping, etc.) are negative reinforcers; i.e., that presenting them following undesirable behaviors will weaken the behavior. Unfortunately, a reprimand may often serve to strengthen rather than weaken the undesirable behavior (e.g., if attracting the teacher's attention is a positive reinforcer for a child) (Becker, Thomas, & Carnine, 1969).

Schedules of Reinforcement

Effective control of behavior is largely a result of the arrangement of consequences. In any behavior-management situation there are rules, either explicitly stated or implicit in the sequence of events, which determine the arrangement of rewards and punishments. These *rules which arrange the relationship between the occurrence of behavior and its consequences are*

Table 2-3

Methods of Influencing Behavior By Using Consequences

	Positive Reinforcer (something you will work to get)	**Negative Reinforcer** (something you will work to avoid)
Present Reinforcer	*Positive Reinforcement* *Effect:* Increase or strengthen behavior which produces reinforcer; acceleration of behavior. *Example* *Behavior:* Child begins assigned seatwork. *Consequence:* Teacher smiles at child and remarks, "Good, I see you've started!" If the child's initial effort at doing his assigned work is consistently given immediate attention and praise by the teacher, the promptness with which he begins his work will likely increase.	*Punishment* *Effect:* Decrease or weaken behavior which produces reinforcer; deceleration of behavior. *Example* *Behavior:* Child destroys paper of other children. *Consequence:* Teacher points at child and shouts "NO!" If the teacher is generally positive, controlled, and soft-spoken in his interaction with the child, but consistently points at child and shouts "NO!" when he begins to destroy another child's paper, child's destruction of papers will likely decrease.
Withdraw Reinforcer	*Punishment** *Effect:* Decrease or weaken behavior which results in loss of reinforcer; deceleration of behavior. *Example* *Behavior:* Child "tattles" to teacher. *Consequence:* Teacher turns away from child (withdraws attention completely). If the teacher consistently and totally withdraws his attention from the child immediately after he begins to "tattle," tattling will likely decrease. *Sometimes called "response cost" because every response "costs" the child something.	*Negative Reinforcement** *Effect:* Increase or strengthen behavior which avoids or escapes the reinforcer; acceleration of behavior. *Example* *Behavior:* Child runs out of the classroom when teased by other children. *Consequence:* Teasing stops. If the child can escape from the teasing by running out of the room, running out is likely to increase when teasing occurs. *Buckling your seatbelt may be maintained by negative reinforcement (avoidance of or escape from an aversive buzzer).

called **contingencies** or **schedules** of reinforcement. A contingency states the conditions under which reinforcement will occur. For example, the child may be required to do a certain *number* of specified behaviors to obtain reinforcement, or he may be expected to complete a task during a certain *time* interval to get a reward.

Although there are many very complicated reinforcement schedules which scientists use in research, they are derived from combinations and modifications of a few basic schedules which may be used in the classroom. Several of these basic schedules are described in Table 2–4. There are two classes of reinforcement schedules: *continuous,* in which every response is reinforced, and *intermittent,* in which not all of the child's appropriate responses are reinforced.

Continuous Reinforcement

It is advantageous to reinforce *every* occurrence of a desirable behavior when it is first being taught. Otherwise, the behavior may not be learned at all or may be learned very slowly. Continuous reinforcement should be offered when a new skill or behavior is being learned; but after it has become firmly established, other schedules may be more effective and efficient. For example, when a child is being taught a new computational skill, it may be best to reward him for each problem completed correctly to maintain his interest in the task and allow him to observe his progress. However, after the child has mastered the new skill, continued reinforcement of every correct response is unnecessary, inefficient, and impractical. Continuous reinforcement after the skill has been learned may result in loss of interest in the reward and a decline in appropriate behavior. Continued interest in the reward and a high rate of appropriate behavior can be maintained by using intermittent reinforcement.

intermittent Reinforcement

Behavior that has been learned can be efficiently maintained by arranging consequences for only a portion of the child's appropriate responses. Reinforcement may be based on the number of responses or on a response completed after the passage of an interval of time, as shown in Table 2–4. When a change is made from continuous to intermittent reinforcement, the requirement for reinforcement must not be increased too quickly or the behavior may be lost. A gradual increase in the requirements will insure a smooth transition without loss of the newly learned response. If the child who has learned a new computational skill for the reward of a star for every problem completed correctly is suddenly expected to complete 50 or 100 problems before earning a star, he may not continue to work for the reward. He will probably continue to work industriously, however, if he is expected to complete first two, then three, then five, and finally ten such problems. Eventually he may be willing to complete 100 problems before receiving his reward. It is likely, in this case, that other natural consequences in his environment (e.g., praise or self-congratulation) are providing intermittent reinforcement for his behavior.

Each specific schedule of reinforcement generally produces a characteristic pattern of response. Reinforcement given on a variable schedule, in which the child cannot predict when the next reward will be available, will usually produce faster and more persistent responding than a fixed ratio or fixed

Table 2–4
An Outline of Basic Schedules of Reinforcement

I. **Continuous Reinforcement**

Every time the behavior occurs, it is reinforced.

Example: Each time the child completes an arithmetic problem correctly he is given a point for his progress chart.

II. **Intermittent Reinforcement**

A. *Ratio Schedules*

Reinforcement is given for every *n*th behavior and depends on the number of behaviors the child performs regardless of time.

1. *Fixed Ratio*

A fixed number of behaviors must occur for each reinforcement.

Example: Every 10th sight word read correctly is rewarded with a piece of candy.

2. *Variable Ratio*

An average number of behaviors must occur for each reinforcement. The number of behaviors required varies around a mean.

Example: On the average, every 5th time the child raises his hand he is called on by the teacher. The actual number of times he raises his hand before being called on varies.

B. *Interval Schedules*

Reinforcement depends on the passage of time *and* the occurrence of a behavior.

1. *Fixed Interval*

A fixed amount of time must pass, after which the next appropriate behavior will be reinforced.

Example: Every 3 minutes during recess the teacher observes the child to see whether or not he is talking to another child. The next time he approaches another child and speaks to him, the teacher pats him on the shoulder and praises him for being friendly.

2. *Variable Interval*

A variable amount of time must pass, after which the next correct response will result in reinforcement. The amount of time required varies around a mean.

Example: On the average, every 5 minutes the teacher observes whether or not the child is writing another correct answer to the questions covering the geography lesson. When he answers the next question correctly, a smiling face is drawn on his paper. The actual number of minutes which elapse before the teacher checks the child's behavior varies.

interval schedule, where the child can anticipate when he will be given the next reinforcer.

In actual classroom practice, teachers usually employ approximations of the schedules of reinforcement described in Table 2–4. That is, a teacher often provides intermittent reinforcement that does not fulfill the *exact* requirements of a particular schedule; reinforcement is given on a variable schedule that depends partly on an unspecified amount of time and an unspecified number - of responses. Too, in everyday life there are not many "true" interval schedules. Typically, the teacher arranges reinforcement to follow a response that is completed before a given amount of time has elapsed. For example, the child may be able to earn a reinforcer for completing a math assignment within 20 minutes or less (or perhaps for completing a reading task before recess). These "deadline" schedules resemble true interval schedules (in which the *first* response *after* the end of an interval of time is reinforced) and are practical for classroom use.

In addition to the schedules of reinforcement described in Table 2–4, there are three other schedules that are particularly useful to teachers. A DRO (differential reinforcement of other behavior) schedule specifies that reinforcement will be given only if a certain behavior has *not* occurred during an interval of time. Thus, a child may be offered reinforcement only if he has not screamed, talked out, or performed some other specified undesirable response for a period of time (which may be a fixed or variable interval). A DRL (differential reinforcement of low rate) schedule specifies that reinforcement will be provided only if the rate of behavior stays below a certain level. A DRL schedule is useful for maintaining a manageable level of behavior when too frequent occurrence of the behavior is the basic problem (see Deitz, 1977; Deitz & Repp, 1973). Behaviors related to biological functions, such as eating, are likely to be appropriate targets for this technique. When the technique is employed, the contingency explicitly states the *maximum* number of behaviors that may be emitted during a specified time interval to obtain reinforcement. For example, the problem with the child who bolts his food is not that he eats, but that his rate of eating is too high. A useful contingency for this child may be that he will obtain a reward by finishing his lunch in no less than 15 minutes or that his reward will depend on his taking less than 5 bites per minute while eating his lunch. For speeding up the rate of a response that is being made too slowly, a teacher may employ a DRH (differential reinforcement of high rate) schedule. In DRH, the child can earn reinforcement only by making more than a specified number of responses during a specific interval of time. For example, Lovitt and Esveldt (1970) set up a schedule in which working math problems faster resulted in the child's earning additional rewards.

Timing of Consequences

Reinforcers are usually most effective when they follow the desired behavior immediately. Adults can often work for distant rewards, as in the case of the prospective teacher working for a teaching certificate. Children, particularly those with learning problems, usually work diligently for more immediate consequences. Praise given immediately after performance of a desirable behavior will be more likely to have the desired effect than a delayed reward. For example, for some children grade cards given daily are more effective in controlling academic responses than grades given every 6 to 8 weeks. As a child's behavior improves, it may be possible to gradually extend the delay between his behavior and its consequences. The temptation to move too - quickly to delayed reinforcement must be resisted. In the analysis of many behavior-management problems, it is found that immediate rather than delayed consequences are controlling behavior. Arranging immediate consequences for behavior usually improves performance.

Shaping Behavior

In teaching children to behave appropriately, teachers must carefully define the terminal goals or behavioral objectives. They must describe in objective and measurable terms how they want children to behave after they are taught. Teachers must also consider in objective and measurable terms how children presently behave. This means analyzing the behavioral goal in relation to the children's present behavior and arranging a sequence of ordered steps or tasks. The teacher must begin by reinforcing a behavior that the child already emits and then gradually increase the requirement for reinforcement. The sequence of steps arranged by the teacher must be **successive approximations** of the ultimate goal. If the approximations are too large, the child is unlikely to learn the behavior or the teaching procedure will be inefficient. The teacher who fails to reward increments of improvement in behavior is not likely to be successful in using behavior modification techniques (Kuypers, Becker, & O'Leary, 1968).

The process of ordered teaching of prerequisite behaviors which are successive approximations of the final goal is called *behavior shaping*. The child who cannot walk cannot be expected to do so until he learns certain prerequisite skills, one of which is standing. Usually, a child must learn to associate letters with sounds before he can learn to read. It would be foolish to expect most children to speak in sentences before they can name objects.

Several examples of behavior shaping in the classroom are presented in Table 2–5. The size of the steps in learning must be adjusted to the learning characteristics of each child. Highly gifted children may be able to make great leaps in learning, omitting successive approximations. Children with special learning problems, on the other hand, may need to take more than the ordinary sequence of steps in learning. The more severe the child's learning disability, the smaller the successive approximations of the final goal must be.

Individual Determination of Consequences

The effective use of consequences to control classroom behavior must be individualized for the child, the teacher, and the situation. Since a reinforcer is

Table 2–5
Examples of Behavior Shaping in the Classroom

behavioral goal	successive approximations
Child will sit at his desk continuously for 20 minutes.	Standing near his desk for a few seconds; touching desk or chair; sitting, leaning or kneeling on his desk or chair; sitting in his chair for a few seconds; sitting in his chair for 3 minutes; sitting for 5 minutes . . . .
Child will complete seatwork assignments.	Looking at assignment, picking up pencil, putting pencil on paper, completing 1 answer, completing 2 answers . . . .
Child will participate fully with class in softball game.	Watching game from a distance, standing behind backstop, keeping score, serving as bat boy, playing a position for ½ inning, playing a full inning . . . .
Child will be able to write the letter *H*.	Writing a vertical line, writing a horizontal line, combining the two lines, making an additional vertical line.
Child will be able to color within the lines.	Holding a crayon, coloring in large areas, gradually decreasing the size of the area until the child completes the desired size.
Child will be able to name his body parts.	Knowing parts making up the body, naming gross features of a stick figure, naming and relating stick figure features to his own body, gradually introducing specific features of human figures and relating to his own body.

defined by its effect on behavior, an event which is reinforcing for one child may be punishing for another. It is the task of the teacher to find and use those events which are reinforcing for a specific child. This can be done by: (a) observing what the child does or seems to enjoy when given a free choice, (b) asking the child what he would be willing to work for, or (c) systematically arranging a consequence for the child and observing its effect on his behavior (see Gelfand & Hartmann, 1975). For example, if the child spends most of his free time working puzzles, it is highly probable that working puzzles will serve as a reinforcer for him. Also, it is simple to ask the child, "What would you like to do when you finish your writing?"

The Premack Principle

A very practical behavior management principle was formulated by Premack (1959). The Premack Principle states that anything a child likes to do more can be used to reinforce any behavior he likes to do less. Thus by observing children's preferences for certain events and activities, the teacher can use more preferred activities to reinforce less preferred behaviors. The greater the difference in preference between two activities, the greater the reinforcing power of the preferred event. This makes it possible to use certain academic and play activities, as well as more "artificial" or contrived reinforcers, as consequences for appropriate behavior. Examples of the application of the Premack Principle are given in Table 2–6. The child's preference for an activity should, if possible, be established through observation; if you guess, you may make a less preferred event contingent upon a more preferred activity. This arrangement would punish desirable behavior. Although rigorous research to support the validity of Premack's law is lacking (Knapp, 1976), the practical utility of using preferred activities as reinforcers is obvious.

Contingency Contracting

Contingencies of reinforcement may be stated in the form of an agreement or contract. Children benefit by an explicit statement of the relationship between their behavior and its consequences. Negotiating a contingency contract involves reaching an agreement that after the child has done something the teacher wants him to do (e.g., spell 20 words correctly), the teacher will provide

---

Table 2–6
Application of the Premack Principle

child's preference	reinforcement arrangement
Child prefers drawing to reading.	Make drawing contingent upon reading.
"Helping the teacher" is preferred to going outside for recess.	Allow going outside for recess to earn the privilege of "helping the teacher."
Child likes to eat candy kisses more than he likes to do arithmetic.	Make eating candy kisses contingent upon doing arithmetic.
Given the choice of doing writing or reading, the child always does reading.	Require writing just before allowing reading.
Writing on the chalkboard is something the child relishes, while writing on paper is something he detests.	Allow writing on the chalkboard only after a writing assignment on paper has been satisfactorily completed.
Child would rather put together a model than spell words.	Arrange to have spelling words written correctly produce permission to work on model.
Child spends every spare moment reading but rarely speaks to anyone.	Make access to reading material contingent upon a specific amount of verbal interaction.

something the child wants (e.g., permission to go to the listening station for 10 minutes). An effective contingency contract must meet the requirements of any good business contract; that is, it must be fair for both parties, be clear in its statement of terms, offer a positive incentive, and be adhered to systematically and honestly (Homme, 1969).

Token Reinforcement

Behavior-management transactions can often be conducted by arranging reinforcing events to follow appropriate behavior immediately. In other situations, it is practical to allow the child to engage in the reinforcing activity only during a specified time period which follows his appropriate behavior by several hours, days, or weeks. For example, a teacher may be able to arrange for a grade of A on a science test to be followed by the privilege of playing a game of ping-pong with the school principal. The teacher may also be able to arrange working with the school janitor, earning small toys or packages of candy, helping in the cafeteria, taking a field trip, visiting his home, watching a cartoon movie, and doing many other activities as reinforcing events for a child or children in the class. The logistics of making these events contingent upon specific behaviors and allowing them to occur immediately following appropriate behaviors is a very difficult problem. But if the reinforcing event does not follow appropriate behavior immediately, its effectiveness in increasing the desired behavior is likely to be lost. One method of solving the logistics and timing problems is to establish a system of token reinforcement or a token economy in the classroom. Points marked on cards or other tokens can be given immediately after an appropriate behavior occurs and exchanged during a specific time period for reinforcing activities. Tokens serve as reinforcers because they can be used to "buy" reinforcing events. Before implementing a token reinforcement system in the classroom, the teacher should read extensively concerning the mechanics of establishing and operating such a system. The details which must be considered in the use of token reinforcement include the problems of supply, demand, inflation, recession, distribution, theft, extortion, and other problems observed in any monetary system. The benefits of a properly functioning token reinforcement program are many, but the pitfalls are equally numerous (see Kazdin & Bootzin, 1972; O'Leary & Drabman, 1971; Payne, Polloway, Kauffman, & Scranton, 1975; Stainback, Payne, Stainback, & Payne, 1973).

Use of Group Contingencies

The classroom teacher will often find it advantageous to manage contingencies of reinforcement for groups of children as well as for individuals (e.g., Greenwood, Hops, Delquadri, & Guild, 1974; Grieger, Kauffman, & Grieger, 1976; Long & Williams, 1973). The teacher who excuses rows of children only when each child is seated quietly is employing a group contingency-management technique. In this example, each member of the group must exhibit appropriate behavior for the group to obtain the reinforcing consequence. When such a contingency is applied, there is considerable group pressure to conform to the teacher's expectation.

It is also possible to make a reinforcing event for the entire class dependent upon the behavior of a single individual. For example, a special treat for each member of the class could be made contingent upon a single child's completion of his work. In this example also, there is likely to be group pressure. Peers may encourage the child whose behavior regulates their reward and distract him as little as possible. When using this group contingency technique, the task must be within the child's capability and positive consequences of his performance must be stressed. Failure of the problem student to perform should *not* result in punishment for the class.

Finally, it is possible to arrange a contingent reward which can be earned by each member of the class individually. For example, any member of the class completing an assignment may be allowed to go to recess 2 minutes early. Care must be taken to provide an appropriate task for each child. With this type of group contingency, group pressure will not increase the probability of appropriate behavior.

Specific consequences for behavior must also be determined by individual teachers. Certain teachers find it difficult or impossible to administer consequences which other teachers consider appropriate. Some teachers can provide visits to their homes, special activities after school, small toys, or treats for children, while others feel that some or all of these events cannot be appropriately offered as rewards. However, unless the teacher is willing to provide *some* effective reward (either social or material) on a contingent basis, classroom management will probably be ineffective.

Other variables also require individualization in the selection of consequences. The constraints of school administrators, parents, or other teachers, or the physical limitations of the school may prohibit the use of consequences which the teacher could otherwise employ very effectively. Unsympathetic principals, parents who demand strict adherence to traditional methods, cynical fellow teachers, and school buildings designed for the past are realities faced by many teachers who wish to implement contingency-management ideas (Kauffman & Vicente, 1972). On the other hand, principals, colleagues, and parents are often invaluable allies in successful modification of children's inappropriate behaviors, and antique features of school buildings can provide opportunities for innovation. The assessment of these situational variables demands no less attention than the consideration of your own feelings and the careful evaluation of the individual child.

CONTROLLING FUNCTION OF ANTECEDENT EVENTS

Thus far we have stressed the use of subsequent events or consequences in classroom management. Although behavior will be shaped and maintained only if it is followed by effective reinforcers, teaching also involves setting the stage for behavior. The teacher must establish appropriate instructional goals, acquire instructional materials, provide a model for the student, schedule a sequence of activities, and give unambiguous signals that behavior should occur. Each of these classes of antecedent events has a significant controlling function in classroom management.

Antecedent events or stimuli increase the likelihood that a specific instance of a behavior will occur. For example, when a second grader is presented with the stimulus $2+2=$ ____, the probability that he will give the response 4 rather than another response is greatly increased. Presentation of the antecedent event, $2+2=$ ____, does not *reinforce* the response 4; it is what occurs *after* the response is given that provides reinforcement. If the teacher informs the child that his answer is correct or offers some other reward for his performance, the probability that the child will give the response 4 the next time the same stimulus is presented is increased.

When reinforcement is consistently paired with a stimulus, the stimulus signals the child that reinforcement is likely to occur. Similar responses which lead to the same consequences will also be increased in probability. Thus, the child may respond to $2+2=$ ____ by writing 4, saying "four," tapping four times with his pencil, pointing to the numeral 4, etc. This tendency to give similar but not identical responses in the presence of a stimulus, all of which lead to reinforcement, is called **response generalization** and is a part of concept formation. It is often necessary to specifically teach response generalizations. Children who have been successful learners tend to be able to respond appropriately in many different ways to an instructional task (i.e., to learn concepts quickly). Children with school learning problems, on the other hand, may need to be taught a variety of appropriate responses.

When stimuli differ perceptibly along a significant dimension or combination of features, a similar response is not considered appropriate and will not be reinforced. The task $2+2=$ ____ calls for a completely different response than $2\times2=$ ____ or $2+$ ____ $=4$. The process of learning to respond differentially to different stimuli is called **stimulus discrimination** and is also a part of concept learning. When a child consistently makes a differential response to a stimulus (e.g., when he consistently responds "cat" to *c-a-t*) he has learned a discrimination. A basic problem in remedial education is teaching appropriate discriminations. Learning to read and do simple arithmetic computations involves learning many discriminations. Learning to behave appropriately in the classroom means that the child must learn to discriminate the stimuli which signal that he will be reinforced for sitting down, for listening, for following directions, and for other behaviors that facilitate academic learning. *Discriminations are learned only when behavior is differentially reinforced in the presence of* **specific** *stimuli*. For example, the child will learn not to talk out if he is consistently ignored for doing so and reinforced for talking when appropriate.

Determination of Tasks: Goals, Rules, and Instructions

The teacher can determine specific instructional tasks for a child only after formulating a behavioral goal. He must define the behavior he wants the child to perform in observable terms. The conditions under which the teacher wants the child to perform the behavior and the criterion for satisfactory performance must also be stated. When adequate goals have been established, instructional tasks for the child logically follow (see chapter 4). It is essential that the task presented to a child be clearly stated in terms of beginning and ending points. It is of utmost importance that the child know what he is to *do* and what constitutes completion of the task. The directive "study your spelling" is not a task which specifies exactly what the child is to do, nor does the task have an unambiguous beginning or end. "Write each of your spelling words five times," on the other hand, is a task which specifies the behavior which the child is to emit.

Clarity in the presentation of tasks allows both the child and the teacher to discriminate the occasions for reinforcement. If the child does not know what to *do* to obtain reinforcement, he is likely to exhibit maladaptive behavior. Analysis of many behavior-management problems suggests that the child is uncertain about what specific behavior the teacher considers desirable at the moment. If the teacher does not know exactly what the child is to do, he will not be able to determine when to provide a reinforcer for appropriate behavior.

There is often ambiguity concerning what behavior the teacher desires during nonacademic activities and between the completion of one academic task and the beginning of another. During these times, the teacher must set clear expectations for nonacademic tasks. The explicit statement of positive rules for behavior is an essential feature of efficient classroom control (Madsen, Becker & Thomas, 1968). To avoid confusion, the number of rules should be kept small. To be effective, the rules must be stated positively and specify behaviors which are incompatible with misconduct. Rules which state what a child should *not* do allow the child to demand another rule to cover each example of misconduct. They are not a guide to reinforcement for the child or the teacher. "Work quietly at your desk" is preferable to "Don't bother others" because it specifies for the child how he is expected to behave and tells the teacher what behavior to reinforce. Positively and explicitly stated rules simplify communication with the child concerning his behavior.

Instructions, when they are effective, are the simplest, most efficient way of changing behavior. Yet instructions have been studied less than any other behavior modification technique (cf. Berman, 1973; Kauffman, 1975; Lovitt, 1977). There is some research evidence indicating that many times if children are just told exactly what the teacher wants them to do, they will do it (Lovitt, 1977; Lovitt & Smith, 1972). Never overlook the possibility that simple, clear, firm instructions about how to behave or how to perform an academic task will solve an apparent learning or behavior problem (Kauffman, 1977).

Use of Models

Stated goals, rules, and instructions are methods of communicating with children. Children also constantly observe the behavior of the teacher and their peers. The behavior of others provides a model or example which the child will tend to follow. Observing the reinforcement of other children who are behaving appropriately tends to induce similar behavior in the observing child. Modeling and vicarious reinforcement, i.e., demonstration of appropriate behavior and its reinforcement, can significantly decrease the amount of time required for a child to learn desirable behavior (see Bandura, 1969; Cullinan, Kauffman, & LaFleur, 1975).

Modeling or demonstration of appropriate behavior is commonly used by teachers in presenting academic tasks (Smith & Lovitt, 1975). Teachers characteristically demonstrate how to solve an arithmetic problem before expecting the child to solve a similar problem. It is less common, however, for teachers to provide models and vicarious reinforcement for nonacademic behavior. Ignoring the miscreant and focusing praise and attention on the children who are behaving well is a highly effective management technique.

The teacher who sets a poor behavioral model for his students will be less effective in controlling misbehavior than the teacher whose behavior should be emulated by his students. Teachers may also provide an academic model for students. Reading for pleasure, searching for information, writing, and applying computational skills to the solution of everyday problems are behaviors every teacher may show in the classroom.

Providing Cues for Behavior

Teachers must give students signals that indicate *when* they are to emit a behavior. Hand signals, special visual or auditory stimuli, facial expressions, touching, and single words can be used to cue performance. To help children learn to discriminate specific behaviors, cues must be systematically followed by consequences. To be effective, cues must be made especially clear and consistent.

Teachers tend to emphasize cues which indicate to a child that he should stop a maladaptive behavior. Nearly every teacher has a well-developed repertoire of "desist signals," such as finger-snapping, bell-ringing, ruler-tapping, frowning, ear-tugging, finger-pointing, shushing, "boys and girls!" These signals are used *after* children have begun to exhibit undesirable behaviors such as disruptive noise making, conversing with peers during study time, moving unnecessarily about the classroom, and talking out of turn. They are often either ineffective or have only a temporary restraining effect on misbehavior because: (a) they are mildly aversive events that children can easily learn to escape or avoid by temporarily behaving well, (b) the children's immediate cessation of their irritating behavior provides negative reinforcement for the teacher, and (c) the attention of the teacher, although intended as punishment, reinforces children's disturbing behavior. Although desist cues can be used effectively and should be part of every teacher's repertoire, their effectiveness will deteriorate if they constitute a majority of the teacher's signals to children.

Few teachers have developed an extensive set of cues which can be used to signal that desired behaviors should occur. Learning to use many such signals, however, is an important skill in behavior management. When teachers emphasize cues for performance of desired behavior rather than desist signals, they are likely to observe an increase in reinforcable behavior. For example, cueing children to speak in a discussion is more likely to achieve the desired result than reprimanding children who speak out of turn.

Programs of Activities

Relatively little attention has been given to the controlling function of programs or schedules of antecedent events. The controlling effects of specific antecedent events themselves have not been studied in classroom situations in great detail, yet the program of tasks presented to children may significantly affect their academic and social behavior. Because many children with school learning problems have experienced inconsistent and unpredictable environments, it is helpful to follow an invariant daily schedule of activities. The child should be able to predict from day to day the sequence of tasks that will be presented to him. As his academic and social responses improve, the routine can be made more flexible and the child can take a greater part in determining his work schedule.

The principles discussed previously provide a guide for programming specific tasks in sequence (see also chapter 5). Generally, the daily schedule should consist of a series of short work periods followed by brief periods of reward. As behavior improves, reward periods can be decreased in length and scheduled to occur less frequently. Work which can be done individually and without movement about the classroom should be emphasized until appropriate patterns of response are established. Subsequently, academic activities requiring social interaction, free movement about the classroom, and group participation can be increased gradually. The child's least preferred work should be scheduled early in the day and his most preferred work late in the day. A child should not be allowed to go on to the next activity until he has successfully completed the task preceding it. Both the first and last activities of the day should be easily accomplished tasks which are pleasant for the child and encourage him to return to school. These programming suggestions are based on the observation that arrangement of antecedent events builds reinforcement into the schedule and makes the occurrence of reinforceable behavior more likely.

GENERAL BEHAVIOR-MANAGEMENT TECHNIQUES

The behavior principles discussed in this chapter have led to the development of thousands of specific techniques for the management of individuals and groups. The principles can be applied to the unique requirements of each problem situation. Classroom teachers and researchers are constantly devising new techniques for behavior-management problems. A number of specific procedures which have been found useful in resolving common behavior problems are listed in chapter 6. Teachers may find some of the techniques listed in Part Two directly applicable to their classrooms, but we cannot emphasize too strongly that knowledge of the general principles of behavior will give the teacher added flexibility in improvising specific management methods which are most effective for his pupils.

Over the years, behavior principles have led to the development of a number of general methods and procedures. These procedures emphasize a highly structured environment in which *clear* directions, *firm* expectations of performance, and *consistent* follow-through are of primary importance. Teacher interaction with the child is kept task centered, and the child is given many success experiences through individualized assignments and behavioral expectations. Unnecessary verbalizations to the child are kept at a minimum. Academic work is evaluated immediately to provide the child with feedback on his performance. Improvement in behavior indicates that teaching has been successful, while failure to improve is regarded as a signal to try different procedures. Punishment is deemphasized as a behavior-control technique, and shaping appropriate responses by successive approximations is stressed. Emotions are evaluated as by-products of behavior rather than as causes of behavior, and it is assumed that as behavior improves the child's feelings about himself and his attitudes toward others will also improve. This structured, directive approach to behavior management has a long and successful history (see Kauffman, 1976), and its twentieth-century proponents have provided ample description of its value (e.g., Cruickshank, Bentzen, Ratzeburg, & Tannhauser, 1961; Haring & Phillips, 1962; Phillips, 1967).

Newer techniques of behavior management, which have been tested empirically in the classroom, provide even more powerful and positive methods of control of behavior problems (see Hallahan & Kauffman, 1976; O'Leary & O'Leary, 1976). There is no guarantee that teachers using these techniques will be successful in their first attempts to change behavior. As in the acquisition of any set of skills or the solution of problems in any field of human endeavor, repeated trials may be necessary. The teacher who at first is not successful must try to determine the reasons for failure and try again. After all, teachers expect no less of children.

General Techniques for Decreasing Unwanted Behavior

The most common classroom-management problems involve talking without permission, getting out of seat without permission, refusing academic work, failing to complete assignments, hitting other children, having tantrums, and crying. Although the management problem may involve the entire class, one or two pupils frequently account for most of the troublesome behavior.

As we suggested earlier, it is self-defeating for the teacher to try to change many troublesome behaviors at once. Concentrating on the one or two most serious problems is much more likely to be successful. When the targets for behavior change have been selected, it is helpful to collect baseline data so that a valid assessment of change can be made. Then, one or more of several general procedures for decreasing the unwanted behavior can be used.

Extinction

As a procedure, **extinction** refers to preventing a behavior from being reinforced. As a process, it means that behavior which is not reinforced will decrease in strength and eventually cease. When observing maladaptive behavior, the teacher must also observe what happens immediately after the behavior occurs which may serve to reinforce it. If the reinforcer can be withheld, the behavior will be extinguished. A very common reinforcer for inappropriate behavior is the attention of another person. Often the child's misbehavior produces attention from the teacher or his peers, usually in the form of reprimands or reminders to behave appropriately. Frequently his misbehavior is followed by attention on an intermittent schedule, which has the effect of maintaining his unwanted responses at a high rate. When using an extinction procedure, it is necessary to make sure that *all* reinforcers are consistently withheld from the undesirable response so that there is no reinforcement.

Most troublesome classroom behavior does not result in permanent damage to persons or property and, consequently, can be ignored. Ignoring misbehavior completely can be an effective extinction procedure. However, extinction will not be maximally effective unless other, more appropriate, behaviors are strengthened.

When using an extinction procedure, the teacher must be prepared for a temporary increase in the behavior before its strength begins to drop. When the usual reinforcer for a response is not forthcoming, the child will at first attempt to produce the expected consequence by escalating the misbehavior.

Reinforcing Incompatible Behaviors

Incompatible behaviors are behaviors that cannot occur at the same time. Sitting is incompatible with walking about the room. Reading is incompatible with sleeping. But sitting in a chair is *not* incompatible with talking, nor is writing incompatible with standing. A more powerful procedure for decreasing unwanted behavior than merely withholding the reinforcer (extinction) is to reinforce a behavior incompatible with the inappropriate response. For example, the child may not only be ignored whenever he is out of his seat without permission, but may be reinforced for sitting in his chair.

Maladaptive behavior sometimes occurs primarily in certain settings which predispose the child to misbehave. A change in the situation in which the behavior is likely to occur may produce marked improvement. For example, being in close proximity to a certain classmate may be the setting in which a child tends to make distracting noises. Changing the seating arrangement so that the two children are away from each other may decrease the inappropriate behavior significantly. Keeping objects such as dolls, balls, small rubber animals, or other objects in their desks may provide the occasion for children's desk-searching behaviors, unwanted noise making, or arguments. Removal of these objects from children's desks may resolve the management problem.

Some children's academic responses can be greatly increased by simple changes in the way in which tasks are presented to them. Presenting fewer problems per worksheet, presenting single pages cut from a workbook, presenting tasks at a faster pace, heightening the stimulus value of the materials with color cues, amplification, or tactile stimuli—all these strategies may accelerate response rate and decrease dawdling, daydreaming, and other behaviors which interfere with instruction.

The effectiveness of reinforcers is determined in part by events antecedent to the behaviors they follow. The probability that a behavior will occur, and its power as a reinforcing event for other behaviors, is constantly changing. One factor affecting these changes is the passage of time. For example, immediately after a full meal, eating food is a less reinforcing event than after several hours with no food. The child who has been deprived of candy is more likely to work to obtain candy as a reward than one who has continuous access to sweets. Thus, the probability that a behavior will occur can sometimes be decreased by allowing it to occur freely or requiring that it occur frequently, a technique which produces **satiation.** For example, children's tendency to tire quickly of a formerly prohibited activity once restrictions are removed is well known.

Forcing a child to behave in a given manner usually produces unpleasant emotional responses. Allowing the behavior to occur freely is usually preferable to forcing repetition of the undesirable response. For example, the child prone to write socially unacceptable four-letter words on the walls may be permitted (not forced) to write them freely on a special sheet of paper. Some prudent restaurant owners control the defacement of their restroom walls by providing chalkboards for graffiti.

Punishment

Historically, American public education has stressed the use of punishment to suppress undesirable behavior, including the use of ridicule and, sometimes, the infliction of physical pain. A behavior-modification approach focuses on positive rather than punitive control (Skinner, 1971). Most classroom behavior problems can be solved without the use of punishment. Excepting cases in which the maladaptive behavior is a serious threat to the health and safety of another person or the child himself, other means of reducing behavior problems should always be tried first. In the few cases in which punishment is necessary, remember that "punishment is not synonymous with physical pain or bodily harm and does not necessarily result in emotional responses" (Hall, Axelrod, Foundopoulos, Shellman, Campbell, & Cranston, 1971, p. 25).

As we have already said, punishment is defined as the systematic use of consequences to decrease the strength of a behavior. It may involve presenting an aversive consequence (negative reinforcer) or removing a rewarding consequence (positive reinforcer) contingent upon the behavior. Thus the contingent removal of teacher attention is an effective punishment technique for many young children. The contingent removal of earned rewards or token reinforcers can also be effective punishment, but this technique must be used with caution to avoid unfair treatment. In some cases, rewards may be presented on a noncontingent basis and then removed contingent upon inappropriate behavior. For example, the child may be given 10 token reinforcers at the beginning of a period, and one may be taken away each time he talks out during the class. Restriction of activity or removal of privileges (being first in line, choosing the game for the day, permission to visit the library, etc.) may also serve as punishment. Frequently, public recording of the maladaptive behavior is sufficient to reduce the problem. "No!" spoken in a loud, firm voice contingent upon the behavior will often decrease its frequency.

A procedure which combines the features of both types of punishment (withdrawal of rewarding stimuli and presentation of aversive conditions) is **time-out.** Time-out refers to a time when reinforcement is not available on any terms; it does *not* mean merely time out of the classroom or time out of the teacher's sight. Unless there is an established, on-going program of positive reinforcement, it is impossible to use a time-out procedure effectively (Gast & Nelson, 1977). When used correctly, time-out involves removing the child from a positively reinforcing situation, such as simply turning away from the child and avoiding any contact with him for a specified time period (usually 30 to 60 seconds) or until he stops his misbehavior. When the child is being managed in a group rather than on a one-to-one basis, other uncomplicated time-out techniques can be used. For example, if a token reinforcement system is being used, time-out may mean that the child cannot earn tokens for a brief specified time period (e.g., 5 minutes). If the child is engaged in a pleasurable play activity when the maladaptive behavior occurs, an effective time-out procedure may be to require the child to stop the activity or "sit out" for a specific length of time (usually 3 to 5 minutes).

Occasionally it is helpful to isolate the child from the teacher and his peers for a brief interval. Ideally, the time-out area to which the child is restricted should be a small, lighted room containing only a chair. The room should not contain objects or other stimuli which might be interesting to the child. Spending more than 1 or 2 minutes in such a room is aversive for most children. When isolation in such a room is used, time-out involves not only removal from a reinforcing environment (the classroom) but presentation of an aversive environment. Special care must be taken to avoid placing the child in a frightening or dangerous situation. Unlighted, frightening, or dangerous isolation rooms cannot be defended ethically, and their use increases the teacher's liability (see Gast & Nelson, 1977; in press).

When an ideal time-out room is not available, one may be improvised by screening off a corner of the classroom. The temptation to place a child in the hallway or send him to the principal's office must be resisted, as these places are likely to provide many interesting and reinforcing events. If the child encounters interesting stimuli during time-out, the value of isolation as an aversive technique is lost.

When punishment is used to suppress undesirable behavior, it will be most effective if its use is restricted to occurrences of a specific behavior. Some teachers tolerate misbehavior until their patience wears so thin that they explode with punitive action for a variety of behaviors. This is clearly ineffective. To be maximally effective, punishment should be administered unemotionally and consistently. *Immediate* action is necessary to prevent reinforcement of the behavior before punishment occurs. Delayed punishment will be as ineffective as delayed reinforcing consequences.

Kauffman (1977), MacMillan, Forness, and Trumbull (1973), and O'Leary and O'Leary (1972) have provided guidelines for using punishment in the classroom. In general, these guidelines indicate that punishment should be:
1. Used only when positive methods have failed and allowing the child to continue his behavior will result in more suffering than the punishment causes;
2. Administered by persons who are warm and loving in their relationship with the child as long as his behavior is acceptable;
3. Administered matter-of-factly, without anger, threats, moralizing, or ill temper after the punishment is over;
4. Administered fairly, consistently, and immediately for specific behaviors that the child knew would result in punishment;
5. Reasonable in intensity and, whenever possible, related to the misdeed (e.g., repairing what was destroyed).

As Kauffman (1977) has stated, "Behavior modification literature clearly supports the assertion that punishment, when carefully and appropriately administered, can be a humane and effective technique for controlling misbehavior. . . . Used clumsily, vindictively, or with malice, punishment is the behavior modifier's nemesis" (p. 195).

General Techniques for Increasing Good Behavior

Teachers must establish priorities for teaching good behavior as well as for reducing behavior problems. After teachers have determined the most important things for their students to learn, they must select effective methods for teaching those skills. At least five alternative general techniques for increasing desirable behavior are available to every teacher.

Stating Rules, Praising Good Behavior, and Ignoring Inappropriate Behavior

Efficient behavior management in the classroom seems to consist of at least three basic techniques which must be used in combination to be most effective (Madsen et al., 1968). Rules for conduct in the classroom must be clearly and positively stated. Children must know how they *are* to behave. It may be helpful to post rules in a conspicuous place in the classroom and review them periodically. Rules alone, however, are not likely to produce appropriate behavior. They are antecedent events which are of little value without the systematic application of consequences for behavior related to the rules.

Teacher attention and praise for rule-following behavior are powerful positive consequences for most children. The teacher must seek out those children displaying appropriate behavior and praise them. In this way, the teacher calls attention to appropriate models and offers vicarious reinforcement for other class members. Teacher attention may consist of nearness or proximity to the child, a touch on the shoulder, assistance with academic work, a wink, or any other sign of recognition. Praise can be given by a smile, a nod of approval, a "happy face" drawn on the child's paper, other nonverbal signals of approval, and a variety of verbal statements. When verbal praise is given, indicate specifically what the child is doing that is praiseworthy. "I'm glad you've started your work already" is preferable as a praise statement to "You're being a good boy this morning," or "Agnes, you're a doll."

In addition to establishing rules and "catching the children being good," ignoring inappropriate behavior will probably increase classroom control. The fallacy of attempting to control misbehavior primarily by criticism or "talking it through" has already been discussed. The more skillful the teacher becomes at totally withdrawing attention from misbehaving children, the more likely he will achieve efficient classroom management.

Criticizing, nagging, rebuking, punishing, and other negative interactions are more tiring than positive interactions such as praising, complimenting, approving, and thanking. This is true whether you are on the giving side or on the receiving end of the transaction. At the same time, negative interactions seem more likely to occur when an individual's energy is depleted. Consequently, teachers who do not waste their energy, and the energy of their students, by attending to misbehavior may successfully avoid a dangerous spiral of unpleasant behavior.

Successful use of this technique depends on the application of the three elements: rules, praise, and ignoring. Without rules, children will not know how to behave. Without teacher attention and praise for good behavior, they will not learn to follow the rules. But without teacher attention as a consequence, misbehavior will likely subside.

Rewarding Approximations

Few complex behaviors are learned in a day. Acquisition of a complex skill requires repeated trials over a period of days, weeks, months, or even years.

The child whose expectation turns to disappointment when he does not learn to read a book the first day of school does not know how learning takes place. The teacher who expects a disturbing child to become a model of perfection immediately will be disappointed because he has lost sight of the principle of behavior shaping. Looking for and rewarding small improvements in behavior is one key to successful teaching. If the teacher waits for perfection, he will probably never have an opportunity to reinforce the child's behavior. If he identifies and reinforces successive approximations of his goal for the child, he will likely see gradual but steady improvements in behavior. Before embarking on a behavior-management program, the teacher should be able to state what actions of the child will constitute improvement.

Strengthening Reinforcers

Children vary greatly in their behavioral responsiveness to reinforcers. Traditional social reinforcers, such as attention and praise, are sufficient to control the classroom behavior of most children. For others it is necessary to provide more effective consequences. This may mean using food, money, toys, personal-care items, special privileges, or special activities as reinforcers (see chapter 6, pp. 141-43, for a list of possible reinforcers). A subsequent event which is not a reinforcer is of no value in teaching appropriate behavior. *It is essential that the teacher find* **what each child will work for** *and employ those things as reinforcers*. Consequences that are more natural should always be preferred to those which are more contrived or artificial. If the teacher must employ more extrinsic or primitive rewards than are necessary for most children, little is to be gained by appealing to the child's "love of learning," lamenting his lack of "maturity," or disparaging his acquisitiveness. Whenever a teacher is unsuccessful in obtaining the responses he wants a child to emit, he should consider the possibility of increasing the strength of the reward. The strength of reinforcers may be determined by observing what children prefer, asking them what they would like to work for, or providing a consequence for behavior and observing its effect. In addition to strengthening the reinforcers themselves, it is often helpful to make the consequences of behavior more explicit by using a contingency contract or establishing a system of token reinforcement.

Making Reinforcement More Immediate

Delayed rewards are effective only for individuals who have a high level of self-control. Children with school learning problems seldom have learned the self-control necessary to work for distant reinforcers. They must be taught the self-control which brings their behavior under the control of future consequences. Until the complex task of self-control is taught, their behavior will remain almost exclusively under the control of immediate environmental consequences. Therefore, a technique for increasing appropriate behavior is to move the reinforcers closer in time to occurrence of the behavior. In general, the sooner a child is allowed to have his reward after behaving appropriately, the more successful the teacher will be. A token reinforcement system helps to reduce the tactical problems of delivering immediate rewards. Tokens can be given immediately after an appropriate behavior without interrupting class-room routine.

Varying the Schedule of Reinforcement

Schedules of reinforcement appear to be as important in behavioral change as the reinforcers themselves. The schedule by which a reinforcer is adminis-tered often determines its power. Although some behaviors apparently are acquired with intermittent reinforcement, learning is more likely to occur when *every* response is reinforced. Continuous reinforcement is not, however, an efficient schedule for maintaining behavior. Furthermore, change to an inter-mittent schedule may produce marked acceleration in response rates. Rein-forcement on a variable ratio or variable interval schedule will maintain a steadier rate of behavior than reinforcement on a fixed ratio or fixed interval. Consequently, the teacher must always choose a schedule of reinforcement which fits his teaching objectives and the child's level of learning. When the child is not responding to a behavior-modification procedure, an appropriate change in the schedule of reinforcement may produce the desired results. It is not uncommon to find that learning has not been acquired because reinforce-ment has been too infrequent or that learning has not been maintained be-cause of failure to shift gradually to an intermittent schedule.

Changing Antecedent Events

Antecedent events which may be modified to produce behavioral change include rules, tasks, cues, models, and setting events. Establishing positive rules for behavior has already been discussed. The tasks presented to chil-dren must be carefully prepared and presented if other elements of behavior management are to be effective (see chapter 4). For children with school learning problems, you may need an individualized instructional program. Chapter 3 provides principles of academic remediation.

Cues and models may be presented for social-emotional as well as academic behavior. The performance of many behaviors can be regulated by appropriate prompts or cues. Normal adults program cues for their own behav-ior by using watches, notes, hand signals, grocery lists, flashing lights, met-ronomes, bells, and a wide variety of other devices. Children's classroom behavior and academic performance often fall short of teacher expectations because the children have no clear cues indicating how, when, or where they are to behave. The child who talks out may do so because the teacher has not developed clear, consistent signals for permission to speak. Children with auditory learning difficulties may have difficulty understanding the verbal prompts of the teacher, especially if the teacher ververbalizes instructions. Sometimes children have difficulty reading the teacher's cues because the postural, gestural, intonational, and verbal signals given by the teacher are not consistent. For example, a teacher may call a child's name, indicating that he is to make a verbal response, but fail to look at the child or turn away. For the child with a history of acting-out behavior or learning deficits, the teacher may need to use more dramatic and abbreviated prompts. Withdrawn children, on the other hand, may respond more readily to subtle prompts.

A behavioral model is invaluable in teaching. When a teacher is attempting to help a child acquire a new skill, he must provide many demonstrations of the final performance. Otherwise, he risks inefficient teaching or needless attention to detail in shaping behavior (see Cullinan et al., 1975). The child who consistently hears a good language model is much more easily taught appropriate language patterns than one who is exposed frequently to models of poor language.

Changes in antecedent events can be used to decrease unwanted behavior. Providing a quiet, uncluttered place to work, attractive and interesting materials, and individualized tasks at which the child can be highly successful will increase learning. Study booths or "offices" in which a child may work without the distraction of other classroom activity may increase the child's attention to the task at hand.

Deprivation of reinforcers, the inverse of satiation, may be used to increase the reinforcing potential of consequences for good behavior. When the child has been deprived of a reinforcer for a period of time, he is more likely to work to obtain it. For example, a child is more likely to work for the privilege of writing on the chalkboard if it is offered as a consequence for good behavior when he has not had the opportunity for several hours. Reinforcement should be offered frequently, but in relatively small amounts so the child does not get satiated.

Changing the program or schedule of antecedent events may be a technique for increasing good behavior. The teacher who would like the child to talk only when called on in class discussions must remember to cue his behavior by calling on him frequently. The child who has completed an academic task can make more responses only when additional tasks are presented. Making certain that the children have ample opportunities to respond appropriately is an essential element of behavior management.

General Techniques for Maintaining Behavioral Gains

Behaviors learned are not necessarily skills retained. Reinforcement is necessary to maintain behavior as well as to acquire it. Teaching a child a new behavior only to see it forgotten or not applied is both inefficient and disheartening. The ultimate goal of classroom management should be self-controlled, highly motivated learners. When artificial or obvious contingencies of reinforcement are necessary to control an individual's behavior, he is perceived as lacking self-control; if consequences native to the individual's environment produce appropriate behavior, he is said to be in control of himself. When frequent reinforcement is necessary to maintain behavior, the child is thought to lack motivation; if he continues to behave as desired under contingencies which result in a low frequency of reinforcement, he is considered highly motivated. Every teacher should try to maintain appropriate behavior by infrequently using reinforcement in the child's natural environment. At least four general techniques for achieving this goal are available (see also Kazdin, 1975).

Gradually Reducing Reinforcement

The frequency and amount of reinforcement may be varied to increase good behavior. After a behavior is learned, reinforcement should be intermittent rather than continuous to make the behavior more resistant to extinction. The shift to intermittent reinforcement must be gradual, and occasional reinforcement of the behavior must continue or the response may be extinguished. Gradual reduction of the frequency of reinforcement will increase the likelihood that the child will adopt a "normal" motivational pattern.

Gradually Delaying Reinforcement

Immediate reinforcement is essential for effective modification of behavior. Once a child has learned a behavior, delayed reinforcement can be effective for maintenance; but you must provide feedback to the child regarding his progress in earning the reinforcer. A child is not likely to continue working toward a long-term goal without recognition of intermediate accomplishments. Token reinforcement is particularly well-suited to the successful use of delayed reinforcement because the child can observe the accumulation of tokens as an immediate consequence. As the child is able to work for rewards which are delayed for a longer time, he will more closely approximate the motivational model of the teacher.

Gradually Fading Artificial to Natural Reinforcers

Natural reinforcers are those that can be viewed as native to the environment of the child, assuming that his environment is not pathological. Thus, tokens, toys, money, candy, and other reinforcers contrived for therapeutic ends may be considered artificial because they are not ordinarily used as classroom consequences. Teacher attention, praise, grades, records of progress, special activities, and so on, are natural reinforcers in that good teachers ordinarily provide such consequences. Natural reinforcers have two distinct advantages over artificial reinforcers: (a) they occur in a wider range of environments, and (b) they are less obvious to the casual observer. As remediation of the child's behavioral deficits progresses, a gradual shift should also occur from artificial, material rewards to natural, social rewards. Remember, however, that reinforcers are natural or artificial in terms of specific behaviors and situations. The successful teacher continues in his profession for both material and social rewards. If either is lacking, that is, if the teacher never receives social reinforcement from his pupils or if his pay is terminated, he will not continue to teach. Material rewards for children's appropriate behavior are sometimes essential, but the emphasis should be on social rewards.

Teaching Self-Control Behaviors

Response to natural reinforcers is not the only characteristic of self-control. Haring and Whelan (1965) have detailed the stages through which a child passes in remediation of maladaptive behaviors. The final stage is one of integration, in which the child not only observes the relationship between his behavior and its consequences but also begins to control his own reinforcers to further improve his behavior. Children can be taught to manage their own behavior through systematic development and reinforcement of the behaviors which constitute self-control. The child who selects an appropriate task for himself, makes a realistic and positive statement about himself or his performance, or establishes his own contingency of reinforcement offers the teacher a clear opportunity for reinforcement of self-control. Failure to respond to such behavior with a positive social consequence is costly for everyone concerned with the child's success as a learner.

Recently, behavior modifiers have become increasingly interested in the cognitive aspects of self-control and have begun to teach children with learning and behavior problems to talk to themselves in order to control their responses (see Bornstein & Quevillon, 1976; Mahoney, 1974; Meichenbaum & Goodman, 1971).

Beyond the Classroom

The teacher does not control all of the consequences for children's behavior. Parents, siblings, other teachers, the school principal, peers, or acquaintances in the community may be able to provide very powerful reinforcers for the child. Teachers will increase their effectiveness as modifiers of behavior if they enlist the aid of other people who control the child's rewards. The coach, the industrial arts teacher, the principal, the janitor, or the cook often can offer powerful school-related incentives for the child. If they agree to assist in providing contingent rewards, they can contribute significantly to modification of the child's behavior.

Other than the classroom teacher, the principal has the greatest potential effect on children's behavior in school. He is responsible for the emotional climate of the school, whether it emphasizes punitive control or the positive control of rewards. The principal's support of the teacher's efforts to establish a climate of positive control may make the difference between success and failure in the implementation of behavior-modification techniques. The principal who responds primarily to misbehavior seems doomed to an ever-widening spiral of unpleasant interactions. The teacher who arranges to send children to the principal for compliments rather than criticism, pats on the back rather than spanks, rewards rather than punishment, can help the principal focus on positive control and increase his own options for the use of positive consequences.

Behavior-modification techniques can easily be taught to parents and other persons outside the school environment (Kazdin, 1975; Krumboltz & Krumboltz, 1972; Madsen & Madsen, 1972). There is little empirical evidence, however, that behavioral improvement at school will necessarily result in positive changes outside the classroom, or vice versa (Wahler, 1969). Remediation should be a joint effort of parents and teachers. Parental use of behavior-modification techniques can contribute significantly to the acquisition and maintenance of learning.

LEVELS OF APPLICATION OF BEHAVIOR PRINCIPLES

Like an artisan selecting tools, the teacher must select techniques for changing behavior. However, just as the tool does not determine the skill of the artisan, the behavior-management technique does not make a good teacher. Behavior-modification techniques must be viewed as precision instruments— useless in the hands of the incompetent and invaluable in the hands of a master. The behavior principles discussed in this chapter have produced numerous techniques which can be applied with varying degrees of precision and sophistication. At least three levels of application can be defined.

Structured Classroom

Good teachers have used behavior principles for centuries (see Kauffman, 1976; Lane, 1976). It is not uncommon for the experienced teacher to remark about behavior modification, "But I've been doing that for years!" When an experienced teacher is having classroom-management problems despite knowledge of basic principles, it is often because he has not applied them consistently and systematically.

The principles of work before play, contingent rewards for good behavior, consistency, firmness, fairness, clarity of instructions, and individualization of expectations seem to be minimum requirements for successful teaching. When these underlying principles of behavior management are employed systematically, a high degree of "structure" is introduced into the classroom.

This structure, or predictability of the classroom environment, has been found to have a therapeutic effect on children's social-emotional and academic behavior (Cruickshank et al., 1961; Haring & Phillips, 1962; Phillips, 1967). The structured classroom makes systematic use of most of the behavior principles discussed in this chapter, but is a more intuitive, less technological level of application than methods currently being researched. A major difference between the structured classroom and more sophisticated levels of application is its lack of emphasis on daily recording of specific behaviors.

Behavior Technology

At a second level of application, greater precision is employed in manipulating environmental variables and monitoring behavioral change. The structured classroom concept is extended to include more explicit contingencies of reinforcement and daily recording of behaviors (Haring & Phillips, 1972; Haring & Schiefelbusch, 1976; Lovitt, 1977). Teachers applying behavior principles at this level are interested in precise measurement of the effects of their teaching procedures on children's behavior. Although it is possible to use behavior principles successfully at a less sophisticated level, teachers should strive to be as precise as possible in teaching and evaluating learning. The application of behavior principles at this level may not be as simple as it first appears (Birnbrauer, Burchard, & Burchard, 1970), but the competent teacher is not likely to find it extremely difficult to learn the use of behavior technology.

Research Designs

Some teachers will want to develop skills in the scientific analysis of behavior change. Many teachers are capable of using basic research designs to explore the extent of their control over the variables influencing learning. Research designs allow the teacher to state with greater confidence whether his teaching is responsible for changes in his pupils' behavior. The efficacy of various teaching procedures can also be compared by using research methods. Discussion of specific research designs is beyond the scope of this chapter, but the teacher who has mastered the basic elements of behavior technology may want to extend his use of behavior principles to more scientific applications (see Gelfand & Hartmann, 1975; Kazdin, 1975).

LIMITATIONS OF BEHAVIOR MODIFICATION

It would be presumptuous to assert that a behavior-modification approach to classroom management represents a limitless solution to educational problems. Likewise, it would be incredibly naive to assume that all intervention approaches to school learning problems are equally valid or useful. No other approach is supported by the empirical research which undergirds behavior modification. Of the alternatives available to classroom teachers, we believe that a behavior-modification strategy is the best point of departure. Certainly, it is important to keep in mind that behavior modification is only a tool that will allow a teacher to serve children's needs more effectively *if* that teacher is sensitively attuned to children as human beings. Behavior modification techniques can be (and sometimes are) used mindlessly to squelch children's individuality or to teach meaningless or unimportant skills. In addition to competence in the application of behavior principles, teachers need skills in listening and talking to children, knowledge of curriculum, and awareness of how they relate to children as persons.

SUMMARY

Behavior modification involves the systematic manipulation of environmental events to produce specific change in observable behavior. The teacher may control events which occur before, during, and after a problem behavior to modify its occurrence. The teacher confronted with a classroom-management problem must first define the problem behavior as an observable action of the child. An objective and reliable baseline record of occurrences of the behavior should be obtained and plotted on a graph. After a baseline has been established, a wide variety of intervention techniques designed to increase or decrease the behavior may be used. General procedures for decreasing undesirable behavior include extinction, reinforcement of incompatible behaviors, changing stimuli which precede the behavior, and punishment. Some general techniques for increasing good behavior include stating rules, praising good behavior, ignoring misbehavior, rewarding approximations, strengthening reinforcers, making reinforcement more immediate, varying the schedule of reinforcement, and changing tasks, cues, and models presented to the child. Behavioral gains can be maintained by gradually reducing the frequency of reinforcement, delaying reinforcement, fading from artificial to natural reinforcers, and teaching self-control behaviors. To be most effective, behavior modification should be extended to the home and other settings outside the classroom. Although behavior modification can be misused and is not a panacea, its effectiveness is supported by more scientific research in the laboratory and classroom than any other approach to behavior management.

3
Principles of
Academic Remediation

Principles of Academic Remediation

Remediating academic difficulties often requires personalized instruction and the use of specialized materials and techniques. Consequently, special teachers, rather than regular classroom teachers, have commonly been assigned the task of remediating the vast majority of school learning problems (Kirk, 1972). We believe, however, that many of the instructional methods employed by remedial specialists can be used in the regular classroom. Furthermore, the principles that apply to the remediation of academic problems are not limited to the special class. The principles discussed in this chapter, and the teaching suggestions outlined in Part Two, are intended for use in both the regular classroom and in specialized remedial situations.

VARIETY OF ASSESSMENT PROCEDURES

Successful instructional programming for children with learning problems depends upon a thorough appraisal of each child's specific learning strengths and weaknesses. Assessment procedures are an essential part of the remedial process, even though individual circumstances and the type of program will affect exactly what is included in the diagnosis, which assessment procedures are used, who will be involved in the process, and when and where the evaluation will take place (Gilliland, 1974).

Unfortunately, the concept of diagnosis has been misunderstood and inappropriately implemented in many schools. Assessment has often been viewed as a very structured and formal situation where the child is given a battery of highly specialized, standardized tests. Generally, these formal evaluations within a school occur in settings other than the regular classroom; and, according to Hammill (1971), the tests are usually administered by an individual other than the person who is actually teaching the child. The assessment data are most often integrated into a written report which is subsequently shared with the classroom teacher and parents.

In contrast to these procedures, we believe that assessment should be an on-going part of the teaching process, one in which the teacher has a responsible and central role. Testing instruments need not be so highly specialized that teachers are excluded from various diagnostic procedures. It seems more reasonable to have teachers play an active assessment role since most teachers are in the best position for appraising children's educational problems (Smith & Neisworth, 1969).

In addition to actively involving the teacher in the assessment process, we believe that a wide variety of techniques should be used to assess children with learning problems. The large number of assessment procedures available are listed in Table 3-1. Three of the more widely used approaches are also discussed below.

Table 3-1
Assessment Techniques

A. Objective tests and standardized measures

1. Standardized tests and measures.
   a. Achievement tests.
   b. Mental and intelligence tests.
   c. Tests of motor skills and abilities.
   d. Aptitude and readiness tests.
   e. Physiological measures and medical examinations.
   f. Personality and adjustment tests.
   g. Interest inventories and attitude scales.
2. Unstandardized short-answer objective tests.
   a. Simple recall or free response tests.
   b. Completion tests.
   c. Alternate response tests.
   d. Multiple choice tests.
   e. Matching tests.
3. Improved essay types of tests consisting of questions so formulated that they can be scored on a fairly objective basis.
4. Scales for analyzing and rating a performance or a product.
5. Tests involving evaluation of responses using projective methods.

B. Evaluation of behavior by less formal procedures

1. Problem-situation tests.
   a. Direct experience.
      (1) Experiment to be performed.
      (2) Actual life situation to be met.
   b. Indirect approach.
      (1) Improved essay-type examinations.
      (2) Expressing judgments about described situations.
      (3) "What would you do?"
2. Behavior records concerning inand out-of-school activities.
   a. Controlled situations.
      (1) Use of checklists, rating scales, score cards, codes for evaluating personality traits, behavior, attitudes, opinions, interests, and so on.
      (2) Self-rating devices, "Guess-Who?"
      (3) Time studies of attention, activities.
      (4) Photographs and motion pictures.
      (5) Stenographic reports.
      (6) Dictaphone and tape recordings.
   b. Uncontrolled situations.
      (1) Log or diary; autobiographical reports.
      (2) Anecdotal records; behavior journals.
      (3) Records of libraries, police, welfare agencies, and so on.
      (4) Still or motion pictures.
      (5) Tape recordings.
3. Inventories and questionnaires of work habits, interests, activities, associates, and the like.

4. Interviews, conferences, personal reports.
   a. With the individual learner himself.
   b. With others, such as parents or associates.
5. Analysis and evaluation of a creative act or product, such as a poem, music, constructions, and so forth.
6. Sociometric procedures for studying group relationships.
7. Evaluation of reactions using projective and expressive techniques.
   a. Psychodrama and play technics.
   b. Free-association tests.
   c. Interpretation of reactions to selected pictures and drawings.
   d. Interpretation of free oral and written expression.
   e. Interpretation of artistic and constructive products.

Source: From *The Diagnosis and Treatment of Learning Difficulties* by Leo J. Brueckner and Guy L. Bond, 1955, 8-10. © 1955 by Prentice-Hall, Inc. Reprinted by permission.

Observation

A large part of the information which will eventually be utilized in planning an instructional program for children with learning problems can often come from observations of the child during daily classroom activities. We feel that regular classroom teachers are provided many different opportunities throughout a school day to observe each child's academic skills. Wallace and Larsen (1978) note that oral reading periods, for example, provide an excellent time to observe a child's word analysis, word recognition, or reading comprehension skills. Similarly, many different language skills can be observed during a child's conversation with other children, during question and answer sessions, and in oral discussion periods.

According to Cartwright and Cartwright (1974), the first step in the process of observation is to *determine the purpose* for observing a particular child. Deciding the types of word analysis techniques a certain child uses might be the teacher's purpose, while in another case the teacher might be interested in the number of times a child is out of his seat without permission during a specified length of time. Once the purpose for observation is determined, Cartwright and Cartwright (1974) suggest that the following guidelines must also be considered:

1. Who will make the observation,
2. Who or what will be observed,
3. Where the observation will take place,
4. When the observation will occur,
5. How the observation will be recorded. (p. 46)

Among the many different approaches to observation, anecdotal recordings have probably been the most widely used in the past. Specific behavioral events are usually described in some detail in anecdotal records. More recently, however, a variety of time-sampling techniques have been used in observing different aspects of children's behavior. Time-sample techniques allow the teacher to determine how often a behavior is occurring during a specified time interval. The teacher who is interested in how often a child is talking out of turn during the social studies period, for example, would probably find a time-sampling technique quite useful.

Rating scales and checklists can also be used during observation periods to help focus the observer's attention on specific behaviors. Nevertheless, we have found that rating scales and checklists tend to limit the observer to the behaviors included on the list. Furthermore, ratings are somewhat difficult to translate into specific instructional practices.

Although we believe that observational data should be included as a part of the total assessment process, there are a number of limitations of observation. In particular, Strang (1969) notes that the potential for bias on the part of the observer should be strongly considered. Some individuals may only look for what is already in their minds about the child. In addition, observers should be careful in interpreting observational data since most observations are only a *sample* of a student's behavior. Finally, observations should be taken in a variety of situations and during differing time periods to validate the behaviors which are observed.

Informal Tests

In addition to the observational data obtained through daily interactions with the child, it is often necessary to administer informal, teacher-made tests (Lerner, 1976). Many informal tests are administered to supplement the information obtained from observation and standardized tests. These specific, task-oriented, informal tests often provide evaluative teaching data which are more valuable than the data obtained through more formalized testing procedures. Most informal tests are also administered by the teacher in the classroom.

Informal, teacher-made tests can be used to assess a wide variety of both specific and broad-range skills. A child's knowledge of certain blends, for example, may be measured by an informal test. On the other hand, a broader range of skills (e.g., knowledge of time tables, phonics knowledge, etc.) can also be evaluated through informal testing. A number of examples of informal tests are provided in Table 3-2. Additional informal tests are listed for each diagnostic question in Part Two of this book.

Informal tests are not intended to be complicated, expensive, or time-consuming. Most of these tests are teacher-made and teacher-administered, and the information obtained is typically intended to provide the teacher with planning data for the instructional needs of individual students. Some of the instruments from which informal tests may be adapted include: (a) seatwork exercises emphasizing *one* specific task, (b) orally administered exercises, (c)

Table 3-2
Examples of Informal Tests

Syllables

Objective: To assess knowledge of syllables.
Directions: Ask the child to draw a line between the syllables.

1.	program	6.	before
2.	sister	7.	letter
3.	little	8.	singing
4.	reread	9.	without
5.	number	10.	concert

Decimals

Objective: To assess knowledge of multiplication of decimals.
Directions: Direct the child to complete the following arithmetic problems.

$$\begin{array}{ccccc} .095 & .59 & .002 & .33 & .70 \\ \underline{\times\ .2} & \underline{\times .3} & \underline{\times .7} & \underline{\times .5} & \underline{\times .7} \end{array}$$

$$\begin{array}{ccccc} .86 & .731 & .662 & .90 & .52 \\ \underline{\times .40} & \underline{\times .59} & \underline{\times .84} & \underline{\times .36} & \underline{\times .53} \end{array}$$

informal teaching lessons assessing various skills, and (d) individually administered written assignments.

We believe that informal tests are uniquely suited to the needs of children with learning problems because of the similarity to on-going instructional programs, the simplicity of design, ease of administration, and the direct involvement of the teacher in the assessment process. Nevertheless, informal tests must be carefully constructed and administered. According to Karlin (1971), informal test items should be carefully selected and sequenced in order of difficulty. In addition, Charles (1976) suggests that relatively simple language must be used in informal tests, along with very concise directions.

Formal Tests

In addition to observational data and informal testing procedures, teachers may also need the supportive data provided by formal published tests. Although formal tests have been widely used in education for a long time, we believe that teachers nevertheless must be careful in selecting various published tests because of the large number of poorly constructed tests presently available on the commercial market. Furthermore, according to Kaluger and Kolson (1978), most formalized tests will provide the teacher with little more than he already knows, especially if informal tests have been accurately administered.

The selection of a formal test should involve very careful planning on the part of the teacher. Most importantly, the teacher should know the specific purpose for administering a test. In addition, the teacher should also know how the information obtained from the test will be used. It is frustrating and inefficient for both the teacher and the child to spend time on assessment instruments that provide little in the way of specific instructional information. A number of additional considerations in selecting published tests for use with children with learning difficulties are discussed by Strang (1969).

Although a significant advantage of standardized tests is the ability to compare a child with the normative sample of a test, it is nonetheless important that test findings not be overgeneralized. Ekwall (1976), for example, points out that many individual placement decisions are made from group standardized tests. He feels that for any individual, group test scores are often so unreliable that it is difficult to place any real confidence in the results.

Finally, when a standardized test is administered, the teacher should administer all aspects of the evaluation within his capabilities. Because formal testing is likely to involve direct individual interaction with the child, teachers sometimes find it difficult to schedule the time for it. Consequently, formal testing is often left to someone other than the teacher. However, we believe that the teacher should attempt to schedule the evaluation during a quiet time in the class, before or after school, or during recess.

A last note involves the administration of more exacting tests that require specific training in interpretation and analysis. It may be necessary to employ a qualified examiner who is trained in the areas of personality or intelligence testing. When this type of service is warranted, the results of these tests should be viewed in conjunction with the data previously obtained by the teacher. Too often, teachers do not use the information accumulated by others because of its indirect implications for instructional programs (Hewett, 1968). There should be closer coordination between informal teacher evaluations and formal test results. Individuals working together should be able to evaluate more accurately the specific instructional needs of children experiencing learning problems in school.

Remediation is likely to be successful only when it is based upon adequate evaluation of the child. Clearly, the best evaluation is ineffectual if the results are not used in planning instructional programs.

USING ASSESSMENT DATA FOR PLANNING INSTRUCTION

In many schools, testing seems to have become an end in itself rather than a means to planning an instructional program. The emphasis upon exacting scores (e.g., grade-level scores, age equivalents, percentiles, etc.) has contributed to the incorrect usage of test results. Few teachers seem to remember that the purpose of educational assessment is to provide data to be used in developing an instructional program for individual children. Consequently, the important information that led to the formulation of the grade or age score is often overlooked.

We obviously believe that using informal tests is one solution for handling the problem of inappropriate test scores. The information pertaining to specific skills which is usually obtained from informal tests provides the teacher with information about what the child can and cannot do in terms of actual academic behaviors. For example, it certainly is instructionally useful to know that John has mastered the names of all the letters of the alphabet, except *c* and *g,* and that he knows only the sounds of the letters /a/ and /m/. In contrast, it is of little value to know that he reads at the equivalent grade level of 1.2. The descriptive information obtained from informal tests actually provides the teacher with basic data for planning and implementing an instructional program. On the basis of this information, teachers can decide *what* needs to be taught, and eventually, with additional information, *how* it should be taught (Stephens, 1975).

The teaching information usually provided by informal evaluation can also be obtained from some formal published tests (Woolbright, 1971). However, administrators must go beyond resulting grade scores or percentiles to the child's actual responses for individual test items (Wallace & Larsen, 1978). In this way, the results are informally studied and analyzed. The information obtained can then be applied to instructional strategies and on-going programs of remediation. The integration of formal test information into instructional practices is illustrated in the case of David.

David

David was a 10-year-old youngster experiencing written language problems and reading difficulties. His teacher also reported that David was having great difficulty in following directions and generally attending in class. David was given the **Gates-McKillop Reading Diagnostic Test** (Gates & McKillop, 1962) with the following results: David knew all of the letter sounds except the short /o/. With regard to the names of the letters, David said /P/ for capital /B/. For the lowercase letters, he called l for i and p for q. He was particularly weak on discriminating final letter sounds, calling /f/ for /v/, /l/ for /k/, /p/ for /b/, /n/ for /b/.

On the Oral Reading subtest, he tended to omit and mispronounce words. He read slowly with poor phrasing and emphasis in a low, often indistinct voice. He appeared to depend mainly on a combination of initial letter sounds and general configuration to attack a word, frequently skipping unfamiliar words. Infrequently, he would name the letters in attacking a word. Finally, on the Spelling subtest, David usually guessed at the remainder of the word after correctly saying the initial sound.

The results of the informal measures and the **Gates-McKillop** provided the teacher with a basis for initiating an instructional program. In David's case, the teacher used a language-experience approach to develop sight vocabulary, word analysis skills, and writing ability. Telephone conversations aided in developing his attending and listening skills. The teacher also used the

Language Master to develop a sight vocabulary and work on medial and final letter combinations. Some of the teaching activities listed in chapter 8 under initial and final letters were used to teach this particular skill.

The *Gates-McKillop Reading Diagnostic Test* is one example of a standardized test that provides the user with "teachable" information. Many other standardized tests (as listed in Part Two) can also be used if the administrator is willing to analyze a test carefully for the needed instructional information. Very often, the teacher must translate test information into instructional processes, since most tests provide few guidelines for this particular purpose. However, this requirement certainly does not preclude using test results for planning a program of remediation. The teacher must know and obtain all the information important for planning an instructional program for each child.

Finally, an important but often overlooked facet of evaluation is the information that clearly points to a child's strengths. What a child *can* do is as important in planning a program as what a child cannot do or does poorly. Learning strengths exhibited both in the classroom and in informal and formal tests will often provide the teacher with the basis for a teaching program. Spache (1976) suggests that administrators should attempt to find ways in which the child *does* learn and which can eventually be strengthened through instructional activities.

In sum, it is important to evaluate *all* available information and use that which will be most helpful in planning for individual children. Data obtained through both informal and formal evaluations serve as a guideline in planning remedial programs. Some of the information (e.g., knowledge that the child reverses letters) can be used directly in the teaching process. Other information (e.g., observation that the child learns motor skills quickly) will be used for total program planning. Wherever the evaluative data are utilized, they serve as a foundation upon which future successes can be built.

CONTINUOUS ASSESSMENT

In planning a program of remediation, the initial evaluation of a child should be viewed as only a starting point for continuous evaluation (Meyen, 1972). All of the information needed to help the child with learning problems will not be obtained in the initial testing at the beginning of the program (Spache, 1976). Some children will continue to experience specific difficulties as they progress academically, while other children will outgrow certain methods and materials. Teachers will sometimes be able to improvise a diagnostic teaching procedure to clarify a particular concept. In other cases, a more detailed analysis of the situation might be required before the teacher can instruct the child successfully. Formal testing and the consideration of other alternatives will often be needed in these situations.

Continuous evaluation is also necessary in the case of the child with difficulties in more than one academic area. Once the child experiences success in analyzing unfamiliar words, for example, it might be wise to consider his difficulties in arithmetic. The emphasis of the remediation will then be transferred from one subject area to another. Nevertheless, teachers should be extremely careful not to abandon successful work in one area to begin remediation of another academic problem. Children with learning problems will require continual success so that original gains are not lost.

Continuous assessment is actually the basis upon which clinical or diagnostic teaching is formulated (Wallace & Larsen, 1978). It is the process of teach-test-teach-test, whereby the teacher is constantly observing the student's behavior, his responses to the approach being used, and the apparent impact upon the child's development (Spache, 1976).

We do not view continuous assessment as a series of formal tests which are administered to the child. Rather, continuous assessment involves the many different opportunities which teachers have throughout a school day to evaluate a child's achievement informally. Written seatwork activities, for example, can actually serve as a good indication of a student's understanding of a unit of work. Similarly, teachers can also evaluate achievement by observing a child during oral reading periods or while working at the chalkboard. As noted by Lerner (1976), continuous assessment actually becomes a part of the entire teaching process through which the teacher continually evaluates units of instruction.

Continuous assessment should also involve program evaluation. In most cases, teachers will be able to informally evaluate the effectiveness of the remedial program through observation and teaching procedures. When a child is not succeeding, it might be necessary for the teacher to change the method, give additional supportive teaching, or reevaluate the effectiveness of the entire remedial process. In the last case, the teacher will be required to reassess his remedial goals and look for possible explanations for a program's failure. When supportive teaching is required, it might be a matter of prolonging the exposure to a particular skill that is being taught or changing the medium of presentation so that the child is exposed to an additional sensory modality. All of this requires some creativity, originality, and flexibility on the part of the teacher. He must analyze the situation and subsequently decide what might be done to clarify a concept for a particular child. As mentioned, evaluation then becomes a part of the teaching process. The teacher must evaluate the effectiveness of his teaching and the learning taking place in the classroom. Ultimately, the success of the remedial program will depend upon this phase of the teaching process.

VARIETY OF MATERIALS AND METHODS

It has been suggested that if there are significant individual differences in the ways children learn, it should follow that teachers should use varied approaches for helping children who are failing to learn (Heilman, 1977). Consequently, we believe that there is no one best instructional material or method for children with academic difficulties. Teachers should be able to handle any number of different learning problems by finding what will work for a particular child. In our experience, the lack of flexibility in teaching approaches is a source of learning problems in some children.

One of the challenges of teaching is adjusting to individual differences among normal children. Even more challenging are the differences presented by children experiencing difficulties in school. Probably the most complex problem confronting the teacher is that of adjusting instruction to individual differences. The ability to adjust instruction requires teachers to have a working knowledge of a wide variety of instructional materials and techniques.

It is difficult for some teachers to use more than one teaching method. It is equally difficult to convince some teachers of the merits of a specific approach for a particular child if the teacher is already convinced of the "advantages" of using a certain material with all children. Nevertheless, we have found that learning is most often enhanced, and the teaching process is less frustrating, when the teacher is flexible in his approach to instruction.

The difficulty of individualizing a program for a few children is frequently mentioned by teachers as an argument against employing a variety of instructional approaches. The ease of using one method with all children is viewed as the corresponding advantage. The obvious flaw in this argument—the amount of extra work entailed in trying to fit a child to specific material or technique not suited to his needs—is rarely considered. The burden is very often lightened when teachers try to match an approach to the learning styles of individual children. The planning for individual children suddenly seems to be much less work when youngsters are learning.

Articulate arguments, and occasionally empirical evidence, can be cited in support of certain materials and techniques. Heilman (1977), for example, reports that virtually every method and procedure described in the literature is reported to have been successful with some children and unsuccessful with others. Furthermore, teachers are likely to be less receptive to other points of view and approaches when they become enamored with one method to the exclusion of others. In short, we believe that successful remediation is based upon *teacher versatility.* Becoming versatile is not an easy task. On the contrary, it requires detailed planning and conscientious study. A particularly difficult aspect of this process is experimenting with different methods and materials for specific children until a successful approach is found. Often a child will continue to fail and lack motivation until a successful teaching technique is found. Understandably, some teachers hesitate to experiment with new teaching methods and materials for fear of continuing the child's failure. Nevertheless, we believe that a variety of teaching methods and materials is absolutely basic to successful remediation.

INDIVIDUALIZATION

Many teachers are convinced that successful remediation depends upon the use of a variety of materials and methods but find it difficult to select materials and determine their effectiveness for particular learning problems (Adamson &

Van Etten, 1970). Selecting materials is one of the most important tasks that a teacher must perform, since successful remediation is often dependent upon the instructional material or approach used. Some of the following questions may be considered basic guidelines for selecting specific materials for individual children:

1. What are the child's strengths? Through which modalities does he seem to learn best?
2. What are the child's weaknesses? Through which sensory modalities does he seem to have the most difficulty?
3. Is the child immature for his age? Does he become frustrated easily? How long does he attend to a task?
4. What is the child's interest level? What are his special interests?
5. What methods and materials have been used in the past? Which have been successful and which have been unsuccessful?
6. Does the child have any physical handicaps that necessitate specialized equipment? (Dumas, 1972)

Selecting Instructional Materials

The process of determining which material to use with a particular child should begin with the questions listed above. Usually a child with a specific difficulty has some patterns that eliminate certain types of materials. For example, a sight word approach to reading instruction would not be an effective choice for a child with visual memory problems. Likewise, a child who has spent 2 years with a particular basal reading series with little academic improvement may profit from using an alternative reading approach. We often have seen children struggling through various academic programs with little evaluation or understanding of their specific difficulties. In many situations, the teacher switches to lower grade-level materials because the child is having difficulty with the material normally used in his class. Here the only consideration is often one of finding "comfortable" or easy instructional materials for the child, rather than evaluating the child's individual needs or deficits.

After an analysis of all available information (test results, informal observations, prior use of certain materials, and individual interests), the teacher should be able to list a number of alternative instructional approaches. Based upon individual teacher judgment, one approach should be chosen and implemented. No magical formula is available at this stage, although Weinthaler and Rotberg (1970) have attempted to specify particular variables to consider during material selection (see also chapter 4). A number of factors complicate the final material selection. The availability of certain materials, the financial status of the school district, administrative policies of the school district, and teacher preference all ultimately affect which material can and will be used with a particular child. Nonetheless, once all these factors have been considered, the final decision rests with the individual teacher.

Adjusting to Individual Differences

Once a specific remedial approach has been selected and the teacher begins to progress with instruction, he will sometimes find that the approach is not meeting the child's needs. The immediate tendency is to consider another method or material; however, this is not always the best procedure to follow. It has been our experience that children who have experienced academic difficulties over a long period of time will need some time to adjust to new methods and materials. With a child who has continually failed, you cannot expect that the difficulties will disappear immediately. Some period of adjustment to the new approach is required. Flexibility in the use of materials is encouraged, but you must give an instructional approach time to succeed. Alternating the approach should be considered only after the teacher has given the method ample opportunity to succeed. Individual differences preclude rigid guidelines, but 2 weeks may be a reasonable minimum for experimenting with a new material. Little can be assumed before this amount of time has been allowed for success.

The inclination of many teachers to switch from material to material without any consistency from year to year can be extremely debilitating for children with learning problems. We have found it discouraging to examine such a child's cumulative folder and discover the number of different programs, approaches, and materials to which the child has been exposed. We usually assume that the changes in instructional materials were apparently of no avail, since many of these children continue to have academic difficulties. Any number of reasons may have caused the continual difficulty, not the least of which may be the lack of appropriate planning for selection of instructional materials.

In many cases one remedial approach will not be sufficient. The more effective formula for success may include using a variety of materials with one child. The severity of a child's difficulties might indicate the use of a specific exercise in learning the mechanics of reading and another type of material in applying the mechanics to textual reading. Similarly, the child with severe written language and reading difficulties might require a number of different materials.

Evaluating Materials

The proliferation of commercially prepared instructional materials has certainly added to the teacher's material-selection dilemma. The hard-sell and the creative packaging of many instructional materials have made many teachers question the effectiveness of many commerically available materials. According to Ensminger (1970), many producers of materials advertise specific materials as being the solution to all a child's problems when in fact the material may be appropriate for only a certain level of development. It is unfortunate that many advertising gimmicks have helped to sell basically inferior materials. Teachers must be aware of packaging and advertising deception (Lazarus, 1971) and judge a material on its intrinsic value and appropriateness to their particular situation.

Much can, however, be said about the number of excellent materials available. Many outstanding newer materials are finding their way into remedial programs and should be both well received and widely used. Many of these materials have been expressly designed for children with specific learning problems. There is an acute need for good materials, since children with learning problems often have failed to respond to programs designed to meet the instructional needs and characteristics of normal children. Specialized approaches and materials uniquely designed for handicapped children serve a very useful purpose in education. They provide the teacher with precise tools to help in remediating academic problems. Using material that is matched to specific difficulties lets the teacher spend more time on other aspects of remediation.

DIRECTIVE TEACHING

Following the evaluation and selection of appropriate materials, the teacher faces the equally difficult task of implementing and organizing the remedial instruction. It has been our experience that children with learning problems will usually respond favorably to an organized classroom situation with the emphasis placed on systematic and direct instruction. The unstructured classroom is often the place that causes the greatest difficulty for the child with academic problems. Situations where children do not know what is expected of them will often reinforce the behaviors that originally contributed to the learning deficits (Kauffman, 1977). A specific program of organization is, therefore, a primary consideration in planning for remediation.

As a first step, the program being used with a particular child should be written down. A format that includes the following information is both functional and less time consuming than the detailed lesson plans that are often suggested.

Date	Skill(s) to be worked on	Method and material to be used	Lesson outcome

This type of planning can be continued throughout the remediation program. It serves as a concise chronology of what a teacher has done with a particular child. At the same time, it provides the teacher with a means for on-going evaluation of both materials and achievement. Teachers have also used this format in reporting pupil progress to parents. If the format is continued over some period of time, it serves as a "remediation diary." The written outline of remediation provides the teacher with an organization plan that lends itself to sequential program planning.

Teaching Directly to the Problem

Once the actual teaching program is initiated, it will be important for the teacher to focus on the specific behaviors that he is attempting to develop (Lovitt, 1977). There is a tendency on the part of some teachers to neglect those aspects of the learning problem that call for direct remedial action. Teachers are often tempted to devote an inordinate amount of time to peripheral skill development and disregard the actual problem. This situation occurs many times in the case of children with reading difficulties complicated by perceptual-motor problems. Teachers can easily spend months perfecting the skill of walking on the balance beam, for example, neglecting the child's deficits in reading. But balance-beam walking is a poor substitute for learning the skills needed for success in reading. In this regard, Lovitt (1977) notes that the available data regarding transfer of training do not support the strategy of developing the proficiencies of one skill by teaching another. On the contrary, children need to be *directly* taught the specific skills they are lacking. Children will learn to read by reading or to calculate by calculating. Obviously, the more time spent in effectively developing any given skill, the greater the chance that the child will learn that skill. In essence, if the objective is to teach a child how to read, then this is where the teacher's emphasis should be.

Managing the Remedial Program

There are several other considerations in planning a remedial program for children with academic difficulties. Children should be aware of the day's plan in terms of what they are expected to do and what they should complete (Cruickshank et al., 1961; Phillips, 1967). Periods of remediation are sometimes so haphazard that children have a difficult time relating what happened yesterday to what will be happening today. The organization of an instructional period and the "why" behind certain teaching materials should be explained to a child who is experiencing learning problems. The child should know what he will be doing during a certain period and how the material at hand relates to the particular skill being developed. Setting clear expectations for completion of the task provides the child with a goal to reach for that day. Reinforcement can be based upon the attainment of specific goals, as suggested in chapter 2.

We believe it is also important to assign each child a permanent seat. The child who knows where he is to sit is more likely to be task-oriented than the child who sits in a different place each day. Permanent seating also provides the child with some stability that may have been previously lacking in his educational experiences. The chances of exhibiting inappropriate behaviors are also lessened when the child has some permanency in a classroom.

Children should know where their materials are located. Children who waste time looking for particular papers or books and asking procedural questions of the teacher could be greatly helped if their materials were always located in the same place with daily written directions for them to follow (cf. Phillips, 1967). Thus, the teacher who is involved with other children will not be interrupted by questions such as "Where is my notebook?" "What do I do?" "What page is the lesson on?" A child should also be told the specific activities in which he may participate after he has completed the assigned work. This provides an answer to the inevitable question, "What do I do *now*?"

In addition, children should know and see that good work produces appropriate rewards. Children who are succeeding after having failed for a long time need to know that they are doing well. Many times success is self-evident. Nonetheless, it is important that these children get some type of overt recognition. Reinforcing events associated with learning provide children the motivation to continually try to do their very best. (Chapters 2 and 6 list appropriate reinforcement techniques.)

Otto, McMenemy, and Smith (1973) also suggest the following guidelines for successful remedial teaching:

1. Secure the learner's cooperation,
2. Offer instruction at the learner's level,
3. Take small steps,
4. Reinforce success,
5. Keep learning tasks and materials meaningful,
6. Facilitate remembering,
7. Encourage pupil discovery of relationships,
8. Guard against motivation that is too intense,
9. Provide spaced practice,
10. Build a backlog of success experiences.

The teacher working with children with academic difficulties will reap obvious advantages from a well-organized classroom. The individualization of programs for particular children necessitates concise organization if remediation is to be effective. Many failures can be partly attributed to the lack of structured programs. A well-organized classroom serves as a prerequisite for effective instruction in any school. This need is doubly important for the child with learning problems.

EARLY IDENTIFICATION AND REMEDIATION

An area of increased concern to professionals in many different disciplines during the past few years has been the early identification and remediation of children with learning problems. One indication of this interest has been the implementation of many early screening programs in school districts across the country. Educators, in particular, have recognized that the prognosis for successful remediation is certainly increased when learning handicapped children are identified and treated at an early age. Furthermore, available evidence seems to indicate that children who receive remedial assistance early exhibit few educational difficulties as they advance in their school careers (Garber & Heber, 1973; Hayden, 1978; Nazarro, 1974).

A crucial point to remember, however, is that early identification must also carry a specified direction or program for treatment (Keogh & Becker, 1973). Early screening programs can be worthless if the identification goes no further than labeling the child. We actually do a considerable disservice to handicapped children if massive screening programs are not followed by well-conceptualized educational programs (Frankenburg, 1973). We believe that there is a critical relationship between early identification and subsequent programs of intervention. It is essential that early screening programs are closely associated with future educational planning. A number of important guidelines for both identifying and remediating learning problems at an early age are presented in chapter 5.

TEACHER INVOLVEMENT

Effective remediation is closely associated with what has simply been recognized as *good teaching.* In other words, effective remediation is directly related to teacher competency. Unfortunately, this principle has been widely misunderstood. Many have suggested that remediation is based upon a set of principles totally different from those adhered to in regular classrooms. Nothing could be more inaccurate. The principles that apply to good teaching are principles that cut across all types of instruction. The child with academic difficulties will be taught in basically the same fashion as the child who is succeeding academically. The only differences are those of degree. The time that is spent teaching a specific skill, the individualization of instruction, and the variability of materials are procedural differentiations. These differences are brought about only because of the uniqueness of the learning problem. The teaching that takes place during the remedial session will differ little from what goes on within a group of "normal" learners.

Effective remediation actually necessitates direct teaching. Unfortunately, materials have been viewed by some as the teaching agent or the means by which a child will learn a certain skill. *Materials cannot teach.* The materials merely facilitate teaching, but nothing replaces the teacher in actually performing his role as the "change agent" in remediation.

Unique materials, aids, and games that are used in a remedial teaching situation should be viewed as temporary teaching devices. At no time should these devices be considered the remedial programs. They should be considered motivators that help a youngster overcome a particular difficulty in understanding a specific concept (Heilman, 1977). Lengthy dependency upon such devices can serve no useful purpose, and, ultimately, only hamper a child's chances for success. The teacher must not depend on these materials to do the teaching job. He must realize that the only way a child will learn to read, or write, or calculate, is by his teaching the child to do so. No instructional material will be able to do this for a teacher. Those who oppose this viewpoint are merely seeking excuses for inappropriate teaching. A conscientious and skillful effort on the part of the teacher is the primary factor in successful remediation.

COMPLEX NATURE OF LEARNING PROBLEMS

The complexity of remediating individual learning difficulties is understandable when you consider the complicated nature of learning and the variety of pressures that are brought to bear upon the child. All children, at some time, are subjected to the pressures of school. Most children are able to cope with the frustrations, anxieties, and confusion that accompany the learning process and suffer little from this encounter. But for the child with academic problems, the situation is different. The pressures that are brought to bear upon this child reduce his ability to respond appropriately and, in many cases, little if any learning takes place. The child who is permitted to remain in such frustrating situations may become so educationally handicapped that he drops out of school at the earliest possible time.

Some children with school learning problems are fortunate enough to be recognized and helped. In some cases, the slightest alteration of instruction may be enough to move the child on his way. Others may require more detailed individualization of instruction over a prolonged time. In the process of remediating the problem, the teacher will often find his task to be complicated. Assessment, materials, organization, reinforcement, and individualization will be important considerations in the remedial program. The child's progress will sometimes be slow, and often frustrating. However, successful cases of remediation seem to make the entire process very worthwhile. In retrospect, remediation does not seem as difficult once a learning problem has been overcome.

An important element in the successful remediation of learning problems is the orderly sequence of skill presentations. Children with school learning problems require much more systematic instruction than the child who is learning without difficulty. There is a tendency on the part of some to neglect the sequences involved in basic academic areas and to emphasize the development of specific isolated skills. The slower paced remedial instruction and the difficulties encountered with specific skills seem to account for this inclination in remedial settings. Skills must be taught in an integrated, orderly fashion. Nothing should be omitted or assumed. Our discussion in chapter 5 provides operationalized principles for sequential skill development.

As we have already said, teachers in regular classrooms have been led to believe for too long that remediation falls entirely within the realm of the specialist. Few classroom teachers have been given the opportunity to exhibit their remedial teaching competencies. However, many children with learning problems can and should be handled in the regular classroom by regular classroom teachers. A substantial number of the suggestions presented in this chapter can be easily adapted to regular class instruction. The principles are also applicable to teachers currently involved in remedial programs. Remediation should be a concern of *all* teachers.

SUMMARY

This chapter serves as a basis for effective remediation in any educational setting. All teachers at some time in their careers are faced with children experiencing academic learning problems. These children often require specialized instruction to overcome their academic difficulties. Successful instruction will depend upon a concisely formulated system of remediation. Basic principles that all teachers should consider in designing a program of remediation have been outlined.

The initial and on-going instructional needs of the individual child should serve as the focus of a remedial program. Formal and informal assessment results must be used in planning programs and evaluating program effectiveness. Successful remediation will depend on the selection of a wide variety of materials, techniques, and methods that are tailored to individual needs. Finally, the difficult aspects of overcoming learning problems in children are directly related to the type of instruction provided for the child. The successful remedial program will essentially be based upon good teaching.

4
Remedial
Teaching
Competencies

Remedial Teaching Competencies

Effective remedial teaching in the regular or special classroom depends on the teacher's mastery of specific instructional skills grounded in the principles discussed in chapters 2 and 3. Specific competencies which make those principles operational include the teacher's ability to:

1. Use diagnostic information to initiate a remedial program,
2. State instructional goals as performance of specific tasks,
3. Analyze tasks to pinpoint learning problems,
4. Present learning tasks to remediate problems,
5. Provide the learner with feedback on task performance,
6. Structure the environment in which the task is performed,
7. Keep evaluative records of teaching and learning.

When children have difficulty in school, it is essential that their teachers attempt to diagnose and remediate their behavioral or academic problems. However, teachers must first analyze their own teaching behavior. Our suggestion that teachers are responsible for children's learning implies that remediation of *teaching* problems must precede remediation of *learning* problems.

Teaching involves constant reevaluation of instructional behavior as well as constant reassessment of pupil performance. The behaviors which comprise teaching are no less open to scrutiny and diagnosis than the behaviors which constitute learning (see Kauffman & Hallahan, 1975). Therefore, teachers must continuously monitor and correct their own behavior in order to be most effective. The remainder of this chapter is an outline of remedial teaching competencies needed by all teachers. It provides a checklist for evaluating teaching problems that may be contributing to the child's learning difficulty.

A COMPETENCY CHECKLIST

I. USE DIAGNOSTIC INFORMATION TO PLAN AN INITIAL REMEDIAL STRATEGY

Diagnostic information should serve one major purpose—that of providing a basis for remediation. Useful diagnostic information comprises two major categories:

Type I—general information, including standardized test scores and case history material, which gives an overall picture of the child and suggests a beginning point in remediation;

Type II—specific information obtained from the child's responses to remedial teaching and provides the basis for further instruction, i.e., direct measurement of the child's performance.

Type I information is the concern of this competency. The use of *Type II* information is discussed under competency VII.

A. *Use all available sources of information*

To get as broad and complete a picture of the child's weaknesses and strengths as possible, no source of useful information should be overlooked. All school personnel, both professional and nonprofessional, should be considered and evaluated as sources of observations of the child's academic and social behavior. School records, parents, peers, and community agencies (e.g., church, scouts, family service, welfare, etc.) are also potential sources of useful data. However, it cannot be stressed too strongly that the classroom teacher is the *best single source* of useful information in teaching the child. By systematically observing the child's behavior, an experienced teacher can accurately formulate an initial remedial program.

B. *Estimate the child's developmental level*

The remedial strategy should be consistent with the child's level of development. Note whether the child's physical development is discrepant from the norm, whether his social behavior is appropriate for his age and sex, whether his academic achievement is within the expected range, and whether the rewards he prefers are characteristic of other children his age. The initial remedial activities should fall within the child's physical capacity, degree of socialization, academic ability, and reward preference.

C. *Eliminate possible health and sensory factors as causes of learning problems*

For maximum learning efficiency, the child must be in good health and all of his senses must be functioning properly. It is particularly important to be aware of indications of a hearing or vision problem which may be contributing to the child's learning difficulty. The child may have a hearing problem if he:
1. Has an articulation (pronunciation) problem,
2. Is delayed in language development,
3. Is inconsistent in responding to oral directions and questions,
4. Is inattentive, hyperactive, or restless,
5. Has frequent ear infections or earaches.

If there is reason to suspect that the child may have a hearing problem, he should be referred immediately to a speech clinician for screening or to an audiologist for evaluation.

The child may have a vision problem if he:
1. Frequently stumbles, runs into objects, and/or walks cautiously,
2. Avoids bright or direct light and/or frequently rubs his eyes,
3. Has a tendency to close or cover one eye or shows a divergence of gaze in one eye,
4. Complains frequently of dizziness, headaches, or pain in the eyes,
5. Has a tendency to hold objects or printed matter very close (less than 6 inches).

If there is reason to believe that the child may have a vision problem, he should be referred immediately to the school nurse for screening or to an ophthalmologist for evaluation.

Disease, malnutrition, and other physical conditions obviously can contribute to learning problems and should be corrected by appropriate professionals as quickly and completely as possible. Nevertheless, the teacher must not use suspected or real physical or sensory defects as an excuse for failing to develop the best possible remedial teaching program.

D. *Observe the methods through which the child learns best*

Normally, academic learning in any curriculum area involves multisensory stimulation and a variety of response modes. The primary channels through which school learning takes place appear to be auditory-vocal and visual-motor. However, the question of primary concern for the teacher should be what methods work best with a given child, regardless of his supposed strengths or weaknesses in modal learning. To know that a child learns spelling words more quickly by tracing them than by hearing them spelled is more useful than to know that he scores high on visual-motor and low on auditory-vocal tasks on a standardized test. From the first moment that they work with children, teachers should begin observing the teaching methods that work best in teaching specific skills to individual children (see Lovitt, 1977).

E. *Integrate Type I information into an initial teaching strategy*

Type I information includes test scores, anecdotal observations, physical status, and other data which are useful in formulating an initial teaching strategy. The value of such a beginning strategy is that it allows the teacher to focus quickly on remedial tasks and teaching methods which have a high probability of success. The integration of Type I information into an initial remedial teaching strategy is illustrated by the case of Ted. The test and observational data were obtained and interpreted by a resource teacher. Note that the recommendations suggest a beginning point for remedial teaching.

──── AN INITIAL TEACHING STRATEGY FOR TED

Background Information

Ted is a quiet but friendly 8-year-old who is in the third grade. He has no history of medical problems and shows no indications of sensory defects. He is of average height and weight but appears somewhat uncoordinated in his movements and is unskillful at athletics; in fact, he appears to be somewhat weak, slow, and clumsy in sports and playground activities compared to his classmates. He is an only child who is pampered by his mother and ignored most of the time by his father. His mother, a high school graduate, works part-time as a hostess in a restaurant; his father, a college graduate, is a business manager for a branch office of a large corporation. During the past year his parents separated for about 6 months, apparently in anticipation of filing for a divorce. Ted's mother moved into an apartment, and during these months of separation Ted and his father interacted much more. They shared chores around the house, and his father took an active interest in Ted's daily activities. However, now that Ted's mother is living at home again, Ted's father pays almost as little attention to him as before the separation. Ted's comments to his teachers have made it obvious that he admires his father and enjoys doing things with and for him.

Ted is not actively rejected socially by his classmates, nor is he a social isolate. However, he has few close friends, mainly because of his lack of skill in active games and sports. He is considerate of others and good natured but seldom invites social contacts and is not a social leader. He typically chooses adult company over play with his peers, and he thrives on praise from adults.

Ted's third grade teacher is concerned about his progress in three areas: reading, motor development, and social development. His progress in arithmetic is very satisfactory; in fact, he is ahead of most of his classmates. If given the opportunity, he would spend almost his entire school day working math problems, looking at pictures, or listening to stories. He seems to be a bright child who has no difficulty comprehending what he hears and grasping quantitative relationships. However, oral and silent reading are difficult for him and hinder his progress in other subjects, such as science and social studies. His attitude toward reading is that he'd sooner not do it—he often dawdles over his reading assignments and complains that the work is too hard. He is not a social failure, but he needs to learn to initiate more social contacts with his peers. His lack of gross motor skills required in active games and sports seems to be a major hindrance to his social development.

Test Results

Ted was cooperative throughout the testing sessions and appeared interested in the tasks. He was tested in October, when his grade placement was 3 — 2. On the **Slossen Intelligence Test,** Ted achieved a mental age of 9 years, 8 months (his chronological age was 8 years, 7 months) and an IQ of 113. He was given the **Peabody Individual Achievement Test** (PIAT), with the following results:

subtest	grade equivalent
Mathematics	4.0
Reading recognition	2.2
Reading comprehension	2.8
Spelling	2.0
General information	4.3
Total test score	3.0

The **Key Math Diagnostic Arithmetic Test** was given, and his overall grade equivalent score of 3.3 was consistent with his teacher's report and his score on the PIAT. On the Berry-Buktenica **Developmental Test of Visual-Motor Integration** Ted scored an age-equivalent of 7 years, 4 months, reflecting his lag in skills necessary for achievement in action games and sports. He was given the **Woodcock Reading Mastery Tests** with the following results:

subtest	easy reading level	instructional level	frustration level
Letter identification	2.6	3.0	3.6
Word identification	1.8	1.9	2.0
Word attack	1.6	1.8	2.1
Word comprehension	1.9	2.4	2.0
Passage comprehension	1.9	2.2	2.6
Total reading	1.9	2.2	2.5

He was given the **Wepman Auditory Discrimination Test** and was found to have average auditory discrimination skills.

Informal Observations

Ted's teacher has a well-controlled, highly structured class. Most of the activity in the classroom consists of individual, teacher-directed tasks; most social interaction between children takes place at recess or on the playground, where Ted is at a disadvantage because of his lack of visual-motor skills. Ted's positive social interactions with his peers occur most often during games and activities requiring little visual-motor skill (for instance, checkers and chess, at which he excels). His oral reading is slow and characterized by many hesitations, repetitions, and errors on small words. He fails to recognize many of the words that are part of his speaking vocabulary. He relies primarily on contextual clues in figuring out words and does not appear to use any other word attack skills consistently. When he is given a silent reading task, Ted typically responds in one of two ways: he either hurries through it, making many careless errors in his slap-dash performance; or dawdles and day-dreams, failing to complete the task. He seldom receives praise from his teacher for his performance on reading tasks.

Initial Strategy

First, there appears to be a serious motivational problem in reading. Because he seems to respond well to social praise and attention, social rather than material rewards for appropriate responses should be tried first.

Second, reading tasks should be kept well within his capability (i.e., he should be able to read the material with 95% accuracy), and tasks should be kept short. Praise for correct performance should be given immediately, and a favorite activity (e.g., math or a game of chess) should be scheduled immediately following reading. However, the reading task must be completed correctly before Ted engages in the preferred activity.

Third, Ted should be asked to read for 1 minute each day from the same reader, and careful records should be kept of his errors and his correct reading rate (i.e., words read correctly per minute). Analysis of his performance on these daily probes will reveal the consistency of his errors and indicate what specific skills he is lacking.

Fourth, instruction should be given in phonetic word analysis skills, and drill should be provided on common sight words.

Fifth, an attempt should be made to obtain the assistance of Ted's father by requesting that he listen to Ted read a short passage (specified by the teacher) every evening and praise Ted for his performance.

Sixth, Ted's father should be encouraged to teach him some of the skills useful in organized games and sports (e.g., throwing, catching, and batting a baseball; dribbling and shooting basketball; swimming).

Seventh, Ted's teacher should be asked to provide small-group activities in which Ted can interact with his peers, and these activities should be ones in which Ted can be highly successful (e.g., projects involving arithmetic problems).

An initial teaching strategy suggests instructional goals. Instructional objectives must be stated explicitly so that teaching and learning can be evaluated.

II. STATE INSTRUCTIONAL GOALS AS PERFORMANCE OF SPECIFIC TASKS

After using Type I information to initiate a remedial program, the teacher must give careful attention to instructional goals. Instructional objectives are of crucial importance because they lead directly to the presentation and analysis of instructional tasks. Establishing adequate goals is the first step in the remedial teaching process itself.

A. *Objectify task performance*

Adequate instructional goals state clearly what individual children will do, the conditions under which they will do it, and the criteria that will be used to judge their performance. If any one of these elements is missing, the goal is not stated adequately (Mager, 1962). Goals stated in performance terms indicate clearly what teachers should teach and help in judging how effectively they are teaching. The following are examples of instructional goals that are inadequate because they are not stated in performance terms:

"To know the seven continents."

"To understand that an adjective describes a person, place, or thing."

"To tolerate other people's points of view."

The following goals are stated in performance terms:

"Given any map or globe, the student will be able to identify each of the seven continents by tracing its outline with his finger."

"Given any printed standard English sentence in which he can read all the words the student will be able to underline the adjectives with 100% accuracy."

"Given a situation in which he is conversing with someone who expresses an opinion or belief different from his own, the student will show tolerance for the other person's point of view by allowing him to speak without interruption and by refraining from physically attacking him."

B. *Determine immediate goals*

Every remedial teaching session should include immediate goals which can be accomplished during the session. It is important to have immediate goals so that time and effort are not wasted on irrelevant activities, so that the pupil can gain a sense of accomplishment, and so that the ultimate long-range goal is not lost.

C. ***Formulate long-range goals***

Immediate goals should constitute successive approximations of long-range goals. Priorities for the child's learning must be established. Long-range goals must be formulated on the basis of the objectives' educational relevance for the child. When relevant long-range goals are established and immediate goals are successive approximations of them, remedial teaching and learning become an orderly progression of relevant tasks. An example of a long-range goal and several immediate goals which are approximations of it could be stated as follows:

Long-range goal

Given any clock or watch face, the child will be able to tell the time shown to the nearest minute.

Immediate goals (approximations)

1. Given a large clock face with arabic numerals, the child will be able to read correctly the o'clock and half-past times for any hour or half hour.

2. Given such a clock face, the child will be able to count the minutes by fives proceeding clockwise from 1 (5) and continuing through 11 (55).

3. Given such a clock face, the child will be able to tell the time as _____ minutes after _____ or _____ minutes till _____ to the nearest 5 minutes for any position of the hands.

Instructional goals suggest remedial tasks. Performance goals provide a guide to the instructional tasks which will remediate the problem.

III. ANALYZE TASKS TO PINPOINT LEARNING PROBLEMS

Instructional tasks are the essence of remedial teaching. By performing instructional tasks, children move closer to mastery of the skills in which they are deficient. Consequently, no aspect of remedial teaching competence deserves closer attention than the analysis of instructional tasks. *Task analysis may be viewed as a sequence of evaluation activities which pinpoints the child's learning problem and guides the teacher in planning an effective remedial sequence of instructional tasks.*

A. ***Specify the task***

A task is something to do. It is an observable behavior, as discussed in chapter 2. It is described by what comes after the phrase "the child will be able to . . ." in the statement of an instructional goal in performance terms. For example, the following are tasks:

"Point to the red ball."

"Write the lowercase alphabet in manuscript letters."

"Copy a square."

"Find the sum of three two-digit numbers."

"Stay seated while taking the spelling test."

More important than defining *a task* is consideration of the task in question. The teacher must specify what it is that the child is to do. Otherwise, both the teacher and the child will become confused about what response is expected. Following oral directions is a different task from following written directions. Pointing to the correct object is a different task from naming it. Tasks must be defined *precisely* before their response requirements can be identified.

B. *Identify the task's response requirements*

A task requires a response. Every response can be broken down into a set of sequential subskills or response requirements which are prerequisites for successful task performance. Identifying the response requirements for instructional tasks is of primary importance in task analysis. Only when the component responses of a task are known can the child's learning problem be pinpointed. The teacher must analyze the instructional task by asking, "What are the things a child must do to perform this task successfully?" For example, when given the oral direction, "Print your name at the top of the paper," the child must be able to:

1. Interpret (understand) the task directions.
2. Find the top of the paper.
3. Hold the pencil in writing position.
4. Form each of the manuscript letters in his name.
5. Print the letters in his name in sequence.

Each of these five response requirements is a task in itself. As a task, it can be analyzed in terms of its own response requirements. Whether or not a response requirement must be further analyzed as a separate subtask depends on the child's performance.

C. *Note the child's errors*

Task analysis requires that the child be directed to perform the task. When the child's task performance breaks down, it is imperative that the teacher pinpoint the difficulty. Thus if a task is not performed successfully, the teacher must analyze the first response requirement on which the child makes an error. In the example, "Print your name at the top of the paper," the teacher must analyze response requirement no. 4 if the child has mastered response requirements 1 through 3 but does not form all of the letters in his name correctly. The teacher must note which letters were not properly formed and identify the response requirements for the tasks of forming those letters. Then the teacher must present the tasks of forming the letters (e.g., "Make the letter *A*"), and note the child's errors on the specific response requirements for those tasks. This process of task presentation and error identification must continue until a task is given which the child can perform without error. Errors on more difficult tasks then clarify the child's performance difficulty.

D. *Describe the learning problem as a performance deficit*

Careful analysis of the child's errors will indicate what the child has not learned that is essential for successful task performance. The learning problem can then be described as a deficiency in performance which can be remediated. What the child should be taught follows logically. To return to the example of the task, "Print your name at the top of the paper," if a child named "Randy" consistently responds to the task by printing "Rnady" at the top of the paper, his performance deficit is that he reverses the order of the letters *a* and *n* in his name. Since it is known that he has mastered all the other response requirements for completion of the task, it is obvious that what he must be taught is the correct sequence of letters. If, on the other hand, a child named "Sue" responds to the task by printing "2d" at the top of the paper, it is clear that the response requirement of forming the letters comprising her name must be analyzed as a set of separate tasks. If an analysis of the task of printing the letter *S* shows that Sue does not visually discriminate "S" from "2," although she reliably discriminates and copies some letter forms (e.g., "t" and "o"), her performance deficit (does not visually discriminate "S" from "2") indicates precisely what must be taught.

Task analysis explicates what is required for performance, what the child can do, where the child's response breaks down, and what sequence of skills must be taught to remediate the problem (see Lovitt, 1977).

IV. PRESENT TASKS TO REMEDIATE THE PROBLEM

The teacher must design and present a sequence of remedial tasks that will help children overcome their performance deficits. The nature of tasks themselves and the manner in which they are presented will determine children's progress in learning.

A. *Organize tasks for efficient presentation*

Tasks must be organized so that the child is not distracted or confused. The necessary instructional materials must be arranged so that tasks can be presented briskly and with a minimum of teacher effort. As soon as one task is completed the next task should be presented, unless the task is to be followed by a break for rest or reinforcement. If the teacher has to search for the needed material or cannot manipulate the material efficiently, the child's attention is more likely to stray from the task. Unneeded teaching materials and other objects which the child may want to manipulate or which may attract attention should be removed from the teaching environment. The child's attention can then be focused more readily on the task to which the teacher wants a response. The teacher must be in a position to direct the responses and manipulate the teaching materials easily; the child should be seated or positioned so that an appropriate response can be made easily. In any remedial teaching situation the teacher must:

1. Select the materials to use in teaching the task(s),
2. Know how to use the materials,
3. Arrange the materials in proper order,
4. Arrange the task environment for efficient presentation and response:
   a. Remove unnecessary materials,
   b. Have necessary materials within easy reach,
   c. Be sure the child has an appropriate desk, table, chair, or other area in which to work,
   d. Stay within easy reach of the child and the materials.

B. *Be directive*

The teacher must assume responsibility for directing the child's attention and responses to tasks. To do this effectively, you must establish a pleasant but controlling relationship with the child. The teacher must know exactly what the child is to do, and must tell the child what to do and when to respond. Questions should be reserved for situations in which the child has a legitimate choice or where the question is intended to elicit a correct answer to a task. For example, the teacher should avoid using questions in the following ways:

The teacher wants the child to put together a puzzle—"Let's put this puzzle together, O.K.?"

The teacher wants the child to read the next paragraph—"Do you want to read the next paragraph?"

If the teacher has determined that the child *should* do these tasks it would be better to direct the child as follows:

"Here's a puzzle to put together. See how well you can do it."

"Now read the next paragraph, please."

The child's task and the teacher's expectation must be made unambiguous. Teaching is most effective when the teacher pleasantly but firmly and clearly assumes the role of director of the learning activities.

Questions *are* appropriate when the teacher wants the child to choose one of two or more alternatives, any one of which is acceptable. For example, "Which do you want to do first, reading or arithmetic?" is an appropriate question when either choice is acceptable. "What is Barney doing in this picture?" is a question for which the teacher can expect a specific correct answer.

When a child does not respond correctly to oral directions, the teacher must take action to help him complete the task. The teacher may do this by repeating and simplifying the directions or by using cues, prompts, and models. Clear, direct instructions are sometimes all that is necessary to remediate an apparent learning problem (Lovitt, 1977).

Repeat and simplify directions

The teacher must be absolutely certain that the child understands exactly what to do. Otherwise, the reason for the child's failure cannot be determined. If the child does not respond promptly and correctly to directions for performing a task, the directions should be repeated. Furthermore, the teacher must be sure that the child understands each part of the direction given. For example, if the task directions are stated as "Draw a straight line from the monkey to the house," the teacher must be sure that the child understands what it means to draw a straight line from one object to another and that the child can identify both the monkey and the house. Before assuming that the child cannot perform the task or prompting the child's response, the teacher should repeat the task directions and, if necessary, simplify the directions to make sure that they are understandable. Directions can be simplified by using simpler vocabulary or by breaking them down into small, sequential steps.

Cue responses

If the child does not respond to repeated or simplified directions, the teacher must take further action. The child may respond appropriately when given a signal or cue. The teacher may cue a response by a word, a gesture, or any other auditory, visual, or tactile signal. For example, if a child tends to respond at an inappropriate time, the teacher may call the child's name, use a hand signal, or touch the child to cue the responses at the appropriate time. If the child is attending to the wrong stimuli (pictures, words, blocks, etc.), the teacher may use a pointing or tapping cue to direct the child's attention and response.

Use prompts

If a child does not respond to the teacher's cue, the response may need to be prompted. When a response is prompted, the teacher physically assists the child in performing the task. For example, if the child cannot perform the task of drawing a square, the teacher may take the child's hand and help him draw the figure. Occasionally, only a partial prompt may be needed, as when the teacher helps the child to draw only three sides of the square. Prompts can be faded out as the child learns the task. A prompt should be faded by gradually dropping assistance *beginning at the point of completion*. For example, the prompt for drawing a square should be faded as follows:

1. Help the child draw all four sides.
2. Help the child draw only the first three sides.
3. Help the child draw only the first two sides.
4. Help the child draw only the first side.

Eventually the prompt may be dropped completely, the child completing the entire task independently.

Provide a model

Children can often learn a task more quickly if they have models to follow (Cullinan et al., 1975; Lovitt, 1977). If a child does not make an appropriate response, the teacher may need to demonstrate how to do the task. For example, if the child does not cut on the dotted line or clap his hands when told to do so, the teacher should demonstrate the correct response. Instructions such as "Watch me" or "Do it like this" should be given when the teacher models the response. In some cases it may be helpful to have another child provide the model.

C. *Present only essential tasks*

The child should be presented with tasks that are directly related to the concept the teacher is trying to teach. Irrelevant tasks should be eliminated. Each task should be an essential step in reaching the next performance goal. As suggested in chapter 3, the teacher must teach directly to the problem. If the objective of instruction is to teach the child to catch a ball, little is to be gained by providing tasks in picture naming. If the teacher wants the child to learn sight words, there is little benefit in asking the child to walk on a balance beam. Picture naming and balance beam walking are legitimate instructional tasks, but there is little reason to expect that competence on one task will generalize to a very different one. Generalization is much more likely to occur among very similar tasks. Therefore, the teacher should present tasks which are prerequisites for reaching the instructional goal.

D. *Present tasks sequentially*

The sequence in which tasks are presented affects the rate at which children learn. Complex tasks are mastered by sequential learning of many simpler tasks (see the discussion of shaping in chapter 2). It is important for the teacher to be aware of the sequential development of academic, social, and perceptual-motor learning so that tasks can be ordered effectively. The teacher should become familiar with the sequential development of skills by consulting other sources. To be effective in remediation, the teacher must be well-organized and directive and present essential tasks in the proper sequence. However, tasks must be followed by feedback if they are to remediate the problem.

V. PROVIDE FEEDBACK ON TASK PERFORMANCE

Competence in remedial teaching demands more than merely presenting appropriate tasks. To learn efficiently, children must be informed frequently, immediately, and clearly of the adequacy of their performance. One of the advantages of programmed instruction and other highly structured teaching systems (e.g., Becker, Engelmann, & Thomas, 1971) is that they provide such feedback. As discussed in chapter 2, what happens immediately after a response determines whether or not that response is likely to occur again. Teachers who fail to give adequate feedback on task performance risk extinguishing the child's appropriate responses.

A. *Give clear feedback*

Ambiguous feedback on performance is worse than no feedback at all. Ambiguity will only heighten the child's anxiety and confusion. When the child makes a response to a task, the teacher's feedback should leave no room for doubt in the child's mind about the correctness of the response. Feedback on correctness might include such statements as "That's perfect," "It's all right except for this part right here," "No, that's wrong," or "Yes, it's a bicycle." The teacher should also give explicit feedback regarding his affective reaction to the response. The teacher can communicate affective reactions clearly by smiles, hugs, pats, winks, and a variety of other physical and verbal responses. It is necessary to give some children extrinsic rewards (e.g., candy, trinkets, stars, tokens, etc.) along with social rewards and knowledge of correctness in order to make the feedback completely clear.

B. *Give corrective feedback*

Positive feedback for appropriate performance is corrective in that it strengthens correct responses to remedial tasks. When the child gives an incorrect response to a task, the teacher's feedback should be corrective in that it tells the child how to improve his performance. "Make this line a little straighter," "You have to put the second number right under the first one," and other such remarks go beyond merely telling the child clearly that a particular response is wrong. Feedback can also be corrective in a third sense—it helps the child evaluate his own performance accurately. By giving corrective feedback, the teacher provides a model which can be incorporated into the child's own self-evaluation. When feedback is adequately corrective, it reinforces correct responses, extinguishes incorrect responses, indicates how task performance can be improved, and provides a model of realistic evaluation.

C. *Give feedback immediately*

Feedback is usually most effective when it is given during or immediately after performance. When the teacher is continuously observing the child's performance, encouragement and praise or correction may be given *while* the child is performing the task as well as immediately after it is completed. When not observing the child continuously, the teacher must establish a structure and routine which allow feedback to be given as soon after task completion as possible.

D. *Give feedback frequently*

Feedback is so vital to learning that very few, if any, responses should go without it in the beginning stages of remediation. Most teachers tend to overestimate the frequency with which they provide feedback and allow the child to make many responses to which they do not respond. This tendency should be corrected if teaching is to be maximally effective. A good rule is **"Give feedback at almost every opportunity."** Feedback should be a consequence for task performance. As a consequence, feedback is an essential element of classroom structure.

VI. STRUCTURE THE LEARNING ENVIRONMENT

In chapter 3 we suggested that remedial teaching must be highly organized. Such organization results in an environment that is structured for learning. A highly structured environment has been found helpful in teaching children with learning problems (Cruickshank et al., 1961; Haring & Phillips, 1962, 1972; Phillips, 1967). Structure includes classroom rules, routines, and consequences of behavior related to the rules. In a well-structured classroom environment, the rules and consequences of behavior are simple, primarily positive, and consistently applied. The structure creates an atmosphere which is conducive to learning and the development of a good teacher–pupil relationship.

A. *Keep the structure simple*

Rules for behavior need to be kept short and simple, as discussed in chapter 2. This suggestion is appropriate for all classroom rules, including those that apply to academic responses and routines. The teacher should determine which rules and routines are essential for efficient classroom operation and concentrate on making them work. Routines for distributing and collecting materials, preparing to leave the room, and following a schedule of activities, as well as rules governing movement about the room, talking in turn, and completing assigned tasks, should not be complicated. When the structure of the classroom becomes elaborate, children are likely to become confused about what is expected, required, tolerated, and prohibited by the teacher.

B. *Build rewards into the structure*

Adults, including teachers, often tend to assume that appropriate performance is its own reward. For many children with learning problems, if not for most, this is not the case. A good classroom structure emphasizes explicit positive consequences for cooperative, productive behavior. The teacher must arrange rewards for good performance as an integral part of the structure. This can be done by scheduling positive consequences for appropriate responses. The consequences need not be extrinsic rewards, such as candy or trinkets, although such rewards might be necessary for some children. Every child has a right to rewards that are meaningful to him, no matter what his level of development. The teacher must develop competence in finding meaningful consequences and helping the child learn to work for rewards which indicate a higher level of maturity.

C. *Adhere firmly and consistently to the structure*

Rewards are effective only when they are kept in the proper relationship to performance. The teacher must be firm and consistent in providing rewards only *after* appropriate responses are made to the structure. The "reward now, perform later" plea of children must be resisted. Likewise, if the structure established by the teacher calls for leveling an aversive consequence for behavior, the teacher must not allow the child to dissuade him. The primary aspects of a structured classroom environment are clear directions, firm expectations, and consistent follow-through (Haring & Phillips, 1962). Remember, however, that consistency does not mean rigidity. There are circumstances under which routines should be varied and rules should be broken. But if the classroom rules and routines are varied at the whim of either the teacher or the children, learning will not be optimal.

D. *Develop a good teacher-pupil relationship*

A good teacher-pupil relationship is based on mutual respect and trust. Many children with learning problems neither respect nor trust teachers. It is the teacher's responsibility to respect and trust children in spite of their lack of reciprocal regard. Children will learn respect if the teacher's behavior is fair, consistent, and task-centered. It is misleading to assume that to be an effective teacher you must first become a confidant of the child. Lasting confidence grows out of a history of predictable interactions. The teacher can develop a sound and productive relationship with children in the following ways:

1. Demonstrating concern for individuals by gearing teaching to specific needs,
2. Remediating learning problems by offering skillful instruction,
3. Making learning enjoyable by exciting interest and providing rewards for appropriate performance,
4. Remaining confident in all children's ability to learn,
5. Being cheerful, pleasant, and fair but firm, consistent, and predictable in interactions with pupils.

A well-structured classroom facilitates learning and development of a sound teacher–pupil relationship. It also simplifies documentation of the remedial process through careful record keeping.

VII. KEEP USEFUL RECORDS OF TEACHING AND LEARNING

Good record keeping is an essential feature of effective teaching (see Lovitt, 1977). Accurate, objective records serve the following purposes:

1. They provide feedback to the teacher regarding the adequacy of instruction.
2. They simplify communication with other teachers and parents.
3. They provide a guide to future instruction.

Teachers should keep two basic kinds of records: logs of teaching activities and charts of children's performance. In addition, teachers should use *Type II* information to plan future teaching.

A. *Keep a log of teaching activities*

A teacher's log should provide a brief narrative account of what instructional tasks were presented, what materials were used, the child's responses to the tasks, and the teacher's evaluation of the outcome (see chapter 3). It is important to date each entry so that the log is a chronology of instruction. Anecdotal records of the child's social-interpersonal behavior, as well as responses to instruction, should be entered in the log so that the relationship between academic and social learning can be observed. The entries in the log, including the teacher's evaluation of instruction, must be kept accurate and objective if the log is to serve its purpose. If the teacher wishes to keep a record of subjective impressions and feelings, it should be kept as a separate set of notes. The log should summarize the teacher's instructional activities so that the child's educational experience can be documented for the child's parents (if they wish to have the information) and future teachers. It is often helpful to append samples of the child's written work. In most cases the log will serve as the teacher's lesson plan. However, the teacher may need to write more detailed plans in some situations.

B. *Chart the child's progress in learning*

The child's progress in learning specific skills and behaviors may be plotted on a graph. The experience of graphing progress can be exciting and motivating for both the child and the teacher. The visual feedback from a graph is more immediate and interpretable than the information obtained from written reports or summary tables. Whenever possible, children should be encouraged to maintain the graph themselves, as graphing is often a reinforcing behavior for children. (See chapter 2 for a discussion of graphing techniques.)

C. *Base future teaching on Type II information*

Type II information is obtained from the teaching process itself. It is the basis for day-to-day and moment-to-moment remedial teaching. It implies that the teacher will continuously monitor the child's responses to instruction and modify the instructional tasks and their presentation to increase instructional effectiveness. Type II information provides corrective feedback in a remedial teaching system. As a system, remedial teaching may be diagrammed as shown in Figure 4–1.

Before beginning remediation, the teacher must use *Type I* information to formulate an initial teaching strategy. On the basis of preliminary observation of the child, test results, and information obtained from other sources, the teacher enters the remedial teaching system.

The teacher must first state a long-range instructional goal and an immediate goal which is an approximation of it. The instructional task presented will follow logically from the immediate goal. If the child performs the task without error, the cycle of stating an immediate goal and presenting the next task in sequence is continued until the long-range goal is achieved. When the long-range goal is achieved, the cycle includes the statement of a new long-range goal. If all the teacher's long-range goals are reached, remediation is no longer necessary and can be terminated.

If the child makes an error in task performance, the teacher must first analyze his own teaching behavior and modify the task presentation, feedback

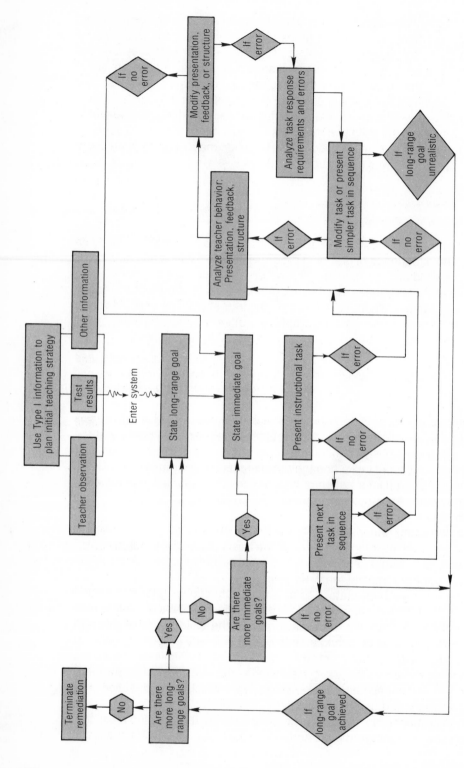

Figure 4-1
Schematic Representation of a Remedial Teaching System

on task performance, and/or the structure of the learning environment. If the child is able to perform the task without error after the teacher corrects his own behavior, the cycle of restatement of the immediate goal and presentation of the next task in sequence is resumed.

When the child's task performance breaks down after the teacher has corrected his instructional behavior, the teacher must analyze the response requirements of the task and the child's errors. If modification of the task or presentation of a simpler task results in adequate performance, the next task in sequence is then presented. If the child continues to make performance errors, the teacher may either reanalyze instructional behavior or restate the long-range goal for the child to make it more realistic.

Using *Type II* information to guide instruction requires both a high degree of technical competence and a high degree of self-awareness and sensitivity on the part of the teacher. Technical competence is demanded in sequencing and presenting remedial tasks. Sensitivity and self-awareness are necessary if the teacher is to analyze the role played by his own behavior in contributing to the child's learning problem.

SUMMARY

Successful remedial teaching, whether accomplished by regular or special class teachers, requires specific competencies based on the principles of academic remediation and behavior management discussed in Part One. These competencies involve assessment, goal setting, task analysis, task presentation, feedback, structure, and record keeping. Mastery of these skills will let the teacher provide an environment in which the child can learn both academic skills and appropriate social-emotional behavior.

5
Prevention of
Learning Problems

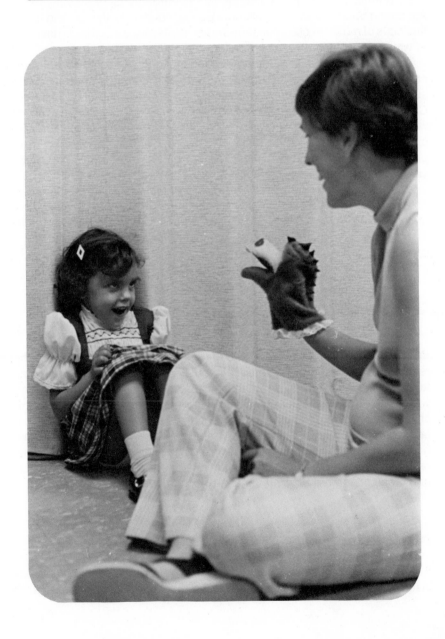

Prevention of Learning Problems

Preventing school learning problems has two basic facets. The first entails developing techniques that preclude or greatly reduce the probability that problems will occur. The second involves using therapeutic teaching methods that minimize existing problems, prevent complications, or provide solutions. Although the first facet is the ultimate goal of education, the second has been the focus of most special education and related services. Schools have tended to wait for problems to develop before taking constructive action.

The value of prevention both to individuals and to social institutions seems obvious. The child and his parents are spared considerable psychological suffering when unnecessary difficulties in the child's learning are avoided. Communities and institutions reap benefits in human and economic resources when learning problems are prevented. Nevertheless, the implementation of preventive programs in the schools is not universally lauded, nor are the preventive efforts of an individual teacher always accepted without controversy (Bower, 1969).

That it is a major responsibility of the school to prevent learning problems is not arguable. Furthermore, nearly all educators agree that two fundamental principles of prevention are good teaching and early detection of problems. There appears to be increasing agreement among educators regarding what constitutes good teaching and what procedures are most reliable and useful in early identification.

GOOD TEACHING AND PREVENTION

Principles of good teaching are based on the assumption that the teacher is responsible for children's learning. Without this assumption, the onus of failure falls on the child, a burden he should not be required to bear, or on "society" for which no remedy can be expected during the crucial learning years of the child's life. The five principles of good teaching listed below are applicable to all educational situations. Consequently, they serve also as basic principles of prevention. As the health-related disciplines have discovered that good health practices are the best prevention of disease, educators have observed that good teaching is the best prevention of school learning problems.

Principle 1:
Good Teaching Means Teaching Specific, Measurable Skills

It is of crucial importance for the teacher to formulate learning goals or instructional objectives for the children he teaches. It is essential that these objectives state what the child will be able to do, the conditions under which he will do it, and the criterion that will be used to judge his performance. Unless specific, measurable skills are taught, it is impossible to evaluate the teacher's effectiveness. High-sounding but vague, subjective goals are of no value in teaching because you can never determine whether or not they have been attained. For example, the teacher very likely will never be able to determine whether or not he has "given the child a life-long love of reading for recreation," but he can easily evaluate whether or not the child "reads during at least 20% of his free time in the classroom."

Principle 2:
Good Teaching Means Continuous Assessment of the Child's Performance

When the teacher has stated adequate performance objectives for the child, each task presented in a teaching program becomes a potential test of the child's learning. Clearly stated behavioral objectives provide the teacher with continuous feedback concerning what has and has not been taught. The teacher is able to modulate his instruction most effectively by taking his cues from the child's responses to the teaching program itself, rather than from responses to standardized tests.

Principle 3:
Good Teaching Means Establishing Priorities

Teaching will not be effective when tasks and concepts are taught in a random order. Effective teaching depends on initially identifying the behaviors which are most important for a child's survival in his environment. It also depends on analyzing specific tasks to precisely determine their response requirements. The effective teacher will waste no time trying to teach tasks for which the child has not learned the prerequisite skills. Neither will he squander his time and effort teaching skills which are of no functional value to the child.

Principle 4:
Good Teaching Means Being Directive

Learning may happen spontaneously, randomly, and erratically, when children are in the presence of individuals who are not trying to teach. But learning will not be efficient or predictable unless the teacher actively controls specific variables which make learning occur. The teacher teaches by arranging tasks, directing attention, prompting responses, differentially reinforcing behavior, and employing other techniques that change children's behavior (Becker et al., 1971). "The focus cannot be on techniques if the teacher begins with the idea that the children are responsible for what they learn and that the teacher is simply a supplier of 'learning opportunities'" (Engelmann, 1969, p. 40). It is the teacher's responsibility to direct the child's behavior; and if a child does not learn, it can only be concluded that the teacher has failed to teach that child.

Principle 5:
Good Teaching Means Using Positive Methods

Efficiency and effectiveness are necessary but not sufficient criteria for evaluating teaching. Good teaching also involves concern for the happiness and emotional well-being of the child. When the teacher concentrates on positive reinforcement, children are likely to learn more efficiently and happily (Madsen & Madsen, 1974). This does not mean that the child's inappropriate responses will go without correction or that punishment will always be avoided. It *does* mean that good teaching consists primarily of positive teacher-pupil interactions and that the teacher is genuinely concerned about the feelings and welfare of the child.

It is the thesis of this book that the teacher must be primarily concerned with instructional and behavior-management variables as etiological factors. It follows that our major concern in the area of prevention is adequate teaching. If the teacher is to be an effective preventive agent, he must commit his professional efforts primarily to the teaching process.

EARLY DETECTION AND PREVENTION

It is reasonable to believe that if children who will have learning problems can be identified early in life, then they can be helped more effectively to overcome their difficulties. Yet, as Keogh and Becker (1973) have pointed out, you must be cautious about the process of early identification. If the child is identified as having a learning difficulty (or even a *potential* learning difficulty) on the basis of a test that has questionable predictive power, then the child may be done more harm than good. The child's feeling about himself and the perceptions others have of him are not going to be enhanced by his identification as a child who has or may have a special problem. Misidentification could, in fact, have tragic consequences. Furthermore, if appropriate remedial help is not immediately available after the child is identified, then the identification process will result in frustration and disappointment for parents and teachers and will be of *no* benefit to the child. Although it is apparent that young children's learning problems can be detected early in their school years (Glazzard, 1977; Hawthorne & Larsen, 1977; Magliocca, Rinaldi, Crew, & Kunzelmann, 1977), we must urge reasonable caution in using early identification procedures.

Given that reliable and valid identification procedures are used, then it is safe to assume that the earlier a child's learning problem is detected the more easily it can be remediated. School systems that are seriously interested in meeting the challenge of prevention should develop strategies and tactics of early identification of learning difficulties. Until very recently, however, few schools have attempted to use any systematic procedures to identify incipient problems, because special services have been available only for those children with most obvious and disturbing learning deficits. There is little point in identifying problems for which no services are available. Identification under such circumstances highlights the inadequacy of the schools and tends to create pressure for inappropriate solutions.

Identification of learning problems must be a systematic and continuous effort of all professionals dealing with children. Teachers should be involved in administering effective, efficient screening instruments and/or carefully observing children. Information obtained should lead directly to diagnosis and a prescription for teaching.

Because the primary responsibility for early identification rests with the classroom teacher, he needs to be familiar with available screening instruments and be acutely aware of behaviors which signal potential learning difficulties.

Screening Instruments

Rating scales, checklists, and other types of tests often help teachers survey the behavior and achievement of their pupils and identify possible learning difficulties. Brief, easily administered tests that sample skills the child needs to succeed at school and for which there is evidence of predictive validity are most useful to classroom teachers. Screening devices are not diagnostic tests but instruments which select children who have a high probability of experiencing difficulty in school. Any child whose performance on a screening instrument indicates a possible learning problem should be evaluated more thoroughly before a diagnosis and prescription are formulated.

The number of rating scales, checklists, and observation schedules available to school personnel is growing. Be careful to select a screening device to meet the needs of particular situations. Here are brief descriptions of several screening tests that may be administered by the classroom teacher.

Boehm Test of Basic Concepts
(Boehm, 1971)

This test is appropriate for use with kindergarteners and first and second graders. The test samples 50 specific concepts (e.g., *top, over, always, half*) in four categories: space, quantity, time, and miscellaneous. The teacher reads instructions aloud (e.g., "Look at the apples. Mark the apple that is *whole*.") and the children mark a test booklet containing pictures and forms. Administration can be handled with small groups of 8 to 12 children and requires 15 to 20 minutes for kindergarten children. The purposes of the test are to measure children's mastery of concepts considered necessary for achievement in the first years of school and to identify the specific concepts on which the child should receive instruction.

CIRCUS
(Anderson, Bogatz, Draper, Jungeblut, Sidwell, Ward, & Yates, 1974)

This instrument is designed to be administered to small groups (5 to 10 children) or individuals in nursery school and kindergarten. It is a battery of assessment scales, including tests and teacher ratings, used to diagnose the instructional needs of individual children. Included are measures of receptive vocabulary, quantitative concepts, visual discrimination, perceptual-motor coordination, letter and numeral recognition and discrimination, discrimination of everyday sounds, auditory discrimination of speech sounds, receptive language, productive language, general information, comprehension, visual and associative memory, problem solving, divergent pictorial production, and teacher ratings of classroom activities, behavior, and the educational environment. Most of the tests are untimed, and each test can be administered independently. The tests are easy to administer and score. The manual provides suggestions for interpreting and using the information obtained.

Evanston Early-Identification Scale
(Landsman & Dillard, 1967)

The Evanston scale is intended for group or individual administration to kindergarten children (ages 5 to 6). The test consists of asking the child to draw a person. The drawing is scored by the teacher on a 10-point scale. Teachers rank the children in three groups on the basis of their scores: low risk (will have no problem in school), middle risk (may have some difficulty in school), and high risk (can be expected to have problems in school and need special services).

First-Grade Screening Test
(Pate & Webb, 1969)

The FGST is designed to be administered near the end of kindergarten or early in the first grade. It identifies children who will probably not be ready for second grade without special help during their first-grade year. Separate forms are provided for boys and girls, and the test is easy to administer and score. It samples general information, body image, self-perception, perception of parental figures, visual-motor coordination, memory, and ability to follow directions.

Meeting Street School Screening Test
(Hainsworth & Siqueland, 1969)

The MSSST is designed for individual administration to children in kindergarten and first grade to identify those "who do not possess the requisite language and visual-perceptual-motor skills and gross motor control to adequately process the symbolic information of the traditional school curriculum" (p. 1). The test can be administered in 15 to 20 minutes. The manual provides cut-off scores for high-risk children and discusses the use of scores in understanding the skills of a particular child with learning problems. It also discusses the problem of planning and carrying out early identification programs.

Preschool Inventory
(Caldwell, 1967)

This screening device is designed for individual administration to children ages 3 to 6. It measures the child's achievement on 64 items which sample basic information and vocabulary; number concepts and ordination; concepts of size, shape, motion, and color; concepts of time, object class, and social functions; visual-motor performances; following instructions; and independence and self-help. The test is designed to be administered by the child's teacher. The PSI provides a percentile rank for the child's raw score based on his chronological age.

A Process for In-School Screening of Children with Emotional Handicaps
(Bower & Lambert, 1962)

This screening instrument has separate forms for primary, elementary, and secondary grade levels. At each level, the child's social-emotional learning is evaluated by teacher rating, self-rating, and peer rating. It is designed to identify children with suspected emotional handicaps.

Rhode Island Pupil Identification Scale
(Novack, Bonaventura, & Merenda, 1972)

The RIPIS is a two-part rating scale for use by teachers who have observed the child in the classroom for a month or more. It is designed for use with children in kindergarten through second grade. Part I of the scale deals with observable classroom behavior, Part II with the child's written work. The teacher rates each item on a 5-point scale ranging from "never" to "always." Examples of items in Part I are "Bumps into objects" and "Has difficulty sitting still." Part II includes items such as "Demonstrates poor handwriting on papers" and "Has difficulty arranging numbers vertically."

Screening instruments have value in that they formalize the teacher's assessment of each child. However, just as adequate informal assessment of learning may eliminate the necessity for formal testing, as discussed in chapter 3, acute awareness of behaviors which indicate learning problems may make screening tests superfluous.

Behavioral Indications of Potential Problems

The potential problem behaviors listed in this section should be viewed from the broad perspective of child development. Every child exhibits some inappropriate behaviors. Furthermore, many normal children temporarily exhibit a number of behaviors characteristic of children with severe learning problems. Maladaptive behavior and academic deficits should be viewed as pathological only when they are demonstrated to a marked extent and over a period of time (Bower, 1969). This does not mean that preventive action should be taken only after the child has shown a severe and chronic learning difficulty. However, it does mean that the child will not be considered to have a serious problem on the basis of an isolated incident or a temporary condition. It also means that the child's behavior must be judged in terms of developmental norms and the demands of the school environment.

Only major categories of problem behaviors are outlined below. Behaviors relevant to preschool and primary-age children are stressed because preventive efforts logically are concentrated at that age level.

I. Indications of Low Self-Concept

A child with school learning problems often reveals that he does not feel good about himself, that he feels incompetent, inadequate, and worthless. The teacher may suspect that the child has such negative feelings about himself if he:

A. Speaks disparagingly of self
B. Is unwilling to attempt new or difficult tasks
C. Is fearful of new situations
D. Is excessively shy and withdrawn
E. Lacks self-reliance; often says "I can't"
F. Shows excessive concern over acceptance by others
G. Is usually unhappy or depressed; seldom smiles; cries or frowns often
H. Demonstrates inability to make everyday decisions
I. Demonstrates inability to accept errors or correct mistakes
J. Shows extreme negative reaction to minor failures
K. Has slovenly, unkempt appearance
L. Is unable to evaluate his behavior realistically; brags or denigrates his accomplishments

II. Disturbed Relations with Peers

Often, the child with learning problems is a misfit in the social group of the classroom, a pariah among his classmates. Problems in relating to peers are noted when the child:

A. Has no close friends or "chums" in peer group
B. Is avoided by children in games and activities
C. Hits, bites, kicks, or otherwise physically assaults peers
D. Is incessantly teasing or teased by others
E. Belittles accomplishments of others
F. Seeks company of much older or younger children
G. Withdraws from group activities

III. *Inappropriate Relationship to Teachers, Parents, and Other Authority Figures*

Constructive relationship to authority is often a special problem for children with school learning difficulties. Adults who are responsible for the child are often in a quandry when he:

A. Refuses reasonable requests
B. Defies direct commands
C. Disobeys classroom rules
D. Encourages peers to disrupt the class or defy adults
E. Strikes, bites, kicks, or otherwise attempts to injure other children or adults
F. Runs away from school or home or leaves the classroom without permission
G. Steals
H. Lies
I. Manipulates adults to his advantage
J. Is overprotected; seldom allowed to enter new age-appropriate situations alone or allowed to take reasonable risks
K. Is overindulged; "spoiled" by being given noncontingent or excessive rewards

IV. *Other Signs of Social-Emotional Problems*

In addition to maladaptive behaviors related specifically to self, peers, and authority, the child with school learning problems may exhibit a variety of other inappropriate responses. The teacher may observe that the child:

A. Exhibits inappropriate behavior for a given context (e.g., laughs when someone is hurt, interprets figures of speech literally)
B. Is overly suspicious or jealous of others
C. Complains of physical symptoms, pains, or fears in mildly stressful situations; complains of every little hurt
D. Is in constant motion; compulsively manipulates objects, moves about the room excessively
E. Engages in repetitive, stereotyped motor behavior, such as tics, nailbiting, thumbsucking, or rocking
F. Talks incessantly; frequently talks out without permission or interrupts conversations

G. Explains inappropriate behavior by rationalization or intellectualization
H. Does not seem to learn from experience; behavior does not improve with usual disciplinary methods
I. Acts impulsively and shows poor judgment; does not consider or understand consequences of his behavior
J. Fails to learn when there is no evidence of intellectual, sensory, or health problems
K. Makes meaningless or "animal" noises
L. Acts impulsively and shows poor judgment; does not consider or understand consequences of his behavior
M. Is easily distracted; cannot concentrate or pay attention for more than a few minutes
N. Has not mastered bowel or bladder control
O. Shows extreme interest in monsters, war, fighting, or gruesome events
P. Is overcome frequently by drowsiness or sleep during the day
Q. Places inedible objects in mouth or shows appetite for inedible materials
R. Has violent outbursts of temper
S. Lacks curiosity
T. Daydreams; sits with a vacant expression, doing nothing productive

V. *Deficits in Speech and Language*

A child's speech and language often betray his emotional status or his intellectual or academic competence in unique ways. You may suspect that the child is experiencing social-emotional difficulty and/or a speech or language problem when he:

A. Does not speak
B. Speaks only when spoken to
C. Speaks with inappropriate pitch; voice too high-pitched or too low-pitched for age and sex
D. Speaks with inappropriate volume; voice too loud or too soft
E. Has irritating vocal quality; voice too harsh, hoarse, nasal, etc.
F. Speaks with marked dysfluency; stutters, clutters, or otherwise interrupts the flow of speech
G. Uses primarily jargon, neologisms, profanity, or other speech inappropriate for a context
H. Misarticulates many words
I. Has difficulty learning signs and symbols
J. Cannot interpret directions
K. Lacks ability to describe persons, places, and things
L. Cannot identify an object from its description
M. Does not comprehend simple sentences or familiar sequences when a part is missing

VI. *Disordered Temporal Relationships*

Orientation in time and ability to sequence events are required for adequate social and academic functioning. The child's behavior may indicate a learning problem if he:

A. Cannot tell a story in sequence
B. Does not repeat sound patterns in order
C. Cannot remember a sequence of events
D. Is chronically late
E. Is absent-minded; often forgets important events
F. Is unable to plan a sequence of events
G. Refuses to talk about the past
H. Cannot shift readily from one activity to another
I. Is easily confused by a change in routine
J. Confuses seasons, months, years, days, and other intervals of time after the age at which most children learn these concepts
K. Cannot acquire basic auditory sequences, such as telephone numbers, alphabet, nursery rhymes

VII. *Difficulties in Auditory and Visual Perception*

The ability of the child to integrate what he sees and hears in a meaningful way is essential for progress in school. The child may have a serious problem in interpreting visual and auditory stimuli when he:

A. Attends to irrelevant details
B. Cannot organize materials
C. Loses place frequently when copying
D. Has difficulty cutting, coloring, or pasting
E. Does not discriminate differences in size, shape, color, or perspective
F. Does not discriminate changes in pitch, loudness, or timbre of sounds
G. Has difficulty recognizing common objects when a part is missing
H. Has difficulty recognizing sounds made by common objects
I. Does not understand positional words, such as *up, down, above, in*
J. Cannot relate pictures to parts of a story
K. Does not understand the meaning of pictures
L. Has difficulty reproducing simple geometric shapes with pencil and paper (e.g., cannot copy a square, circle, rectangle)
M. Is unable to recognize rhymes or give rhyming words
N. Makes poorly formed or reversed letters; poor handwriting
O. Has difficulty drawing corners or angles
P. Has difficulty spelling phonetic units or words
Q. Makes facial contortions when doing visual tasks

VIII. *Poor Quantitative Reasoning and Computational Skill*

Quantitative reasoning and computational skills are considered to be basic components of intelligence. They are a vital part of school learning and necessary for independent functioning in our society. When a child has a learning problem in this area, it is often found that he:

A. Has difficulty with concepts of inequality (e.g., more-less, larger-smaller, heavier-lighter)
B. Does not understand one-to-one correspondence
C. Is unable to count to a number appropriate for age
D. Has marked difficulty learning basic number facts
E. Does not understand the value of coins
F. Is unable to understand place value (cannot regroup for borrowing and carrying)
G. Can make necessary computations but is unable to organize information from a "story problem"
H. Relies excessively on finger or bead counting for simple computations

IX. *Deficits in Basic Motor Skills*

The child's fine and gross movements often indicate his learning characteristics or adjustment to school. A problem in motor learning may be suspected when the child:

A. Is unable to balance on one foot
B. Has an unsteady, awkward, or unusual gait
C. Is unable to throw and catch a ball
D. Does not hold a pencil or scissors normally
E. Has poor coordination; clumsy and inaccurate in movement, often accidentally breaks things
F. Cannot tie shoes, button, or zip clothing
G. Avoids physical activities or sports

SUMMARY

Prevention of learning problems may entail teaching methods that preclude or reduce the probability that problems will arise or therapeutic teaching to minimize existing problems and prevent their complication. In most schools, the primary responsibility for preventive action is likely to fall on the classroom teacher. Two fundamental principles of prevention are good teaching and early detection. Good teaching means teaching specific measureable skills, continuously assessing the child's performance, teaching first things first, being directive, and using positive methods. Efforts to detect learning problems early carry the dangers of misidentification, negative perceptions of the child, and lack of appropriate services following identification. Early detection may be aided by screening instruments, but acute sensitivity of the teacher to behaviors which signal possible problems is the single most important factor.

A Guide to Teaching Activities

Sound principles are needed to guide teaching practice, but sound practice goes beyond the mere repetition of principles. It is not enough for a teacher to know, for example, that behavior that is reinforced is more likely to occur again or that remedial teaching involves continuous assessment of the child's performance. The teacher must know how to assess the child's performance, how to present instructional tasks, and how to reinforce appropriate behavior. A major purpose of this book is to provide the teacher with an array of specific behavior-management and instructional activities which have proven their value in the classroom.

Chapter 6 suggests techniques for dealing with social-emotional problems in the classroom. Chapters 7 through 11 contain suggested instructional activities for remediating specific learning problems in the curriculum areas of reading, written language, spoken language, arithmetic, and visual-motor skills. Each of the chapters includes a brief statement of the major skills the child must learn to perform adequately in that curriculum area. This statement is followed by suggestions for diagnosis of the child's problems, including teacher observation, informal assessment techniques, and formal tests. Teaching suggestions are organized under diagnostic questions designed to help the teacher identify the child's learning problem. Instructional programs and additional readings at the end of each chapter provide a guide for in-depth study of learning problems and teaching methods.

We have attempted to organize our teaching activities within chapters according to the sequential development of skills. You should recognize, however, that a full exposition of sequential skill development in any curriculum area goes far beyond the skeletal framework on which our chapters are organized. Hopefully, our outlines of sequential learning will provide a beginning point for further study and analysis.

Many basic skills that children learn are relevant to several academic areas. For example, form discrimination is a skill which is prerequisite for success in reading, written language, and arithmetic. Because of interrelationships among basic academic tasks, many of our teaching suggestions can be adapted for use in curriculum areas other than the one for which they are given.

Most of our teaching activities are intended for use with elementary school children who are deficient in very basic skills. The teacher who works with older children will need to adapt many of our suggestions to meet the needs and interests of children of junior high or high school age. Teaching suggestions that are most appropriate for older children are starred.

The source of some of our remedial activities is our own teaching experience. Many of the activities, however, did not originate with us. The sources of those suggestions, or of slight variations of them, have been cited wherever possible. In many cases the original sources of "tried-and-true" activities could not be found.

**6
Social-
Emotional
Problems**

Social-Emotional Problems

The social and emotional growth of the child is equally as important as academic growth. In fact, social-emotional learning is inseparably linked to the acquisition of academic skills. Inappropriate social and emotional responses seriously limit the child's chances for success at school; conversely, school failure often prompts undesirable social and emotional responses. Many children who have learning problems are not distinguished by their good work habits, productivity, cooperativeness, and social graces (see Kauffman, 1977). Frequently, it is necessary to establish good work habits and eliminate interfering social behaviors before academic remediation can be accomplished. The objectives of behavior management should be to prepare the child for academic learning and increase the efficiency and effectiveness of instruction. As suggested in chapters 2 and 4, the teacher must teach work habits and adaptive social behaviors directly. Teachers must concern themselves with two basic problems:

1. What academic response patterns prevent the child from learning efficiently?
2. What social-emotional behaviors interfere with the child's learning?

ASSESSMENT

Screening and Formal Tests

Screening instruments (several of which are described briefly in chapter 5) and rating scales are available for identifying major problem areas. Hewett (1968) has developed a hierarchy of educational goals and a useful inventory of behaviors related to academic and social tasks. Walker (1969) has outlined a model for assessment of deviant behavior. However, effective management of specific problem behaviors depends on observational diagnostic methods which are more precise than rating scales and inventories. A precise definition of the behavior and an analysis of antecedent and consequent events are essential, as we will discuss later.

There are few useful formal tests available for diagnosing behavior-management problems. Although the disciplines of psychology, neurology, and psychiatry have developed a wide variety of personality measures and neurological tests, they provide little information which can be used in teaching. As Hewett (1968) has stated:

> It is not that the multi-disciplinary maps or viewpoints of psychiatry, clinical psychology, or neurology are inaccurate or irrelevant but that they seldom are truly useful in bridging the gap between description and diagnosis and practical classroom application. . . .(p. 78)

Diagnosis of social-emotional problems depends primarily on teacher observation and analysis of the child's behavior. The teacher must obtain baseline data and analyze the factors which control the child's behavior, as discussed in chapter 2. Appropriate diagnostic methods have been described in detail by Lovitt (1967, 1977), Gelfand and Hartmann (1975), Worell and Nelson (1974), and others.

It is helpful to conceptualize the child's behavior in terms of excesses and deficits. When the teacher is diagnosing behavioral excesses, he must answer the following questions:

1. What does the child do that is maladaptive?
2. How often does he do it under present conditions?
3. What environmental events serve to maintain his behavior?
4. How can I remove the events that support his undesirable behavior?

Essentially, diagnosis of behavioral deficits must answer the following questions for the teacher:

1. What do I want the child to do?
2. How often does he do it under present conditions?
3. What approximations of what I want the child to do can I identify?
4. What reinforcers for the child can I identify that are at my disposal?
5. How can I provide reinforcers for successive approximations of what I want the child to do?

Adequate diagnosis requires that the teacher observe not only exactly what behavioral excesses and deficits the child exhibits, but also exactly what happens just prior to and just after the child performs the response. This type of observation is often referred to as an *ABC analysis*—and it is this type of diagnostic procedure that provides the most useful information for managing social-emotional problems.

ABC Analysis

An ABC analysis requires that the teacher consider *A—**the antecedents of the behavior,*** the events that occur immediately before the behavior and seem to "set it off" or provide the occasion for it; *B—**the behavior itself,*** exactly what it is that the child does, defined precisely enough that it can be observed and measured reliably; and *C—**the consequences of the behavior,*** what happens immediately after the behavior occurs and seems to reinforce it.

First, it is necessary to consider exactly what the child does that is a problem: What does he do or what does he say that can be observed and recorded? When did the child last exhibit this behavior? How often do you estimate that the behavior occurs? Does the problem seem to be getting better, worse, or staying about the same?

Second, it is necessary to consider the situations in which the behavior occurs: Does it occur at school, at home, or in both settings? If it happens at school, in what locations or activities does it occur? Can particular events that trigger the behavior be identified? Who is usually with the child when he exhibits the behavior?

Third, it is necessary to consider what happens as a consequence of the child's behavior: How do you respond? How do other children respond? Does the child usually get his own way, receive someone's attention (even if it is negative attention, such as reprimands, criticism, or teasing), or obtain some other reinforcer?

Finally, it is necessary to consider what attempts have been made to modify the behavior: What methods have been tried? For how long, by whom, and with what success? What range of methods *can* be tried, given the child, other children, the adults, and resources in the situation?

After considering these questions, the teacher must observe and record the child's behavior, as we discussed in chapter 2. The direct daily measurement of the child's behavior will indicate the magnitude of the problem and provide a means of judging success in resolving it.

Following are a number of suggestions for managing specific social-emotional problems. Each sugestion is based on classroom experience, but remember that its successful use with a certain child depends on adaptation of the technique to meet the unique requirements of the individual.

INTERFERING SOCIAL BEHAVIORS

Social and emotional behaviors which interfere with learning must be brought under control before academic problems can be remediated. The child must learn to:
1. Attend school willingly and regularly.
2. Accept the authority of the teacher and other school personnel.
3. Work cooperatively and constructively in the classroom.
4. Establish positive relationships with his peers.
5. Exhibit behavior indicative of a positive self-image.
6. Exhibit appropriate behavior outside the classroom.

Diagnostic questions, informal assessment, and management suggestions for interfering social behaviors are listed in the following section.

DOES THE CHILD ATTEMPT TO ESCAPE OR AVOID SCHOOL?

Does the Child Resist Coming to School?

Informal Assessment   Keep careful records of the child's tardiness or absence. See if you can identify specific things that happen at home or on the way to school that account for the problem. What happens after the child comes to school late or when he stays home? Does he "miss" anything that is reinforcing, or does he actually get reinforced for avoiding school (does he get to watch TV, go fishing, or do something else he prefers)?

1. Have a special treat or activity waiting for the child each day when he comes to school. *Management Activities*

2. If one parent brings the child to school, arrange to have the other parent bring the child until he is able to walk or ride the bus by himself.

3. Award every child a star for each day's attendance at school. Have a party on Friday for all children who have had perfect attendance during the week.

4. Start a "club" in the area of greatest interest to the child (science, math, reading, music, etc.). Make participation in the weekly meetings depend on at least four days attendance since the last meeting.

5. Try to get the parent's cooperation in withholding reinforcement when the child stays at home and in stating to the child matter-of-factly each morning that he must go to school.

6. Have the school principal stop by the classroom each morning to compliment the child on his presence at school (Copeland, Brown, & Hall, 1974).

7. Let children earn the privilege of going to a special monthly party by regular attendance during the preceding month (Barber & Kagey, 1977).

*8. Find a person in the community who is able and willing to provide an activity (e.g., riding horses and helping out around the stables, working at the service station) contingent on the child's attendance at school (Tharp & Wetzel, 1969).

*9. Write contingency contracts specifying the rewarding activities the youngster can earn by attending school regularly and behaving appropriately (MacDonald, Gallimore, & MacDonald, 1970).

Does the Child Frequently Run from the Classroom?

Count the frequency with which this problem behavior occurs and note the circumstances under which it tends to occur (time of day, activity, things that happen immediately before he runs out). What *Informal Assessment* happens when the child runs? Do you or others go after him? Where does he go, and what does he do that he might find reinforcing? Is he running away from an unpleasant (aversive) situation or to get something he likes (something reinforcing, such as a chance to play on the playground, the pleasure of being the center of attention and of being chased)?

Management   **10.** Increase your positive attention to the child when he is in the
Activities   classroom. Keep your interaction with the child outside the classroom at a minimum (Haring, Hayden, & Allen, 1971).

*11. Tell the child that if he does not leave the room without permission you will
spend 20 minutes working with him on a favorite activity (e.g., sewing, model
building, reading).

DOES THE CHILD CHALLENGE AUTHORITY?

Does the Child Disobey Directions or Requests?

Informal   How often is the child directed or requested to do something? Is he
Assessment   being badgered? Are the directions given clearly and firmly? Are the
requests reasonable? Does the child respond to no one or to
selected individuals? Does the child finally comply, after he is directed or
requested several times? Will the child eventually comply if the request or
command is given only once and the teacher waits but does not nag? Keep a
record of requests and commands and the child's compliant and noncompliant
responses.

Management   **12.** If the child refuses to recite in class, allow any child who does
Activities   recite to bring a book or magazine of his choice to class for a specified
period of private reading at the end of the class (Madsen & Madsen,
1970, 1974).

13. Provide the class with several specific examples of "good attitude." Include
examples of obeying commands and complying with teacher requests . Later,
praise the child by commending his "good attitude" when his behavior approximates obedience and compliance (Madsen & Madsen, 1970, 1974).

14. Arrange a time-out area in the room. If the child does not obey a direct
command within 15 seconds, place the child in the time-out area for 5 minutes.
After 5 minutes allow the child to leave the time-out area only if he is willing to
follow your directions. Praise the child when he does obey commands.

15. Ignore the child when he disobeys a direction given to the class. Do not
allow him to comply with your next command to the class until he follows the first
directive. Compliment the child for obedient behavior whenever he follows your
directions.

Does the Child Argue with the Teacher?

Exactly what does the child tend to argue about? With whom does
he argue? What happens if people simply refuse to respond with
counterarguments? Count the number of arguments or disputes
each day.

*Informal
Assessment*

16. If you are certain that your judgment is correct, tell the child
only once that his answer is unacceptable. Do not respond in any
way to protestations or complaints that you are wrong (Hall, 1971).
Remember that you can make errors, and give the child the benefit of the doubt
if an issue is unclear.

*Management
Activities*

*17. Whenever the child begins a dispute concerning an assignment or
direction, stop all interaction with him by turning and walking away. If the child
begins an assignment or follows a directive without arguing, praise him with a
positive statement (Hall, Fox, Willard, Goldsmith, Emerson, Owen, Davis, &
Porcia, 1971).

IS THE CHILD UNCOOPERATIVE OR DISRUPTIVE IN THE CLASSROOM?

Is the Child Often Out of his Seat Without Permission?

Count the number of times the child is out of his seat without
permission during a specified time period. During what activities
does the behavior occur with the greatest frequency or cause the
greatest problem? Where does the child go, and what does he do when he
gets out of his seat? Are the rules for getting up and moving about the room
clear and explicit? Is the child actually out of his seat more than other children?
(You may want to record the behavior of several other children for purposes of
comparison.)

*Informal
Assessment*

18. Make an explicit rule concerning movement about the classroom. Ignore children who do not follow the rule. Praise children
who observe the rule (Madsen et al., 1968).

*Management
Activities*

19. Allow any child who has remained in his seat during the work period to
play musical chairs, eraser tag, seven-up, or some other game involving
movement.

20. Shuffle a deck of playing cards and let the child select a suit. For each academic task completed, allow the child to turn a card face up. If the card turned face up is a member of the chosen suit, let the child get a drink of water from the fountain, visit the game corner for 1 minute, or make some other specific, quiet movement about the room. If the child gets out of his seat without permission, require him to forfeit his next card-turn (see Kauffman, Cullinan, Scranton, & Wallace, 1972; Kauffman & Hallahan, 1973).

21. Set a timer for varying brief intervals. If the child has remained in his seat during the interval, give him a small piece of candy and praise him for sitting.

22. Set a timer as in #21 above, but take care to hide it from the child's view. Have the child record whether he is in or out of his seat each time the timer rings.

*23. Mark off an area of the floor around the child's desk with heavy tape. Make explicit rules about the child's movement out of his "area" or "territory" and other children's movement into his "private space." Reinforce children for compliance with the rules about "territorial rights" (Nay, Schulman, Bailey, & Huntsinger, 1976).

Does the Child Talk Out or Interrupt Conversations?

Informal Assessment Count the frequency of interruptions. Are the rules for conversation clear to the child? Is the child successful at interrupting (i.e., does he get the attention of those he interrupts)? Does the child have many opportunities to speak? When he waits his turn to speak does he get the undivided attention of his listeners? Is the child often interrupted himself when he is talking?

Management Activities **24.** The suggestions provided in #18 under "out-of-seat" behavior can also be used effectively for talking out behavior (Madsen et al., 1968; Hall, Fox, Willard, Goldsmith, Emerson, Owen, Davis, & Porcia, 1971).

25. For each 30-minute period during which the child does not talk out, allow him 5 minutes to play with a "magic slate" or some other educational toy (Hall, 1971).

26. When the child talks out without raising his hand or interrupts a conversation, do not recognize him in any way. Turn your back or walk away if the child attempts to get your attention by tugging at your sleeve or standing in front of you. When the child does raise his hand and wait his turn to speak, recognize him immediately and compliment him.

*27. If there are fewer than five talk-outs during a 40-minute study period, allow the class a 10-minute break for casual conversations.

*28. Move the child's desk away from children to whom he tends to talk, and near children with whom he is unlikely to converse.

*29. Award the child a point for each 5-minute period during which he works quietly without talking. When he has accumulated ten or more points, allow him to exchange them for minutes during which he "interviews" other pupils and tape records the conversation for replay to the class.

*30. Give the child a slip of paper on which he is to record his own talk-outs during the study period. Have him return the slip to you at the end of class (Broden, Hall, & Mitts, 1971).

Does the Child Ask Inappropriate or Unnecessary Questions or Change the Topic of Conversations?

Under what circumstances does the behavior occur? How do people respond to the questions or attempts to change the topic of conversation? Keep a careful record of how often the behavior occurs.   *Informal Assessment*

31. Handle this problem similarly to talking out or tattling; ignore the inappropriate or unnecessary questions and attend to the child when his are appropriate and necessary. Do not respond to attempts to change the topic of conversation.   *Management Activities*

*32. If the questions or changes of topic fall below an agreed-upon level for several days, allow the class a "free Friday" when they may discuss anything they wish or engage in any appropriate behavior of their choice (Deitz & Repp, 1973).

Does the Child Make Distracting Noises?

Make a frequency count of the noises. When do they occur most frequently? Does the child make the noises in response to specific interactions or events? How do other children and adults respond to the noises?   *Informal Assessment*

33. Ignore the child's noise making and praise children who are being quiet. Give the noise-maker positive attention and praise when he exhibits quiet behavior (Hall, 1971).   *Management Activities*

34. If the child continues to make excessive noise with an object after he has been warned, take the object from him for a short, specified period of time.

*35. For each 15-minute interval during which the child does not make the distracting noise, give the child a point. Let him take roll the next day if he accumulates ten or more points (see Wulbert & Dries, 1977).

Does the Child Have Frequent Crying Spells or Temper Tantrums?

Informal Assessment   Under what circumstances do the crying and tantrums occur? How do other children and adults respond? Does the child get his own way by exhibiting this behavior? Are unreasonable demands being placed on the child? Can any health problems be identified that might contribute to the inappropriate behavior (for instance, lack of adequate food or sleep)?

Management Activities   **36.** Tell the class that as long as the child is not crying, they must call him by his "big" name, e.g., *Fred*. Whenever he cries, they may call him by his usual though nonpreferred name, e.g., *Freddy* (Kaufhold & Kauffman, in Worell & Nelson, 1974).

37. When the child begins a temper tantrum, immediately place him in an isolation or time-out area of the classroom. Be firm but unemotional in dealing with the child. After the child has been quiet for 5 minutes, allow him to leave the time-out area.

38. Give no attention to the child when he is crying or tantruming. Attend to the child only when his behavior is appropraite.

39. Observe the child's tantrums carefully. Notice the first behavior the child exhibits when beginning a tantrum (e.g., desk-hitting or foot-stomping). Tell the child to repeat the behavior more forcefully for a specific number of times (e.g., "That's it, stomp really hard five times." Tell the child to repeat the behavior until he says he would like to stop.

40. At the beginning of class, give the chilld five coloed slips of paper with his name written on each. Each time the child whines, cries, or complains during the class period, take one name slip away from him. Warn him that this is what you are going to do (Hall, Axelrod, Foundopoulos, Shellman, Campbell, & Cranston, 1971).

Does the Child Destroy Property of Others?

Informal Assessment   Exactly what has been destroyed? When and how was it destroyed? Is there a pattern to the targets of the child's destruction? What happens to the child as a consequence of destroying something? Keep careful records of what is destroyed and the consequences.

Management Activities   **41.** The child should wash desks and walls that are defaced by pen or pencil marks, under close supervision, until the teacher is satisfied (Madsen & Madsen, 1970, 1974).

42. When wads of chewing gum are found under desks, establish gum-chewing privileges for Monday, Wednesday, and Friday. If an individual is caught chewing gum on Tuesday or Thursday, he loses one day of gum-chewing privileges and also has to remove five wads of gum from under a desk (Madsen & Madsen, 1970, 1974).

*43. If a child destroys another child's property, require him to replace it with an equivalent or better item (Foxx & Azrin, 1972).

*44. If the child steals or extorts tokens, invalidate all of the tokens he currently possesses and let him earn only distinctively marked tokens.

Does the Child Swear in School?

How often and in what situations does the child swear? Does the child get a "shock" reaction from other children and adults?   *Informal Assessment*

45. Give the student a list of ten alternative words to swearing. Tell the child that each time he has the urge to swear, he should use a word from the list.   *Management Activities*

46. Set a kitchen timer for successive 30-minute periods. Praise the student for each 30-minute period in which he does not swear. (For some children, the time periods may need to be as short as 1 minute.) After the student shows the ability to refrain from swearing for a given period of time, gradually increase the length of the time period.

*47. Record the number of swears per hour, period, or day. Tell the child that swearing is inappropriate in the school and that it is his responsibility to eliminate this behavior. Have him record his swears on a graph. Praise him for a reduced number of swears per hour, period, or day.

*48. Prepare a tape recorder so that it is ready to operate at a time when the child is likely to swear. Secretly record his swearing. In a private conference with the student, play the tape and have him comment on the appropriateness of his language.

*49. Some children may reduce their level of swearing if they are given a time out for saying swear words (Lahey, McNees, & McNees, 1973).

Does the Child Use Lewd Gestures or Write Inappropriate Messages?

Exactly what gestures or messages are involved? With what frequency and under what circumstances do they occur? How do other children and adults react to these gestures or messages?   *Informal Assessment*

Management   **50.** Establish a special 10-minute recess for the class. Place a set
Activities   of cards numbered one through ten on the base of a desk calendar.
Each time a lewd gesture is seen or reported, turn a card, which
reduces the special recess by 1 minute (Sulzbacher & Houser, 1968).

*51. Make a rule that if students are caught passing notes or secret
messages, a special privilege will be withdrawn. Remind the students that
notes and secret messages may be passed during a special 3-minute
communication period (Madsen & Madsen, 1970, 1974).

Has the Child Failed to Learn Polite Social Behavior?

Informal   How is politeness defined in the child's home and community?
Assessment   What models of polite social behaviors has the child observed?
Does the child infrequently exhibit appropriate social responses, or
does he never do so? What is the reaction of others to the child's lack of social
amenities?

Management   **51.** When distributing materials, praise the children who say
Activities   "thank you." Also praise those students who request material with
the word "please."

53. Role play polite behaviors with the children. Praise the children who
exhibit those behaviors at times other than role playing.

54. If you are certain the child has the appropriate skills and knows he should
use them, give him a gentle reminder and do not respond to his request until he
asks politely.

HAS THE CHILD ESTABLISHED NEGATIVE
OR INADEQUATE RELATIONSHIPS WITH HIS PEERS?

Does the Child Hit or Otherwise Assault Other Children?

Informal   Is the child provoked into aggressive responses by others? Does he
Assessment   attack smaller and weaker children? How do his victims respond?
Who usually gets the attention after a fight, the victim or the aggres-
sor? What consequences do the adults in the situation provide for the child's
aggression? Does the child usually "get away with it" or are there unpleasant
consequences? Do adults respond with hostile counteraggression?

55. Completely ignore the child who did the hitting—do not reprimand him, scowl at him, or attend to him in any way. Go immediately to the child who was hit and give him positive attention, care, or comfort. *Management Activities*

56. Count the number of times the child commits an act of overt aggression against another person during a specified time interval, such as the recess period. Show the child the record of his behavior over a period of several days. Award points each day that the record indicates zero acts of aggression or fewer than the average for the previous days. Let the child exchange the points earned for special activities or treats.

57. Arrange a chair in a corner of the room which is away from any interesting objects or other children. Each time the child hits, kicks, pinches, or otherwise hurts another child place him immediately and unemotionally in the chair and tell him he must sit there for 5 minutes. After 5 minutes let him rejoin the group. Be sure to tell the child what you are going to do before initiating the strategy.

58. Observe the activity during which the most fighting takes place (e.g., music or recess). For each day that no fighting occurs during the chosen activity, allow the child to visit with the principal for 5 minutes. The principal must be willing to chat pleasantly with the child contingent on the child's good behavior (Madsen & Madsen, 1970, 1974).

59. Ignore aggressive behavior unless there is serious threat of bodily harm. Show approval and praise frequently for peaceful and cooperativ e behavior.

60. Give attention to the victim of the child's aggression (Brown & Elliott, 1965; Pinkston, Reese, LeBlanc, & Baer, 1973).

*61. Time-out (immediate, brief, matter-of-factly applied social isolation) is typically the best method of handling aggression, especially in older children (see Gast & Nelson, 1977, in press, for specific guidelines).

Does the Child Tease Other Children too Frequently?

How does the child perform the teasing? Who are the targets of his torment, and how do they respond? Count the number of instances of teasing each day. *Informal Assessment*

62. Do not reprimand the teasing child. Arrange with the child who is being teased that he will earn the privilege of helping you for 2 minutes after school each time he is teased but makes no response. *Management Activities*

63. When the teasing begins, go immediately to the child who is being teased, turn him physically away from the teaser, and engage him in a pleasant conversation before he reacts to the teasing. Ignore the child who is teasing.

64. Tell the child who teases that he may not tease his peers but he may tease you. Encourage him to tease you when he "feels the urge" and react dramatically to his teasing. Tease him appropriately in return. However, if he teases another child, give him a brief but firm reprimand.

65. Have the teased child record the number of times he is taunted but makes no response to his tormentor. Check the reliability of his recording at frequent intervals. Give the child one valentine candy for each occasion on which he makes no response to teasing. For each ten candies, let the child earn an "I can take it" certificate; and after five certificates present him, with great ceremony, the "Medal of Bravery." The certificate and medal may be made from construction paper.

Does the Child Interrupt Other Children Who Are Working?

Informal Assessment
Who does the child interrupt? Exactly how does he do it? How frequently and under what circumstances does this behavior occur? How do other children respond, and what is the reaction of the teacher?

Management Activities
66. For each 10-minute interval during which the child does not bother anyone else in the class, allow him, during a specified time, to spend 1 minute visiting socially with another child.

67. Make a small isolation booth in a corner of the room by using a coatrack, bookcase, or other movable furniture. Each time the child interferes with the work of a classmate, send him to the time-out booth for 10 minutes (Madsen & Madsen, 1970, 1974).

*68. Let the child earn points to "buy" a preferred or larger size desk or permission to move his desk to a preferred location for a day if he refrains from interrupting others.

Is the Child Reinforced by his Peers for Misbehavior?

Informal Assessment
Is the child reinforced by attention from the entire class or a small group of peers? In what ways other than misbehaving does the child get attention from his peers?

69. Discuss the problem briefly with the class. Explain that for each   *Management*
work period during which the usual miscreant does not misbehave,   *Activities*
the entire class will have a 10-minute break.

70. Each time the child misbehaves and is reinforced by his peers, make a tally mark on the chalkboard. Reduce the usual free time or recess period by 15 seconds for each mark given. Praise the child for working without distracting his peers.

*71. Arrange for one or more of the child's peers to pay attention to his appropriate behavior and ignore him when he is misbehaving. Try to enlist the aid of peers who have high social status. It may also be helpful to arrange for the misbehaving child to "tutor" a younger child and teach him how to behave appropriately (see McGee, Kauffman, & Nussen, in press).

Does the Child Seldom Talk to Peers or the Teacher?

Under what circumstances and to whom will the child talk? Is the   *Informal*
child approached socially by peers? Is the child listened to when he   *Assessment*
talks?

72. Let the child record his own voice on a tape recorder and replay   *Management*
the tape immediately. Praise the child for recording his voice and   *Activities*
gradually require more and more conversational speech from the
child.

73. Give the child a penny each time that you observe him talking with another child or he talks spontaneously to you. At first, give the penny even if only one word is spoken. When the child has begun making frequent one-word responses, gradually demand longer responses to earn the reward. Praise the child for talking when you give him the penny.

74. Arrange to have the child's parents reward him for bringing home a daily "report card." Have the child keep a folded piece of colored construction paper with him at all times. Whenever you observe him talking appropriately to someone or he talks to you, draw a "happy face" on his report card. Review his card at the end of the day. Have him return it the following day with a parent's signature.

*75. Let the child work with an especially friendly child on a special project (e.g., building a model car) during a 15-minute period each day. Obtain the cooperation of the child's friend in asking him questions and responding positively to his comments. When conversation between the two children is established, add a third child to the group and let them begin a new project.

Is the Child Rejected Socially by his Peers?

Informal Assessment   Does the child exhibit behaviors his peers find noxious or unpleasant? How does the child respond to social advances from other children? Does the child receive extra attention from the teacher when he is engaged in solitary activities? Record instances of social rejection.

Management Activities   **76.** When rewards (e.g., candy) or highly desired materials (e.g., art supplies) are distributed to the class, have the isolate child be the distributor (Kirby & Toler, 1970).

77. Keep the rejected child close to you. Let the other children observe you interacting pleasantly with him. Give special attention to children who imitate your model. Ignore children who overtly reject or avoid the child, and give attention to the child who is rejected.

78. Choose desirable behavior of the rejected child (e.g., looking at a book, writing neatly). Comment positively on his behavior within the hearing of the entire class and make it the occasion for a special "fun" activity (singing a song, taking a break, giving extra time at recess, etc.).

*79. Set a kitchen timer to ring at 15-minute intervals. When the timer rings, go to the child and give him feedback (privately) on his behavior during the 15-minute interval (see Drabman & Lahey, 1974).

Does the Child Cling to Adults, Avoid his Peers, or Spend too Much Time in Isolate Play?

Informal Assessment   How much time does the child spend with adults versus peers? Record the percent of time spent with adults and with peers. Is the child ignored by adults when he is playing with his peers and given attention when he approaches adults unnecessarily?

Management Activities   **80.** Ignore the child when he attempts to interact unnecessarily with you or another adult. Attend positively to the child when he is playing or working with other children (Allen, Hart, Buell, Harris, & Wolf, 1964).

81. Comment positively on the cooperative behavior of specific children at frequent intervals. Make certain that the isolate child hears your comments.

82. Have children role play characters in a story which demands that they interact socially with peers (Strain & Wiegerink, 1976).

Does the Child Spend Long Periods Daydreaming?

Record the frequency and duration of the child's daydreaming episodes. What is the child supposed to be doing during these episodes? Is the work he is given too easy or to hard? What are the consequences of his daydreaming?

Informal Assessment

83. Make sure that the work is neither too easy nor too difficult for the child.

Management Activities

84. Make the task more interesting by giving novel directions or requiring an unusual mode of response (e.g., let the child "print" the answers to arithmetic problems involving two-digit sums by using a library date stamp).

85. Set a timer to ring at brief random intervals. Explain that when the bell goes off, the child will be allowed to pull an item from a "fun box" if he is working hard. To make the fun box, write directions on slips of paper and fasten them to strings. Put them in a box with only the ends of the strings showing. On the slips, write a wide variety of directions such as "Give one chocolate candy to every person who is working and take ten for yourself," "Go back to your work until you can earn another try," "Take this note to the principal and he will give you five cents," "Choose six other people to play one game of seven-up right now."

Does the Child "Tattle" on Others?

Record how often tattling occurs and what the tattler reports. Who listens and responds to the tattling?

Informal Assessment

86. Ignore the tattling or simply say, "I don't care to hear about it."

Management Activities

*87. When a child tattles, change the topic of conversation abruptly and continue as if the tattling had not occurred.

DOES THE CHILD'S BEHAVIOR INDICATE IMMATURITY OR A NEGATIVE SELF-IMAGE?

Does the Child Appear Sloppy or Dirty?

Exactly what grooming problems does the child exhibit? What factors at home contribute to the child's undesirable appearance? Has the child been taught specific grooming skills?

Informal Assessment

Management   **88.** Make a life-size cut-out of a boy and girl with hair combed, hands
Activities   clean, fingernails clean, teeth brushed, shirt tucked in, and shoes
shined. Have a morning grooming check, and post the name of each
child who approximates the appearance of the cut-out.

89. If you are using a token system in your classroom, the store should contain a
number of self-care items (e.g., soap, comb, toothbrush, aftershave lotion,
perfume). Don't overprice these items. Have frequent sales.

90. Model appropriate grooming skills for the children. Let the children watch
you wash your hands, comb your hair, use a fingernail brush to clean your nails.
Compliment children who imitate your model of good grooming.

*91. Set up a style show for students to model clothes. Make participation in the
style show a reward for good grooming.

Does the Child Suck his Thumb or Fingers?

Informal   Under what circumstances does the behavior occur? Record the
Assessment   duration of thumbsucking during specific time intervals.

Management   **92.** Ignore the child when he is sucking his thumb and give attention
Activities   and praise for behaviors other than thumbsucking (Skiba et al.,
1971).

93. During story time, stop reading to the child immediately when he puts his
thumb in his mouth, and do not resume reading until he removes it. (Note: This
procedure may also be suggested to parents. See Kauffman & Scranton, 1974;
Knight & McKenzie, 1974).

Does the Child Exhibit Repetitive, Stereotyped, or Self-injurious Behavior?

Informal   In what situations does the behavior tend to occur? Does the child
Assessment   receive extra attention when engaging in this behavior? Does the
behavior interfere seriously with the child's development?

Management   **94.** Enlist the assistance of several responsible pupils. Have the
Activities   pupils sit next to the child who is grimacing or gesturing and praise
him when his behavior is appropriate. For example, "Good, Ogden,
you're not gnashing your teeth now" (Gallagher, 1971).

95. When the child begins a self-injurious behavior, shout "STOP IT" as loudly as possible. Make your shouting as aversive as possible for the child. Do not soothe the child or comfort him while caring for his wound if he purposely hurts himself. Give the child a great deal of positive attention when he is not engaged in self-injurious behavior. (See comments on the use of punishment in chapter 2.)

*96. Let the child earn points for refraining from engaging in the undesirable behavior. The points can be exchanged for prizes, such as toys, games, or models (Wulbert & Dries, 1977).

DOES THE CHILD EXHIBIT INAPPROPRIATE BEHAVIOR OUTSIDE THE CLASSROOM?

Does the Child Refuse Many Foods at Lunch?

Keep a record of exactly which foods the child refuses. Has the child been introduced to or sampled the foods he refuses? Are other foods readily available to him?

Informal Assessment

97. Plan a unit of instruction on foods of another culture. For example, have a series of lessons on foods of the Orient and let the children wear coolie hats that they have made, on the days when chop suey is served (Cooper, Payne, & Edwards, 1971).

Management Activities

98. Let the children who have eaten all of their food add a part, such as a leaf on a tree or a cotton ball on Santa's beard, to a special bulletin board (Cooper et al., 1971).

99. Let the child observe you eating and enjoying foods which he does not eat.

100. Provide treats and praise for children who eat nutritional foods (Madsen, Madsen, & Thompson, 1974).

Is the Child too Active or Noisy at the Lunch Table?

Notice the children with whom the child sits at the lunch table. What are the consequences of rowdy lunch-time behavior?

Informal Assessment

101. Arrange with the parents that you will send home a daily report of the child's lunchroom behavior. The report will simply state whether or not he has earned the privilege of staying up for an extra

Management Activities

30 minutes before bedtime. Give good reports contingent on improved behavior.

102. Seat the children in boy-girl-boy-girl order at the lunch table. Reward children who are talking quietly and using good manners with attention and praise.

*103. Arrange special activities in which children may engage if their behavior during lunch is appropriate (special activities might include gym time, movies, outdoor play, TV, card games, model building, story time, clay modeling). Withdraw the child's privilege of engaging in these activities for infractions of specific lunchroom rules. If a child persists in misbehaving, require that he write an essay on the following: What did I do *wrong*? What happens that I don't like when I _____? What *should* I do? What pleasant things happen when I _____? (MacPherson, Candee, & Hohman, 1974)

Is the Child Disruptive on the Bus?

Informal Assessment   How are reports of disruptive behavior on the bus received? What consequences for disruptive and appropriate behavior can be applied by the bus driver, the parents, and the teacher?

Management Activities   **104.** Record several sing-along songs on a cassette tape recorder. Have a responsible student operate the recorder en route to and from school. The use of recorded songs stimulates children to sing rather than fight while they ride (Payne, Finegold, & Cooper, 1971).

*105. Have the child carefully observe what is happening on the bus. Have him write what he sees on a special piece of paper given to him by the bus driver. Reward him for the number of words that he uses to describe the activities on the bus.

*106. If a token system is operating in the classroom, the bus driver can be given tokens to dispense for good behavior on the bus.

ACADEMIC RESPONSE PROBLEMS

To be a successful learner in any area of the curriculum, the child must make appropriate academic responses as directed by the teacher. Specifically, the child must:

1. Accept the tasks provided by the teacher.
2. Complete the tasks within a reasonable amount of time.

3. Work neatly and accurately.
4. Participate in group activities.

Following is an outline of diagnostic questions, informal assessment, and management suggestions to remediate commonly observed academic response problems.

DOES THE CHILD ACTIVELY RESIST ACADEMIC TASKS?

Does the Child Refuse Academic Tasks?

What percentage of work assigned does the child attempt? Are the tasks appropriate for his level of skill? What happens as a consequence when the child refuses his work?

Informal Assessment

107. Present the child with two or three alternative tasks which involve similar skills (e.g., $4\sqrt{12}$, $12 \div 4$, $12/4$, divide 12 by 4). Let him choose the one he prefers.

Management Activities

108. Ignore comments such as, "I don't want to" or "I ain't goin' to do this stuff." If the child destroys his work, be prepared to give him another identical task. Do not allow the child to participate in another activity until he has begun the task. As soon as the child has begun the task, comment positively on the fact that he is doing it.

109. Require only a small amount of academic work, after which the child is immediately allowed to make his next move in a checker game which you are playing with him. Gradually require more work for each move.

*110. Record the number of times the child verbally refuses work each day and plot the data on a graph. At the end of a week, show the child the graph of his refusals. Then have him begin to record his own refusals daily. If he has fewer refusals than the day before, present him with a smiling face.

Does the Child Destroy his own Work?

How does the child destroy his own work? How often does he destroy it? When he does destroy his work, what happens as a result?

Informal Assessment

111. Give the child a decorative sticker or decorative seal for each paper completed and turned in (not destroyed). Let the child keep the stickers or seals in a special notebook (Gallagher, 1971).

Management Activities

*112. For each paper completed but not mutilated or defaced, allow the child to work on an art activity for 10 minutes (drawing, painting, cutting, etc.).

Does the Child Fail to Follow Directions?

*Informal
Assessment*
How frequently are directions given? What percentage of the time does the child follow directions? Are the directions clear to the child? Are they written or oral? If the child does not follow directions, what happens?

*Management
Activities*
113. Present the directions in the form of a "code" or secret message (e.g., "NO EGAP 12 FO RUOY HTAM KOOBKROW OD YLNO EHT TSRIF EERHT SWOR. DOOG KCUL, XAM. TNEGA 99.") Challenge the child to demonstrate that he has "cracked the code."

114. Simplify the directions. Give each step in the directions separately and praise the child for following each step.

115. Record the directions on the tape recorder. Let the child listen to the directions at the listening station.

Does the Child Fail to Return Promptly to Task after a Break?

*Informal
Assessment*
Just how long does it take for the child to return to the task? (Time him.) What tasks is he most reluctant to return to? When he does not return promptly, is he given reminders or ignored? When he does return promptly, is he rewarded?

*Management
Activities*
116. Shuffle a deck of playing cards and show them to the child. Have him pick a suit, for instance, clubs. Explain that if he returns to his work within 2 minutes after the end of his break (recess, free time, etc.), he will be allowed to cut the deck. If he turns up a club, he may have an additional 5 minutes of free time immediately (Kauffman et al., 1972).

117. Five minutes before the break is over, give the child a warning signal. As each minute passes, inform the child of how many minutes are left before the break will be over.

118. Arrange to have the child's favorite seatwork activites (e.g., cutting, coloring, crosswords, reading, math puzzle) following the break. Give the seatwork in two parts, one of which the child may do immediately after the break and one of which he may do only after he has completed the usual task which he tries to avoid.

*119. Allow the children who quickly return to their work to listen to their favorite popular music at the listening station.

*120 Establish the time at which children must return to the room after recess. Post a chart on the bulletin board and record daily the name of each child who returns to the room on time (Hall et al., 1970).

DOES THE CHILD FAIL TO COMPLETE ACADEMIC TASKS?

Is the Child Slow Getting Started on Work?

Record just how long it takes the child to get down to work. Once he begins his work, does he complete it quickly? What types of academic tasks present the greatest and the least problems? Is the child ignored or given frequent attention and reminders when he dawdles?   *Informal Assessment*

121. Record how many minutes pass after the task is assigned before the child actually begins the work. If the child begins sooner than the day before, award a point. When he accumulates five points allow the child to engage in a favorite activity or have a special treat.   *Management Activities*

122. When the task is assigned, set a kitchen timer for 1 minute. If everyone in the class has begun the task when the bell rings, allow the class an additional 5 minutes of recess time.

123. Ignore the child until he completes some small portion of the task. As soon as he begins, praise him for having begun his work and reduce the assignment by 50% or more. Gradually lower the reduction in work as the child learns to begin immediately.

124. Have the child begin his work at a desk where there are fewer distractions. When he has completed the first part of the task, let him return to his own desk.

125. Play "working chairs." Set a timer for variable intervals ranging from 30 seconds to 3 minutes. Make the rule that any child who is working when the timer goes off may move to the next chair if he wishes. Children should rotate around the classroom. Those who are not working must remain in their chairs or go to a time-out chair.

126. Make crossword puzzles shaped like several worms. "Early birds" (children who begin their work immediately) get the worms. Other special activities, such as pictures to color or forms to cut and paste, may be substituted.

*127. Give the child a simpler or shorter task than usual and note whether he begins more quickly. If he does, continue giving the easier task until the child establishes a pattern of beginning immediately. Then very gradually increase the difficulty or length of the task.

Does the Child Begin but not Complete Tasks?

Informal Assessment   Compare percentage of tasks attempted to percentage of tasks completed. Is the completed work done correctly? Are the assignments too long? Does the child dawdle in the beginning and rush to try to complete his work? What is the consequence of failing to complete the assignment?

Management Activities   **128.** Break the task down into smaller units (e.g., assign one row of math problems or an individual problem rather than a page). As the child completes each part of the task, praise his accomplishment and assign another small unit. Gradually lengthen the assignment.

129. If you are certain the task is one which the child is capable of doing, do not allow him to engage in any other activity until the task is completed. As soon as the task is completed, praise the child and allow him to engage in a favorite activity. Avoid nagging the child to finish the task. State the arrangement positively (e.g., "You may go to recess when you have finished your reading").

*130. Allow the child to check his own work as soon as he finishes it.

*131. Give five points for each completed task. When the child has earned 15 points, allow him to skip the next similar assigned task.

*132. Make up a daily "report card" on which you report number of tasks assigned and number of tasks completed. At the end of each day send the child to the office with his report card. Arrange to have the principal talk with the child for a few minutes if the report card is better than the day before. If the report card shows a decrease, the principal is to say "I'm sorry, but I can't see you today," and send the child back to the room.

Does the Child Work too Slowly after He Gets Started?

Informal Assessment   At what rate does the child work (compute rate by dividing responses by time in minutes)? How does his rate compare to that of other children? Is his work mostly correct? Are the tasks at an appropriate level of difficulty? Is there an incentive for working faster?

133. Record the child's rate of work (problems completed correctly   *Management* per minute or words read per minute, etc.). Have him plot his rate on a   *Activities* graph each day.

134. Have the child choose a partner with whom he would like to compete. Make "speedometer" charts by drawing a speedometer dial on a sheet of paper. Do not include the indicator. Let the children draw the indicator on the speedometer to show their rate of correct work for the day. The child with the highest speed wins.

135. Find the speed of various animals (e.g., turtle, goose, cheetah, horse, dog). Post cut-outs of each animal and its speed on the bulletin board. Compute the child's rate of correct work for the day and allow him to wear the cut-out that most closely approximates his rate. (Note: The child's rate of response per minute should be considered the animal's speed in miles per hour in most cases.)

136. If the child completes his assignment by the end of the work period, allow him to be "Mercury" for the day and take messages to the office or other teachers.

*137. Children in the intermediate grades often are fascinated by measures of rate. Compute the child's rate of working each day. Provide one point for reaching a minimum rate and additional points for working at progressively higher rates. For example, give the child one point for doing his math assignment at the rate of three problems per minute, three points for a rate of five problems per minute, ten points for eight problems per minute, etc. Let the child exchange his points for special activities, treats, or privileges (Lovitt & Esveldt, 1970).

*138. Posting children's best work, timing their performance, and providing feedback and praise are sufficient to improve some children's rate of work (Rainwater & Ayllon, 1977; Van Houten, Hill, & Parsons, 1975).

Does the Child Resist Working Independently?

How often does the child request help? What tasks or activities will   *Informal* he attempt on his own? Are there incentives for working indepen-   *Assessment* dently? Is the child capable of doing the work on his own?

139. Break the task into very small work units (e.g., one math   *Management* problem or operation, one comprehension question). Require the   *Activities* child to complete the first small unit on his own. When he has done that, work with him while he does the next unit. Alternate short, independently completed tasks with tasks on which you give assistance. Gradually require more independent work before giving help. (Note: Make certain that the child has the prerequisite skills to do the work independently.)

140. Talk with the child about the need to work independently. Measure the child's height in inches. For each 10-minute period that he works independently, let him color in 1 inch toward his total height. When he reaches the goal of his total height, let him have a special privilege.

Does the Child Resist New Tasks?

Informal Assessment   How different from previous tasks must the new ones be to elicit resistance from the child? Does the child successfully avoid new tasks by noncompliance or tantrums?

Management Activities   **141.** Assign some very small portion of the new task (e.g., one simple subtraction problem) which must be completed before the child goes on to an old, familiar task (e.g., several addition problems). Gradually increase the ratio of new tasks to familiar tasks.

142. Discuss with the child his unwillingness to attempt new tasks. Make an "adventurer" badge and explain that he may wear it for a specified period of time if he attempts a new task without hesitation. When he earns five badges, give the child his choice of an explorer's helmet or showing an "adventure" film strip.

143. Make a "Look What I Tried" scrapbook in which is written each new task the child has tried. Let the child illustrate each new task and take the scrapbook home.

DOES THE CHILD'S WORK LACK ACCURACY AND NEATNESS?

Is the Child's Work Inaccurate?

Informal Assessment   Is the work too difficult for the child? What percentage of the child's work is done incorrectly? What are the consequences for doing inaccurate work?

Management Activities   **144.** If the child's work reaches a predetermined level of accuracy, allow him to be a "supervisor" and help other children with their work.

145. Have the child verbalize each math problem before writing the answer (Lovitt & Curtiss, 1968).

146. Allow children to go to their play areas only when their writing reaches a reasonable standard of accuracy (Salzberg, Wheeler, Devar, & Hopkins, 1971).

147. For each day's assignment, compute percentage correct. Have the child plot his percentage correct on a graph each day.

*148. Divide the class into two "teams." Compute the average percentage on the assigned work for each item. Designate the team with the greatest accuracy the "Eagles" and let each member of the team wear an Eagle badge for the day. Allow the Eagles to choose the game to be played during a special 10-minute recess.

*149. Corrective feedback and reinforcement will improve some children's accuracy, even if they are diagnosed as having severe perceptual-motor disorders (Lahey, Busemeyer, O'Hara, & Beggs, 1977).

Is the Child's Work Done Sloppily?

Establish measureable criteria for neatness. In what specific academic areas is the child's sloppiness the greatest problem? What are the consequences for doing sloppy work?   *Informal Assessment*

150. State specific criteria for neatness (e.g., all letters formed on the line, heading in the proper place on the paper, no numerals touching each other). Post papers which approximate the criteria under a heading on the bulletin board. Gradually increase the standard for posting work and add additional criteria. (See Helwig, Johns, Norman, & Cooper, 1976.)   *Management Activities*

151. Establish a level of neatness and accuracy for completed work. Praise the child for meeting the criterion and allow him to engage in a favorite activity immediately. If the criterion is not met, do not allow the child to engage in the activity. Set the criterion slightly above the child's usual level of performance and gradually require better work (Hopkins, Schutte, & Garton, 1971).

*152. If a child improves the neatness of his work, allow him to be a "secretary" and write "messages" which you dictate to him. These may be complimentary comments on the work of other pupils, notes to the principal or other teachers, letters ordering materials, or a complimentary note to his parents.

*153. Do not allow the child to use a pen for any work until he meets a reasonable standard of neatness. Then allow him to use a pen (or a special pen which you provide) unless the neatness of his work deteriorates.

DOES THE CHILD AVOID GROUP PARTICIPATION?

Does the Child Respond Infrequently in Class?

Informal How many opportunities does the child have to respond? Under
Assessment what circumstances will he respond? When he does respond, how is
his response handled by his peers and the teacher? Count the
number of responses he makes each day.

Management **154.** Ask several class members to give positive feedback (smile,
Activities make a complimentary comment) to the child whenever he makes a
response in class. It is important that the class members be taken
into your confidence and that they are liked by the child who seldom responds.

155. If a child responds well in the presence of one other pupil, plan activities in
which he has ample opportunity to do so. Then add a second peer to the group,
later a third, and so on, until the group approximates the entire class.

156. Begin by asking simple questions that require only a yes or no answer
(e.g., "Are you ready to go to recess?"). Don't allow the child to engage in the
activity until he answers the question. When a one-word response is firmly
established, gradually require two words, then three, then a phrase, and
eventually a complete sentence.

*157. Have the child record the number of times he volunteers an answer in
class and plot the results on a graph. Check the reliability of his record by
occasionally counting his behavior over a given period of time (Gallagher,
1971).

*158. Frequently send the child on errands which require that he talk to
someone (e.g., deliver messages, request materials, make announcements).

159. See also the suggestions in chapter 7, "Spoken Language Problems."

Does the Child Resist Cooperating with Peers in Group Work?

Informal With what peers does the child work best? In what activities is he as
Assessment good as or better than his peers? How do his peers respond to his
efforts? Is he able to avoid work by complaining that he does not want
to work with others? Can any peers be identified who have a particularly strong
relationship to the child or who would be willing to try to work with the child?

160. Make the child a group leader and assist him, if necessary, in   *Management*
obtaining the cooperation of his peers. Praise him for approxima-   *Activities*
tions of good leadership. Gradually introduce situations in which he
must cooperate with another group member who is a temporary leader.

161. Teach the child specific group skills (e.g., listening to others, contributing
suggestions, offering help) in a role-playing situation. Record his cooperative
behaviors in actual group situations and let him plot them on a chart. If
necessary, begin by planning situations in which he must work cooperatively
with only one other child and gradually increase the size of the group.

162. Ignore the child when he is not cooperating with his group (except to stop
destructive behavior), and give him positive physical contact and praise for
successive approximations of cooperation. Cue his peers to respond to him in
the same way. Reward the entire group with praise when the child is
cooperating.

POTENTIAL REINFORCERS

Listed below are some activities that may serve as reinforcers for children.
Remember that for any given child, a specific activity may or may not be a
reinforcer. Additional lists of potential reinforcers may be found in Madsen and
Madsen (1970, 1974) and Gallagher (1971).

1. Helping in the cafeteria.
2. Assisting the custodian.
3. Cleaning the erasers.
4. Erasing the chalkboard.
5. Using colored chalk.
6. Watering the plants.
7. Leading the Pledge of Allegiance.
8. Decorating the bulletin board.
9. Leading the line to recess or the lunchroom.
10. Using a typewriter.
11. Running the ditto machine.
12. Stapling papers together.
13. Feeding the fish or animals.
14. Giving a message over the intercom.
15. Writing and directing a play.
16. Picking up litter on the school grounds.
17. Cleaning the teacher's desk.
18. Taking the class roll.
19. Carrying messages to other teachers.
20. Holding the door during a fire drill.
21. Serving as secretary for class meetings.

22. Raising or lowering the flag.
23. Emptying the wastebasket.
24. Carrying the wastebasket while other children clean out their desks.
25. Distributing and collecting materials.
26. Using an overhead projector.
27. Operating a slide, filmstrip, or movie projector.
28. Recording his own behavior on a graph.
29. Writing with a pen or colored pencils.
30. Correcting papers.
31. Teaching another child.
32. Playing checkers, chess, *Sorry,* tiddlywinks, or other table games.
33. Choosing a game to play.
34. Being captain of a team.
35. Working with clay.
36. Doing "special," "the hardest," or "impossible" teacher-made arithmetic problems.
37. Reading the newspaper.
38. Reading or drawing a road map.
39. Listening to the radio with an earplug.
40. Arm wrestling.
41. Reading or writing poetry.
42. Learning a "magic" trick.
43. Lighting or blowing out a candle.
44. Being allowed to move desks.
45. Sitting beside a friend.
46. Going to the library.
47. Helping the librarian.
48. Writing to the author of a favorite book.
49. Looking at a globe.
50. Making or flying a kite.
51. Popping corn.
52. Making a puppet.
53. Carrying the ball or bat to recess.
54. Visiting with the principal.
55. Making a book.
56. Recording time taken to do a task.
57. Having a spelling bee.
58. Doing a science experiment.
59. Telling the teacher when it is time to go to lunch.
60. Sharpening the teacher's pencils.
61. Opening the teacher's mail.
62. Sitting next to the teacher at lunch.
63. Doing crossword puzzles or math puzzles.
64. Sweeping the floor of the classroom.
65. Weighing or measuring various objects in the classroom.
66. Reading a wall map.

67. Giving a spelling test.
68. Adjusting the window shades.
69. Sewing.
70. Having an arithmetic contest at the chalkboard.

PROGRAMS FOR TEACHING SOCIAL-EMOTIONAL SKILLS

Most social and emotional skills are learned as part of the everyday interaction of children with each other and with adults. There is no substitute for a well-managed environment in which naturally occurring social rewards shape and maintain appropriate behavior. When behavior becomes maladaptive, it is often most effective—even expedient—to rearrange the demands of the child's everyday world and the reinforcement he or she receives for particular behaviors. However, there are commercially available instructional materials designed to teach children social and emotional responses that will be useful to them in understanding themselves and getting along with others.

The Self-Control Curriculum

This curriculum, in the form of a small book (Fagen, Long, & Stevens, 1975), is designed to teach elementary-age children the component skills involved in self-control: selection (i.e., selective attention), storage (i.e., memory), sequencing and ordering, anticipating consequences, appreciating feelings, managing frustration inhibition and delay, and relaxation. Although the curriculum was developed from a "psychoeducational" viewpoint rather than within a behavioral framework, there are instructional units with specific goals and activities. Many of the unit activities involve skills that may be integrated with a behavior-modification approach. A number of the activities are similar or identical to those suggested for the remediation of perceptual, perceptual-motor, or academic difficulties (e.g., identifying foreground objects and hidden-figure tasks for mastering figure-ground discrimination). Some of the major goals of the curriculum are to reduce disruptiveness, improve school adjustment, prevent learning and behavior disorders from developing, and promote a balance between cognitive and affective development.

The Social Learning Curriculum

This curriculum, in the form of an instructional kit (Goldstein, 1975), is designed for use with mildly retarded, learning disabled, and emotionally disturbed children. The primary goals are to teach children to think critically and act independently to such an extent that they can become socially and occupationally competent. Instructional units range from managing personal affairs (e.g., money, leisure time, communication, travel, health) to independent living. The curriculum is organized into 10 phases, each phase containing 15 to 20 lessons.

Behavioral objectives, detailed lesson plans, and instructional materials are included for each lesson. The 10 phases of the curriculum are: perceiving individuality, recognizing the environment, recognizing interdependence, recognizing the body, recognizing and reacting to emotions, recognizing what the senses do, communicating with others, getting along with others, identifying helpers, and maintaining body functions.

Developing Understanding of Self and Others (DUSO)

These instructional kits (Dinkmeyer, 1970, 1973) are designed to help elementary-age children understand and cope with social–emotional behavior. DUSO D-1 is intended for use with kindergarten and primary-age children; DUSO D-2, with youngsters at the upper primary and fourth grade levels (ages 7 through 10). Each kit contains instructional units and materials, including records or cassettes, posters, role playing activity cards, puppet activity cards, and puppets. The eight unit themes in DUSO D-1 include understanding self; feelings; others; independence; goals and purposeful behavior; mastery, competence, and resourcefulness; emotional maturity; and choices and consequences. In DUSO D-2, units include self-awareness and positive self-concept; peers; growth from self-centeredness to social interest; personal responsibility; personal motivation; accomplishment; stress; and values. The kits are structured so that the teacher can make them a part of daily instruction throughout the year or select only specific activities for particular needs.

Toward Affective Development (TAD)

This instructional kit (Dupont, Gardner, & Brody, 1974) is an activity-centered program for use with students aged 8 to 12 (grades three through six). There are 5 sections, 21 units, and 191 individual lessons. The activities are planned to be integrated into the typical classroom schedule. Units focus on experiences ranging from self-awareness to working with others. The kit includes a variety of materials, such as picture cards, posters, duplicating masters, and cassettes.

ADDITIONAL READINGS

The following books will provide additional technical information and case studies in the use of behavior modification in the classroom:

Gelfand, D. M., & Hartmann, D. P. *Child behavior: Analysis and therapy.* New York: Pergamon, 1975.

Givner, A., & Graubard, P. S. *A handbook of behavior modification for the classroom.* New York: Holt, Rinehart & Winston, 1974.

Glavin, J. P. *Behavioral strategies for classroom management.* Columbus, Ohio: Charles E. Merrill, 1974.

Hallahan, D. P., & Kauffman, J. M. *Introduction to learning disabilities: A psycho-behavioral approach.* Englewood Cliffs, N.J.: Prentice-Hall, 1976.

Kazdin, A. E. *Behavior modification in applied settings.* Homewood, Ill.: Dorsey, 1975.

Lovitt, T. C. *In spite of my resistance . . . I've learned from children.* Columbus, Ohio: Charles E. Merrill, 1977.

Madsen, C. H., & Madsen, C. K. *Teaching/discipline* (2nd ed.). Boston: Allyn & Bacon, 1974.

O'Leary, K. D., & O'Leary, S. G. (Eds.) *Classroom management: The successful use of behavior modification.* New York: Pergamon, 1972.

Stephens, T. M. *Implementing behavioral approaches in elementary and secondary schools.* Columbus, Ohio: Charles E. Merrill, 1975.

Stephens, T. M. *Directive teaching of children with learning and behavioral disorders* (2nd ed.). Columbus, Ohio: Charles E. Merrill, 1976.

Stephens, T. M. Teaching skills to children with learning and behavioral disorders. Columbus, Ohio: Charles E. Merrill, 1977.

Worell, J., & Nelson, C. M. *Managing instructional problems: A case study workbook.* New York: McGraw-Hill, 1974.

7
Spoken Language Problems

Spoken Language Problems

The spoken aspects of language are unique to man and are acknowledged to be one of man's greatest achievements (Lerner, 1976). The close relationship between language and learning has often been recognized as extremely important (Freud, 1953; Piaget, 1952; Skinner, 1957). Some children with language problems are handicapped in understanding and using the spoken word. Consequently, many of them have difficulties in acquiring basic academic skills.

Deficits in spoken language can be very complex. Many children require specialized remediation by highly trained language therapists. The development of oral language skills must, nevertheless, be recognized as an important goal for the classroom teacher. The teacher must be aware of the three basic aspects of language acquisition and the difficulties usually associated with each of them.

1. What inner language disorders prevent the child from acquiring basic language skills?
2. What receptive language problems interfere with the child's ability to comprehend the spoken word?
3. What expressive language difficulties preclude the development of adequate spoken language?

ASSESSMENT

Teacher Observation

Observations of children during both formal and informal school activities will provide the teacher with important instructional data. Spradlin (1967) feels that observations of oral language skills often provide information that can be obtained in no other way. Long-term daily interaction with a child gives the teacher ample opportunity to observe all facets of a child's oral language development. A number of behavioral symptoms with which the teacher should be familiar have been listed by Myklebust (1954). Detailed grade-level competencies in oral language are listed by Otto, McMenemy, & Smith (1973) and Wallace and Larsen (1978).

Informal Assessment

Specific skill development can be informally measured by the classroom teacher through teacher-made tests. Based upon his observations, the teacher may more closely evaluate a child by having the child answer particular questions, complete skill worksheets, or participate in evaluative games and exercises. The classroom teacher may also use informal oral language scales, based upon chronological age levels, which have been developed by Zimmerman, Steiner, and Evatt (1969) and Hammill and Bartel (1978). Additional informal tests are described in subsequent sections of this chapter.

Formal Tests

There are many standardized language tests currently available. However, a large number of these tests require specialized training for proper administration. Furthermore, most standard testing procedures have the disadvantages of restricting both the settings and type of language which is sampled (Spradlin, 1967). Nevertheless, the data provided by these tests can be useful in planning individual instructional programs. Some of the more widely used published language tests are described below.

The Houston Test for Language Development
(Crabtree, 1963)

This test measures the language development of children from 6 months through 6 years of age. Part I of the test is intended for very young children (6 months to 3 years) and consists of a checklist which must be completed by an adult informant. Categories of language included on this portion of the test are vocabulary, sound articulation, gesture, and grammatical usage.

Part II of the test is designed for children with chronological ages of 3 to 6 years. It requires the eliciting of spontaneous speech. Vocabulary, syntax, auditory judgments, and self-identity are included in this part of the test.

Illinois Test of Psycholinguistic Abilities
(Kirk, McCarthy, & Kirk, 1968)

The ITPA is an individually administered diagnostic test designed for children of chronological ages 2 years, 4 months to 10 years, 3 months. The test measures psycholinguistic ability through three dimensions: levels of organization (representational and automatic); psycholinguistic processes (receptive, organization, and expression), and channels of communication (auditory-vocal and visual-motor modalities). Ten subtests and two supplementary tests actually constitute the entire ITPA. Although the test is used extensively with children handicapped in learning, the ITPA has been increasingly criticized because it does not give specific language proficiency information (Wiederholt, 1978). Specific age scores and a global psycholinguistic age and psycholinguistic quotient are obtained from the test.

Northwestern Syntax Screening Test
(Lee, 1969)

> This is an individually administered test designed to estimate a child's receptive and expressive level of syntactic development. Normative data are provided for children 3 years, 11 months to 7 years, 11 months of age. Receptive development is measured by having the child select the most appropriate of four pictures following a sentence spoken by the administrator. The expressive items require the child to repeat sentences spoken by the administrator while the administrator points to various pictures.

Peabody Picture Vocabulary Test
(Dunn, 1965)

> Single-word receptive vocabulary is measured in this widely used test intended for children 2 years, 3 months to 18 years, 5 months. The administrator provides a stimulus word orally and a series of plates which contain four pictures. The child is asked to select the picture which best represents the stimulus word. The PPVT also provides an IQ on the basis of the results; however, we believe the test is best used as a measure of receptive vocabulary.

The Test of Language Development
(Newcomer & Hammill, 1977)

> This highly standardized test of language functioning is intended for children 4 years to 8 years, 11 months of age. The test consists of five subtests (Picture Vocabulary, Oral Vocabulary, Grammatic Understanding, Sentence Imitation, and Grammatic Completion) and two supplementary tests (Word Discrimination and Word Articulation). The test can be easily administered by most teachers in approximately 40 minutes. A child's performance on the test will reveal intraindividual strengths and weaknesses, and further identify the specific skill areas requiring additional assessment and remediation.

The Utah Test of Language Development
(Mecham, Jex, & Jones, 1967)

> This instrument is designed to measure the expressive and receptive verbal language skills of children ranging from 1 to 15 years of age. Test items include naming common pictures, repeating digits, copying designs, vocabulary, and reading. The results serve as a useful checklist for normal language development. Test scores may be translated into language-age equivalents. The test is probably best used as an estimate of a child's language development.

INNER LANGUAGE DIFFICULTIES

Inner language disorders have been described as the most complex of all language difficulties (Johnson & Myklebust, 1967; Lerner, 1976). *Inner language* can be defined as the language which one uses to communicate with oneself (Goldstein, 1948) or the language with which one thinks (Johnson & Myklebust, 1967). Inner language development is dependent upon the child's ability to:
1. Establish verbal imagery for sounds, words, concepts, etc.
2. Use the complex maze of skills needed in a logical thinking process.
Diagnostic questions, informal tests, and teaching suggestions for developing inner language skills are listed below.

HAS THE CHILD MASTERED THE SKILLS PREREQUISITE FOR ADEQUATE INNER LANGUAGE?

Does the Child Have Difficulty with Verbal Imagery?

Read a short sentence to the child (e.g., "The sun was very bright"). Have the child draw a picture illustrating the dictated sentence. — *Informal Assessment*

1. As words such as "book," "nail," and "water," are introduced, provide the child with the object to hold, feel, smell, taste, etc. Have the child perform the action for more abstract words such as "hop," "run," and "kick." — *Instructional Activities*

2. Point to and name objects during a walk around the school grounds (e.g., door, flagpole, table). Eventually, point to particular objects and have the child provide the name.

3. Provide the child with pictures of objects or animals that produce particular sounds (dogs, cats, telephone, fire truck, etc.). Record the sounds on a tape recorder. Play particular sounds as the child is looking at the matching picture. Gradually, have the child match sounds with the picture or vice versa.

4. Provide the child with a wide variety of experiences such as going on field trips, constructing models, and playing with manipulative toys. Name and discuss items which are unfamiliar to the child.

5. Select one child in the class and provide the other children, with eyes closed, a one-sentence description of this child (e.g., "It wears glasses"). "It" (the child) repeats one word from that sentence (e.g., "wears"), and the other children try to guess the identity of "it" (Wagner, Hosier, & Blackman, 1970).

6. Use finger plays or *Simon Says* to give the child the opportunity to use parts of the body while listening to directions.

*7. Present pairs of objects (e.g., a guitar and a violin; a ruler and a tape measure) and point out the similarities and differences. Provide experiences where the child can use the objects.

*8. Play "charades" where the child is asked to act out a role, such as a swimmer diving into the water or a carpenter hammering a nail (Bush & Giles, 1977) or have the child guess the role being acted out.

Does the Child Have Difficulty with Thinking Skills?

Informal Assessment   Myers (1965) suggests asking some of the following questions:

"How could a blind person know when food on the stove is burning?"

"How are a turtle and a fish alike? How are they different?"

"Why may it be easier to make a dress shorter than to make it longer?"

9. Provide the child with a series of pictures with one part missing from each picture. Ask the child to find the missing part.

10. Provide the child with a collection of pairs of items which have something in common but which are somewhat different in appearance (e.g., a watch and a clock; a shoe and a boot; a glass and a cup). Ask the child to find two items used in the same way, or give the child one item and ask him to look for the related item (Karnes, 1968).

*11. Read a series of analogies to the child and have him complete each sentence. For example:

"A banana is to an apple as squash is to _____ ."

"A boy is to a girl as a _____ is to a woman."

"A ring is to a _____ as a bracelet is to a wrist."

*12. Read a series of three words to a child and have him choose the two words that are related. For example:

"dog, cat, apple"

"chair, table, knife"

"milk, stone, water"

*13. Bush and Giles (1977) suggest asking questions like these to develop logical relationships:

"Does a bird have wings?"

"Do you read with your ears?"

"Would you go to a grocery store to see a movie?"

"Do you lick an ice cream cone with your knees?"

*14. Read a story to the child and stop before finishing it. Ask the child to think of an ending for the story.

*15. After reading a story, ask the child specific questions which require interpretation and imagination. For example, ask the child to imagine he was the hero. Would he have acted differently? Or what would happen if the story took place in a different country, season, or century?

*16. Use simple riddles to describe familiar people, places, animals, etc. Ask the child to guess the identity based upon the description. Have the child think of riddles to be asked of other children.

*17. Karnes (1968) suggests asking two children to stand before the class. Have one child think of ways in which he and the other child are alike (e.g., "We both wear glasses," "We are both boys").

*18. Ask the child to list all the things that he can think of that have wheels, that are smaller than an ant, or that have hair (Smith, 1974).

RECEPTIVE LANGUAGE DIFFICULTIES

Receptive language is the ability to understand the spoken language of others. The child with difficulties in this area hears what is said but is unable to comprehend it. Adequate receptive language involves the ability to:

1. Auditorally perceive speech sounds,
2. Comprehend concrete and abstract words,
3. Understand the linguistic structure of sentences,
4. Follow directions,
5. Listen critically and make judgments.

Diagnostic questions, informal tests, and teaching suggestions for developing receptive language skills are listed in the following section. Teaching suggestions for auditory memory, an important skill for developing receptive language, are listed in chapter 8.

HAS THE CHILD MASTERED THE SKILLS PREREQUISITE FOR ADEQUATE RECEPTIVE LANGUAGE?

Does the Child Have Difficulty Understanding Various Speech Sounds?

Informal
Assessment
Present isolated speech sounds to the child. Ask the child to listen for a specific sound, such as /m/. Present a sequence of sounds, such as /m/, /p/, /t/, /s/, /m/, /v/, /k/, /m/, /n/, /s/, /m/, and ask the child to raise his hand each time the /m/ sound is heard.

Instructional
Activities
19. Introduce pairs of sounds (e.g., /m/ and /b/) and ask the child to tell if the sounds are the same or different. The child may respond by shaking his head, raising his hand, or with any other agreed-upon cue.

20. Have the child listen for a particular sound at the beginning of words read aloud. Present words that are phonetically very different at first, and eventually present words with beginning sounds that are more alike. Final and medial sounds can be introduced in a similar fashion.

21. Introduce blends, digraphs, and vowel sounds using somewhat the same procedure suggested in #20. The sequence should progress from isolated speech sounds to listening for the sounds in words.

22. Provide picture clues and objects for those children who need additional help in associating speech sounds with letters and words.

23. Give the child a picture which contains many objects, such as an advertisement. Ask the child to point to an object that begins with the same sounds as a stimulus sound you provide (Heilman, 1968). This procedure can also be used for final sounds, rhyming, blends, etc.

24. Lerner (1976) suggests having the child identify objects, pronouncing the name of the object by separating the individual phonemes. For example: "Pick up the p-ĕ-n."

25. Provide children with experiences in listening for rhyming words. Prepare a worksheet with pictures of different objects. Present a rhyme to the children and ask them to circle the picture that would make the complete sentence a rhyme. For example, read "The man was holding a _____ " and use worksheet pictures of a dog, fan, book, and baby.

*26. Play bingo with children who recognize some letter sounds, using initial consonants or other speech sounds for the bingo squares. Call out different words and have the children cover appropriate squares.

*27. Pronounce words and ask the child to determine the number of syllables in each word by holding up the appropriate number of fingers, clapping or tapping out the number of syllables, etc.

Does the Child Have Difficulty Comprehending Words

Place three or four objects before the child and ask him to point to the one that you name. If the child is able to correctly point to an object, encourage him to say its name.

Informal Assessment

28. Johnson and Myklebust (1967) advise that only meaningful words should be taught and that words are meaningful only "when the individual has the experience with which they are to be as sociated" (p. 87).

Instructional Activities

29. Begin training by working with real objects or pictures. Give the child a chance to feel and play with the object. Say the name of the object a number of times while the child has the object or picture before him.

30. Have the child match an object, such as a banana, with a picture of a banana or have the child match similar objects or pictures.

31. Have the child match an object to another object which is basically different in form and physical features but belongs to a similar catagory. For example, ask the child what you do with a lock. Provide him with a nail, key, and cork to select from (Eisenson, 1972). As the child progresses, have him match pictures instead of objects.

32. Have the child classify words into categories such as people, food, and animals by sorting pictures and words into groups.

*33. Teach more abstract words, such as verbs, by having the child perform the activity. Jumping, walking, and so forth can be repeated until the child understands the meaning of the word.

*34. Smith (1967) suggests having the child clap for various reasons when he is being read to. For example:

"Clap for every word that describes something."

"Clap for every person's name."

"Clap for every word that rhymes with _____ ."

*35. Have the child follow simple directions. For example:

"Give me the book."

"Stand next to the door."

"Show me the paper."

"Jump up and down."

*36. Have the child match objects that produce particular noises with the actual noise. Eisenson (1972) suggests using telephone rings, the vacuum cleaner whir, drum beats, bell clangs, or toy animals that approximate the sounds of the live animal.

*37. Teach descriptive words by providing the child with a variety of pictures and having the child pick out the happy boy, the sad clown, the dirty towel, etc.

*38. Provide the child with contrasting sets of experiences to teach the attributes of objects such as hot and cold water, rough and smooth stones, little and big animals (Lerner, 1976).

Does the Child Have Difficulty Comprehending Sentences?

Informal Assessment   Have the child respond yes or no to the following questions (Bush & Giles, 1977):

"Do flowers grow?"

"Do dogs bark?"

"Do rabbits hop?"

"Do you have four ears?"

Instructional Activities   **39.** Gradually add verbs to nouns (e.g., "throw ball," "eat candy") and adjectives to nouns (e.g., "a small truck," "a sad girl") by having the child choose the correct picture or perform the action (Eisenson, 1972).

40. Read a short sentence to the child and ask him a series of questions about the sentence. Children may respond by shaking their heads or merely saying yes or no. For example:

"Jean and Jeff go to the ocean and mountains during the summer."

"Do Jean and Jeff go to the mountains during the winter?"

"Do Jean and Jeff go to the ocean during the summer?"

41. As the child progresses, you can read longer and more detailed sentences and paragraphs. Questions may be provided before the story is read to enable the child to listen for specific answers.

42. Read a list of sentences to the child, and have him sit with his thumbs up. As soon as the child hears a sentence that answers the question "how?" he puts his thumbs down. Sentences that answer "when?" "where?" and "who?" could also be read (Wagner, Hosier & Blackman, 1970). Sentences that answer "how?" include:

"The boys run fast."

"Virgil eats slowly."

"Joyce looks pretty."

43. Prepare a worksheet with various drawings. Ask the child to perform specific directions. For example:

"Draw a circle around the truck."

"Put an X on the little girl."

"Draw a line under the house."

44. Ask questions which require comparisons. For example:

"Who wears dresses, boys or girls?"

"Who shaves every morning, mother or father?"

"Who barks, a rabbit or a dog?"

"Who puts out fires, a police officer or a firefighter?"

45. Johnson and Myklebust (1967) suggest preparing a worksheet with a series of pictures and reading sentences of varying difficulty according to individual needs. Ask the child to follow a specific direction after hearing the sentence. For example:

"Mother bought some apples at the store."

Circle what mother bought at the store.

46. Pass objects out to each child in the class. Ask children to stand if they have the object that is described. For example:

"Stand if you have the animal that meows."

"Stand if you have the object that cuts meat."

"Stand if you have the toy truck that delivers milk."

47. Provide a signal to attract a child's attention to cue him to listen for directions that will be given. For example, flick the lights, play a few notes on the piano, hold up an arm over the head, say "Listen." Use one particular signal consistently for a group of children.

*48. Lerner (1976) suggests having the child listen to a sentence and supply the correct word. For example:

"I am thinking of a word that tells us what you eat soup with."

*49. Zigmond and Cicci (1968) recommend having the child select the word in a sentence that does not make sense. For example:

"It snows during the summer."

"We drink milk out of a book."

"We use a ball to write."

*50. Read a poem or story with obvious missing words. Have the child supply the missing part. For example:

"Chuck built a snowman with _____ . He used a carrot for the _____ and coal for the snowman's _____ . When the sun came out, the snowman _____ ."

Does the Child Have Difficulty Following Directions?

Informal Assessment Play *Simon Says,* and have the child perform simple motor tasks which gradually become more complex as the child progresses.

Instructional Activities **51.** Give the child step-by-step directions for folding a piece of paper to make a certain number of squares or rectangles, or provide him with precut geometric shapes and direct him to assemble step-by-step an ice cream cone or a balloon (Karnes, 1968).

52. Call children to reading groups or dismiss children for recess or lunch by using row numbers, clothing colors, first-name initials, or other specific directions.

53. Ask a particular child to repeat directions that were given to a class or a reading group. This procedure provides an immediate check before the child proceeds with an assignment.

54. Have two children play *Master and Robot* by appointing one child the "Master" who gives directions (e.g., go to the blackboard, draw a circle, turn around, sit in your chair) to the child appointed the "Robot." Have the children change places after a period of time (Wagner, Hosier, & Blackman, 1970).

*55. Provide each child with a paper. Call out various directions for the child to complete on the paper. For example:

"Draw a circle in the upper right-hand corner of the paper."

"Make a triangle in the lower left-hand corner of the paper."

"Write the number 7 in the circle."

"Make a square in the middle of the paper."

You could also record the directions on a tape for the child to complete by himself, using earphones.

*56. Direct the child to a specified place in the school building by providing him with a series of directions to get there. For example:

> "Go out the door and turn left. Walk straight down the hall and take your first right. At the gymnasium, turn left. Go through the first door on your right."

*57. Read directions for making a kite, baking cookies, or building a model. Have the children perform the activity by following the step-by-step directions.

*58. Prepare a series of direction cards for children who can read. Allow the child to continue choosing cards from a pile as long as he is able to follow the commands. The cards might include:

> Go to the library table and find a brown book.
>
> Hop over to the door, turn around, and skip to the window.
>
> Pass out a pencil and the math workbooks to all the children in the first three rows.

Does the Child Have Difficulty Listening Critically and Making Judgments?

Wagner, Hosier, and Blackman (1970) recommend reading several statements to the child and asking him to decide if a statement is fact or opinion. For example:

Informal Assessment

> "George Washington was our first president."
>
> "Thomas Jefferson was our greatest president."
>
> "There were eight dogs in Tom's boat."

*59. Prepare a worksheet with a list of words. Describe a word and direct the child to place a number before that word. For example:

Instructional Activities

> "Write the number 1 before the word that tells us it is the cold time of the year." (*winter*)
>
> "Write the number 2 before the word that describes a fruit that is long and yellow." (*banana*)

*60. Read a list of statements and ask the child to tell whether the statements are true or false. For example:

> "Elephants can fly in the air."
>
> "We swim during the summertime."
>
> "We run with our hands."

*61. Have one child stand in front of the room while the children sitting at their seats describe another child in the room. The child in front must guess the identity from the description provided by members of the class (Wagner, Hosier, & Blackman, 1970). The clues might include:

"He has freckles."

"He rides a bike to school."

"He is wearing a blue shirt."

*62. Smith (1967) suggests reading a short paragraph containing several words that have similar meanings. Ask the child to pick out the words that mean the same thing.

"Soon the little man came to a small dining room. He peered through the tiny door and saw a lovely petite room all set up with miniature furniture. There were even minute dishes on the dining room table." (p. 88)

*63. Read a list of nouns that fit in a particular category (furniture, fruit, animals, etc.). Direct the child to clap his hands when a noun is read that does not belong to a specified category. For example:

"chair, desk, man, couch, table, apple, . . ."

*64. Use the flannel board while telling a story and plan for obvious errors between what is placed on the board and what is said. Ask the child to find the mistake (Lerner, 1976).

*65. Have children arrange scrambled oral sentences in the correct order without using pencil or paper.

*66. Read a short story and stop periodically, asking the child to predict what will happen next.

EXPRESSIVE LANGUAGE DIFFICULTIES

Expressive language is the spoken language the child uses in communicating with others. To have adequate expressive language, the child must have meaningful experiences and must develop comprehension (Johnson & Myklebust, 1967). In addition, the child must be able to:
1. Produce various speech sounds,
2. Formulate words and sentences,
3. Use correct grammatical and syntactical language patterns,
4. Exhibit an adequate spoken vocabulary.
Diagnostic questions, informal tests, and teaching suggestions for remediating expressive language problems are listed below.

DOES THE CHILD HAVE THE PREREQUISITE
SKILLS FOR ADEQUATE EXPRESSIVE LANGUAGE?

Does the Child Have Difficulty Producing Speech Sounds?

Pronounce each of the following sounds and ask the child to repeat the sounds: /m/, /p/, /b/, /k/, /g/, /n/, /t/, /d/, /l/, and /r/.

Informal Assessment

67. Johnson and Myklebust (1967) recommend taking an inventory of movements and phonemes the child can produce. Use *these* sounds to make the child aware of movements and sounds.

Instructional Activities

68. Encourage the use of any vocal utterances which have some meaning to the child to provide him with a process of communication and to motivate him to learn more symbolic language. Gradually require vocal productions which more closely approximate the sounds of words or part of words.

69. Begin training by facing a mirror with the child and slowly articulating a sound in isolation. Have the child imitate your movements. The first isolated sounds to be established, according to Eisenson (1972), should include /m/, /p/, b/, /k/, /g/, /n/, /t/, /d/, /l/, and /r/.

70. Place the child's hand on your throat or face as you make sounds so he can feel the movements. Then have the child place his hand on his own throat.

71. Manually guide the child's tongue or lips to produce certain sounds if he is unable to imitate a sound by observing. A tongue depressor may be used for appropriate tongue movements.

72. Provide children with verbal cues if they are needed. For example, Johnson and Myklebust (1967) suggest "close your lips and hum" for *m* or "bite your lip and blow but do not use your voice" for *f* (p. 128).

73. Have the child practice various tongue and mouth movements such as opening the mouth wide, placing the tongue behind the teeth, and moving the lips to a whistling position.

*74. Provide pictures of the tongue and mouth positions that are used for particular sounds. Hold the picture up to a mirror, and have the child imitate the position.

*75. Have the child close his eyes while he is making certain sounds, so that visual memory may be used as a basis for recalling the movements made for the particular sounds (Eisenson, 1972).

*76. Gradually blend known sounds together, as the child progresses in learning isolated sounds. Provide consonant-vowel and consonant-vowel-consonant combinations for the child. Use many of the same procedures suggested above.

Does the Child Have Difficulty Formulating Words and Sentences?

*Informal
Assessment*

Provide the child with familiar objects to name. Use fruit, clothes, toys, and so on. Say the words and have the child repeat them.

*Instructional
Activities*

77. Work on classifying pictures into categories (animals, furniture, food, etc.).

78. Facilitate word recall by teaching word association through pairs of words (e.g., hard–soft, salt–pepper, hot–cold). Pictures may be used to supplement the words (Johnson & Myklebust, 1967).

79. Build known words into sentences by using repeated phrases. For example:

"This is a dog."

"This is a chair."

"This is a boy."

"This is a book."

80. Bereiter and Engelmann (1966) expand upon repeated phrases by asking questions (e.g., "Is this a book?") and by adding second-order statements (e.g., "This book is red"). They also introduce "not" statements (e.g., "This is not a book").

81. Prepare a series of sentences with key words missing. Read a sentence to the child and ask him to supply the key word. For example:

"A dog makes noise by _____ ."

"Bicycles have _____ wheels."

"We have _____ fingers."

82. Expand upon the "Show and Tell" period by asking the child specific questions about an object that he brings from home.

83. Prepare a grab bag of familiar objects. Have the child choose one object and describe the object in as much detail as possible. Permit other children to guess the object being described.

84. Have the children paint pictures at easels. Ask particular children to describe their pictures to the rest of the class.

85. Have children repeat familiar nursery rhymes while following a record. Eventually have the child recite the rhyme without the record.

86. Use play telephones, tape recorders, or walkie-talkies to have the child focus upon using words and sentences as a means of communication.

87. Provide puppets for the child to use during free play and more structured periods. Cheyney (1967) provides instructions for making puppets out of various materials.

*88. Show a picture to a child and ask him to describe what is happening in the picture. More direct questions, specific to a particular picture, can also be asked. Smith (1974) also recommends having the child tell what went on before the picture was taken, and what happened afterward.

*89. Provide children with a set of sequence pictures or a comic strip cut into frames. Ask a child to "tell the story" by describing the sequence of events.

*90. Smith (1974) suggests having the child respond to questions emphasizing verbal fluency where nearly any response a child gives is acceptable. For example:

"What would happen if we didn't have electricity?"

*91. Give the child practice in using articles and prepositions by providing him with certain key words (e.g., house, boy, door) and having him build a sentence around these words.

*92. Karnes (1968) recommends asking the child "Tell me how," "Why do we," or "Tell me where" questions. For example:

"Tell me how . . .
   you tie your shoes.
   you play kickball.
   your father washes the car."

*93. Gather a number of kitchen utensils or tools. Have a child describe the use of one utensil or tool without using gestures.

Does the Child Have Difficulty Using Correct Grammatical and Syntactical Forms?

Prepare a series of sentences with missing words. Read these to the child and have him supply the omitted word. Plurals, adjectives, prepositions, etc., can be emphasized with this activity. For example:

Informal Assessment

"We went _____ the store."

"The boat is _____ the water."

"The plane is _____ the sky."

"This is John's jacket. It belongs to _____."

"Last summer we _____ to the beach."

94. Use choral speaking to emphasize correct language usage. Bryan (1971) lists over 100 original verses that can be used in the primary grades.

95. Display a picture before the child and describe the picture in a sentence. For example, "This boy is running." Have the child repeat the sentence. Eventually, omit certain words for the child to insert as he repeats the sentence.

96. Have the child describe an activity as he is jumping, skipping, etc. For example, "I am jumping." Upon completion have the child say, "I jumped very high" or "I jumped over the box."

97. Provide the child with two different sized tin cans, a red poker chip, and a white poker chip. Place the red chip in the large can. Ask the child "Is the red chip in the large can?" Gradually have the child verbalize different situations. Vary the manipulations and questions, or verbalize incorrect statements and let the child catch your errors (Karnes, 1968).

98. Have the child repeat words and sentences emphasizing plurals, verb tense, and so on, using the *Language Master*. As the child progresses, let him use a tape recorder to make statements about pictures, objects, etc.

99. Provide the child with pictures showing single and multiple units of different objects. Ask the child to point to the girl in one picture or the girls in another picture. Eventually, have the child make a statement about the pictures, such as "The girls are playing ball" (Karnes, 1968).

100. Wedemeyer and Cejka (1970) recommend preparing small cards with nouns, verbs, and adjectives written on them. Group the noun cards on one ring, the verbs on a second, and the adjectives on a third. Attach the rings to a folded cardboard stand so the cards can be flipped over easily. Have the child form appropriate sentences (e.g., "Rabbits are soft").

101. Provide phrases (e.g., "the big dog," "to the mountains," "under the house"). Have the child build a sentence using the phrases in the standard syntactical form.

*102. Correct grammar and syntax errors by providing the child with the correct usage. Osborn (1968) recommends telling the child to "Say it the way I do," or "This is the way you say it in school."

*103. Encourage the child to respond in sentences. Incorporate a child's one-word responses into a sentence, and have the child repeat the entire sentence. Groups of children can also repeat particular sentences together.

*104. Provide pictures which illustrate past, present, and future tense of verbs. Sequences of an individual about to do something, doing something, and completing the same act can be described and discussed (Johnson & Myklebust, 1967).

*105. Give the child an eraser and instruct him to place it in various places. Have the child describe each situation. For example:

"The eraser is on my head."

"The eraser is in the desk."

"The eraser is under the chair."

*106. Use the flannel board to demonstrate situations to which the child is required to respond. Stress plurals, prepositions, and other syntactical structures. Permit the child to create flannel board situations which he might verbally describe.

*107. Write a sentence on the chalkboard with the words in an incorrect order and have the child arrange the words in the correct order. Flash cards containing single words can also be arranged into sentences.

*108. Bush and Giles (1977) suggest reading a number of sentences to the child, leaving out a word, and having the child fill in the correct ending. For example:

"I have many dresses but I have only one blue _____."

"Yesterday we played ball, and today we will _____ ball."

"I like to jump rope, but after I have been _____ for a while I get tired."

Does the Child Have an Inadequate Oral Vocabulary?

Ask the child to name all the objects in a room or a picture during a specified time limit. Keep a graph to note improvement (Lerner, 1976).

Informal Assessment

109. Provide children with experiences to stimulate vocabulary development and word usage. Field trips, reading stories, and oral discussion can all be used to develop vocabulary.

Instructional Activities

110. Collect colorful and exciting pictures, cartoons, paintings, etc. Have the child describe the action by listing descriptive words. Discuss the words with the entire class.

*111. Have the child build a list of words from one common root, such as "ball" or "man." Assign a point for each word. The child with the most points wins the game.

*112. Have the child list the possible synonyms for particular words such as "cars," "babies," and "days" (Smith, 1967).

*113. Play *hangman* where children fill in the blends of a word by guessing letters. For each letter guessed incorrectly, additional parts of the body are added until the loser is "hung."

*114. Write any 10 letters on the board and have children compose a 10-word telegram using the letters on the board as the initial letters for the ten words. Vary the activity by specifying the nature of the telegram (Platts, 1970).

*115. Stop periodically while reading a story and have the child supply a word that fits with the context of the sentence.

*116. Provide the child with a sentence (e.g., "It rained very hard last night"). Ask the child to say the same thing in as many different ways as possible. Encourage him to use unusual words.

*117. Read a story to the child, and have him retell the story to another child. Encourage the child to retell the story in his own words.

*118. Introduce a "word of the day" and encourage children to use the word throughout the day. Permit particular children to choose the word on certain days (Platts, 1970).

*119. Provide children with a word that has multiple meanings, such as "run." Have each child in turn use the word in a sentence, employing a different meaning each time.

SPOKEN LANGUAGE PROGRAMS

In addition to informal teaching aids, a number of commercially available language programs are also used with children who have spoken language difficulties. Four widely used programs are briefly described in this section.

DISTAR Language
(Engelmann, Osborn, & Engelmann, 1969)

This program was originally conceived to teach language concepts to educationally handicapped children. Aspects of language are directly taught to the child in a highly structured and sequential fashion. The program includes prepositions, plurals, pronouns, categories, and verb tense. Daily lesson plans are provided with explicit directions for administering the program, giving feedback to the child, and using specific groupings. The program is appropriate for preschool and primary age children and older students with specific language disturbances.

Goldman-Lynch Sounds and Symbols Development Kit
(Goldman & Lynch, 1971)

This program is designed for children at the kindergarten level through third grade. The chief purposes of the kit are to develop ability (a) to produce speech sounds accurately, (b) to recognize visual symbols for these sounds, and (c) to understand and use the sounds of the language in words, sentences, and contextual speech. The 64 lessons vary in length from 30 to 40 minutes, and may be used in groups of 20 to 25 children. The program includes a very comprehensive teacher's manual, along with story books, cassettes, puppets, and flash cards. Students workbooks can also be purchased separately.

The MWM Program for Developing Language Abilities
(Minskoff, Wiseman, & Minskoff, 1973)

This language program is based on the ITPA model and includes the following areas of remediation: auditory reception, visual reception, auditory association, visual association, verbal expression, manual expression, auditory sequential memory, visual sequential memory, grammatic closure, auditory closure, visual closure, and sound blending. The program consists of a very comprehensive teacher's manual, an inventory of language abilities, and numerous teaching materials including workbooks, puzzles, and tape recordings. This well-organized program is primarily intended for children 3 to 11 years of age.

Peabody Language Development Kits
(Dunn & Smith, 1965, 1966, 1967; Dunn, Horton, & Smith, 1968)

The four *Peabody Kits* are intended for use with preschool and primary age children or older children with language difficulties. Each kit consists of 180 carefully designed lessons with a wide range of materials for developing receptive, associative, and expressive linguistic processes, and various other intellectual skills. The daily lessons do not require reading or writing, nor is any seatwork involved. The kits can be used by classroom teachers without specialized language training. Specific lesson plans are included with each individual kit.

ADDITIONAL READINGS

Bereiter, C., & Engelmann, S. *Language learning activities for the disadvantaged child*. New York: Anti-Defamation League of B'nai B'rith, n.d.

Bereiter, C., & Engelmann, S. *Teaching disadvantaged children in the preschool*. Englewood Cliffs, N.J.: Prentice-Hall, 1966.

Berry, M. F. *Language disorders in children: The bases and diagnoses*. New York: Appleton-Century-Crofts, 1969.

Bryan, R. *When children speak*. San Rafael, Calif.: Academic Therapy Publications, 1971.

Bush, W. J., & Giles, M. T. *Aids to psycholinguistic teaching* (2nd ed.). Columbus, Ohio: Charles E. Merrill, 1977.

Cheyney, A. B. *Teaching culturally disadvantaged in the elementary school.* Columbus, Ohio: Charles E. Merrill, 1967.

Eisenson, J. *Aphasia in children.* New York: Harper & Row, 1972.

Goldstein, K. *Language and language disturbances.* New York: Grune & Stratton, 1948.

Gray, B., & Ryan, B. *A language program for the non-language child.* Champaign, Ill.: Research Press, 1973.

Heilman, A. *Phonics in proper perspective.* Columbus, Ohio: Charles E. Merrill, 1968; 3rd ed., 1976.

Johnson, D. J., & Myklebust, H. R. *Learning disabilities: Educational principles and practices.* New York: Grune & Stratton, 1967.

Kaliski, L., Tankersley, R., & Iogha, R. *Structured dramatics for children with learning disabilities.* San Rafael, Calif.: Academic Therapy Publications, 1971.

Karnes, M. B. *Helping young children develop language skills.* Arlington, Va.: The Council for Exceptional Children, 1968.

Lerner, J. *Children with learning disabilities* (2nd ed.). Boston: Houghton Mifflin, 1976.

Linn, S. H. *Teaching phonics with finger puppets.* San Rafael, Calif.: Academic Therapy Publications, 1972.

McGrady, H. J. Language pathology and learning disabilities. In H. R. Myklebust (Ed.), *Progress in learning disabilities* (Vol. 1). New York: Grune & Stratton, 1968. Pp. 199–233.

McNeill, D. *The acquisition of language.* New York: Harper & Row, 1970.

Menyuk, P. *The development of speech.* Indianapolis: Bobbs Merrill, 1972.

Myers, G. C. Creative thinking activities. In *Highlights handbook.* Columbus, Ohio: Highlights for Children, Inc., 1965.

Myklebust, H. R. *Auditory disorders in children: A manual for differential diagnosis.* New York: Grune & Stratton, 1954.

Myklebust, H. R. Childhood aphasia: An evolving concept. In L. E. Travis (Ed.), *Handbook of speech pathology and audiology.* New York: Appleton-Century-Crofts, 1971. Pp. 1181–1202.

Myklebust, H. R. Childhood aphasia: Identification, diagnosis, remediation. In L. E. Travis (Ed.), *Handbook of speech pathology and audiology.* New York: Appleton-Century-Crofts, 1971. Pp. 1203–1217.

Newcomer, P. L., & Hammill, D. D. *Psycholinguistics in the schools.* Columbus, Ohio: Charles E. Merrill, 1976.

Osborn, J. *Teaching a teaching language to disadvantaged children.* Mimeograph paper, University of Illinois, Urbana, 1968.

Otto, W., McMenemy, R. A., & Smith, R. J. *Corrective and remedial teaching* (2nd ed.). Boston: Houghton Mifflin, 1973.

Platts, M. E. *Anchor: A handbook of vocabulary discovery techniques for the classroom teacher*. Stevensville, Mich.: Educational Service, 1970.

Smith, J. A. *Creative teaching of the language arts in the elementary school*. Boston: Allyn & Bacon, 1967.

Smith, R. M. *Clinical teaching: Methods of instructhe retarded* (2nd ed.). New York: McGraw-Hill, 1974.

Smith, R. M. (Ed.). *Teacher diagnosis of educational difficulties*. Columbus, Ohio: Charles E. Merrill, 1969.

Spradlin, J. Procedures for evaluating processes associated with receptive and expressive language. In R. Schiefelbush, R. Copeland, & J. O. Smith (Eds.), *Language and mental retardation*. New York: Holt, Rinehart & Winston, 1967. Pp. 118–136.

Steiner, V. G., & Pond, R. E. *Finger play fun*. Columbus, Ohio: Charles E. Merrill, 1970.

Wagner, G., Hosier, M., & Blackman, M. *Listening games: Building listening skills with instructional games*. New York: Teachers Publishing, 1970.

Wallace, G., & Larsen, S. C. *The educational assessment of learning problems: Testing for teaching*. Boston: Allyn & Bacon, 1978.

Wedemeyer, A., & Cejka, J. *Creative ideas for teaching exceptional children*. Denver: Love, 1970.

Wedemeyer, A., & Cejka, J. *Learning games for exceptional children*. Denver: Love, 1971.

Wiig, E. H., & Semel, E. M. *Language disabilities in children and adolescents*. Columbus, Ohio: Charles E. Merrill, 1976.

Wood, N. E. *Delayed speech and language development*. Englewood Cliffs, N.J.: Prentice-Hall, 1964.

Wood, N. E. *Verbal learning*. San Rafael, Calif.: Dimensions, 1969.

Zigmond, N. K., & Cicci, R. *Auditory learning*. San Rafael, Calif.: Dimensions, 1968.

Zimmerman, I. L., Steiner, V. G., & Evatt, R. L. *Preschool language manual*. Columbus, Ohio: Charles E. Merrill, 1969.

8
Reading Problems

Difficulties in learning to read have been called the most important single cause of school failure (Strang, 1969). Many children with reading difficulties also have academic problems in other areas of the curriculum. Smith (1974), in fact, regards reading as the most significant common denominator for adequate achievement in areas such as communication and social-personal adjustment. The skills involved in learning to read adequately are many and quite varied. It is important that teachers in particular be aware of the specific skills with which an individual child is experiencing difficulty. Teachers must also be aware of methods and materials to alleviate the reading problem. Among the general reading problems with which the teacher must be concerned, the following are most basic:

1. What visual skills in reading prevent the child from reading adequately?
2. What auditory skills in reading prevent the child from reading adequately?
3. Does the child comprehend the material that he reads?

ASSESSMENT

The classroom teacher can and should obtain a substantial amount of diagnostic data. As previously suggested, the diagnostic evaluation may involve teacher observation, informal assessment, and formal tests. Appropriate instruction stems from the information obtained during each kind of assessment.

Teacher Observation

Daily observations and contacts with individual children can provide valuable diagnostic information. Little is required in the way of diagnostic materials. Moreover, the *normal* classroom setting gives the teacher the opportunity to clearly observe the characteristic behavior of an individual child in many different instructional situations. Oral reading, silent reading, group discussion of reading material, seatwork activity, and selection of library books are but a few of the situations in which teachers can informally obtain diagnostic data.

Essentially, the teacher must seek answers to the following questions:

1. How does the child approach reading tasks?
2. How does the child attack unfamiliar and difficult words?
3. How does the child respond to instructional help?
4. How does the child feel about reading?

5. What are the child's specific difficulties?
6. What progress is the child making?
7. What are the child's reading interests?
8. What is the child's reading potential?
9. What conditions are causing the child's reading difficulty?
10. Which of these conditions can be modified?

Informal Assessment

Numerous informal tests may be used to assess specific skill development. Informal tests are usually teacher-made and, therefore, are inexpensive, flexible, rapidly administered, and relatively easy to construct. Many informal tests may supplement standardized tests. Informal tests combine the diagnostic values of observation with content that is closely geared to instruction. In addition to the examples provided in this chapter, further informal tests may be found in Wallen (1972), Silvaroli (1973), and Wallace and Larsen (1978).

Formal Tests

Many standardized reading tests are available for use with those children for whom additional information is required. An important consideration in selecting a standardized test is the direct applicability of the information to instruction. As discussed in chapter 3, *teachable tests* provide the classroom teacher with useable instructional data.

Five individually administered diagnostic reading batteries which we believe provide instructionally useful information are described in this section.

Botel Reading Inventory
(Botel, 1966)

The three subtests which comprise this battery include Word Recognition, Word Opposites, and Phonics Mastery. The Word Recognition subtest consists of 20 words for each of eight reading levels from preprimer to fourth grade. Word Opposites is designed to estimate a child's comprehension by having him find the opposite of the first word in a line of five words. The Phonics Mastery subtest is presented in four levels, each measuring a number of different phonics principles. The entire battery is widely used to informally measure a child's instructional, free reading, and frustration reading levels, in addition to appraising the child's phonics proficiency.

Durrell Analysis of Reading Difficulty
(Durrell, 1955)

This battery consists of a series of subtests in Oral and Silent Reading, Listening Comprehension, Word Recognition, and Word Analysis. Supplementary tests are also available for Visual Memory and Auditory Analysis of word elements, spelling, and handwriting. The tests are primarily designed for children at the nonreading through sixth grade reading level. Grade level scores are provided, along with many excellent suggestions for organizing remedial teaching. A checklist for instructional needs also helps focus the teacher's attention on specific reading deficits noted on the test and in the classroom.

Gates-McKillop Reading Diagnostic Test
(Gates & McKillop, 1962)

This complete battery is composed of subtests in Oral Reading, Flashed Presentation of Words, Untimed Presentation of Words, Flashed Presentation of Phrases, Knowledge of Word Parts, Recognition of the Visual Form of Sounds, and Auditory Blending. Supplementary tests are available in Spelling, Oral Vocabulary, Syllabication, and Auditory Discrimination. The battery can be used with any student severely handicapped in reading, and not all subtests need to be administered to each child. The *Gates-McKillop* is probably recognized as one of the most complete diagnostic tests of word analysis skills currently available.

Diagnostic Reading Scales
(Spache, 1963)

This is a series of integrated tests consisting of three word-recognition lists which assess word recognition and word analysis skills, 22 reading passages of graduated difficulty from grades 1.6 to 8.5, and eight supplementary phonic tests. The reading passages are used to determine the child's instructional, independent, and potential reading levels. The phonic tests are intended to provide detailed data concerning phonics proficiency and various word analysis skills. The battery may be used with elementary age children, and older students with reading problems.

Woodcock Reading Mastery Tests
(Woodcock, 1974)

The five subtests comprising this battery include Letter Identification, Word Identification, Word Attack, Word Comprehension, and Passage Comprehension. The two forms of the test are specifically designed for students from kindergarten to grade 12. Results are combined to provide a composite index of overall reading skill. Traditional grade scores and age equivalents are also available. The *mastery scale* is intended to predict the child's relative success with reading tasks at different levels of difficulty.

VISUAL SKILLS IN READING

Many children who have normal visual acuity have difficulties differentiating, interpreting, or remembering different shapes, letters, or words. Basically, children with visual skill deficiencies must learn to:

1. Discriminate sizes and shapes,
2. Discriminate specific letters,
3. Discriminate the directionality of specific letters,
4. Remember letter names and words,
5. Remember particular words learned mainly by sight,
6. Recognize structural parts of words.

Diagnostic questions, informal tests, and teaching suggestions for remediating visually oriented reading problems are listed in this section.

HAS THE CHILD LEARNED THE VISUAL SKILLS NECESSARY FOR READING?

Has the Child Mastered the Skills Prerequisite for Visual Discrimination of Letters?

Display a number of buttons of different sizes (or nails, blocks, pieces of the same color paper, etc.) in front of the child. Instruct him to match the buttons according to sizes or shapes.

Informal Assessment

1. Place a number of objects (cup, pencil, ruler, block, eraser, nail, etc.) in front of the child. Display a duplicate object, such as pencil or block, and ask the child to pick up the similar object. Initially, include only three or four objects. As time progresses and the child improves in this skill, increase the number of objects.

Instructional Activities

2. Match pictures of objects with the actual objects. Variations of this activity could include allowing the child to cut pictures from magazines to match actual objects or matching pictures to pictures.

3. Give children various shapes of macaroni to sort. Initially, the child may group the various macaroni according to shape and place them in small boxes. Later, the macaroni may be colored and sorted according to shape and color.

4. Show the child a picture with missing parts. Direct the child to draw in the part that is omitted. Some examples include:

    a. A tree without a trunk,

    b. A cup with handle missing,

c. Faces with various parts missing (nose, ear, etc.),

d. A child without a shoe,

e. A house without a door.

Begin by requiring the child to draw in parts to match the sample drawing. Gradually make the missing parts less obvious.

5. Display three triangles and one square. Ask the child to identify the shape that is unlike the others. Various geometric shapes may be included. As you proceed, increase the number of shapes to be discriminated. Shapes of different colors may be used after the child learns color discriminations.

6. Encourage the child to become aware of sizes and shapes. Cut out different sizes of squares, circles, triangles, etc. Explain to the child that a square is still a square even though it might be smaller than others. This activity might be extended by having the child find all of the square shapes in a room or all of the circle shapes in a magazine.

7. Describe an object that is very familar to the child. Ask the child to find that object among four pictures (or objects) that are presented to him. For example, "I am thinking of something that is round, that bounces up and down, and that you need to play baseball."

8. Have children complete dot-to-dot pictures of familar objects, animals, etc. Gradually increase the detail of the pictures and ask the child to describe them.

9. Present the child with different arrangements of blocks, geometric shapes, familiar objects, etc. Ask the child to choose the one arrangement that is different from the others and to explain why. For example,

2. Can the Child Discriminate Among Letters?

Informal Assessment   Present rows of four- or five-letter cut-outs to the child. Ask the child to circle the same two letters in each row.

Instructional Activities   **10.** Have the child match capital and lowercase letters: Aa, Mm, Pp, Bb, . . .

11. Play *Letter Bingo* with small groups of children. Cards with different letters printed on them are passed to each child. The teacher or another child covers the appropriate letter. The first child to fill a card is the winner.

12. Have children trace various letter templates and stencils.

13. Let the child use the typewriter to find specific letters. Children can be instructed to find certain letters in a given amount of time.

14. Present letters of varying size to the child and ask him to match the same letters. A large M can be presented with a very small *M*, along with a medium size, lowercase *m*.

15. Pictures that closely correspond to the shapes of individual letters can be presented with the letter as a memory device for children. For example, a wiggly snake can be presented with the letter *S*, a telephone pole with the letter *T*, a wheel with the letter *O*.

16. Present children with partially completed letters and ask them to identify and/or complete them. For example, $C V \backslash \xi S$

17. Show the child the alphabet with specific letters omitted. Ask the child to fill in the missing letters. For example, ab __ d __ fgh __ __ k __ m. . . . Increase the number of missing letters as the child progresses.

18. Tape an individual alphabet to each child's desk to provide a quick reference and guide.

19. Dot-to-dot pictures may be used with letters. The teacher can direct this exercise by instructing the child to: "Draw a line to the letter *p*, now a straight line over to the letter *s*, down to the letter *b*, ..." This activity can also be planned so that the lines are drawn in the exact sequence of the alphabet.

Does the Child Reverse Letters?

Present children with a stimulus word and four choices from which to choose the matching word. For example,

Informal Assessment

pot	otp	top	tip	pot
lap	pal	pil	lap	alp
war	row	war	raw	awr

20. Have the child make an association for letters that are reversed. For example, a child with a freckle on the left hand could remember that a *d* points in that direction. Likewise, a child who

Instructional Activities

wears a ring on one of the fingers on the right hand could associate the ring with the direction of the letter *b*.

21. Print frequently reversed letters on oak tag strips. These letters should also be outlined on tracing paper. Let the child match the tracing paper letter with the oak tag strip by placing the tracing paper over the letter.

22. Give children words with missing letters accompanied by matching pictures. This exercise may emphasize frequently reversed letters. For example,

*23. Instruct the child to trace specific letters on sandpaper, salt trays, etc. Be sure that the child says the name of the letter as he traces it.

*24. Describe a letter and have the child find that letter among three or four placed in front of him. For example, "I am thinking of a letter that is a straight line up and down and another line straight across."

*25. Place words that are frequently reversed on flash cards and use them for periodic drills. Arrow cues may be added for help. For example,

*26. Place words on flash cards and present them to the child by covering up all but the first letter. Slowly uncover additional letters until the child correctly pronounces the word. This activity emphasizes left-to-right orientation. An overhead projector may also be used.

3. Does the Child Remember Visual Stimuli, Including Letters and Words?

Informal Assessment　　Write a number of letters on the chalkboard. While the children's eyes are closed, erase one letter. When the children open their eyes, ask them to identify the missing letter. Words can also be used for this activity.

Instructional Activities　　**27.** Place several articles, such as eraser, block, pencil, and chalk, in front of the child. Allow the child a short time to view them. After you have removed the items, ask the child to recall as many of them as possible. This activity can be varied by removing one or two articles at a time and asking the child to tell what is missing.

28. Present the child with an uncluttered picture of an object known to him. Allow the child a short time to study the picture. After you have removed the picture, ask the child to describe what he saw.

29. Flash a picture of geometric design on a screen through an opaquenor overhead projector or tachistoscope. Instruct the child to match the flashed form with a similar form on a worksheet.

30. Present pictures with missing parts to the child and ask him to either draw in the missing part or tell which part is missing.

31. Allow children to view a pegboard, marble board, or bead design for a short period of time and then ask them to duplicate the design. Children working in pairs may also construct their own designs.

32. Encourage children to use a toy telephone to learn the telephone numbers of their friends.

33. Print letters or words on removable gummed labels on the squares of a checkerboard. Let the children play checkers but require them to name a letter or word before they make a move.

34. Paint the alphabet on a piece of oil cloth. Place the cloth on the floor and have one child walk at random from one letter to another. Ask other children to reproduce the sequence. This activity may be varied by walking through letters that spell specific words. Ask children to reproduce the letter and say the word.

35. Letters or parts of words may be color cued for memory. For example, in the word raining, the *ing* may be color coded red.

36. Printing words with a rubber stamp set provides an interesting activity for some children. This activity calls attention to the sequence of letters.

37. Children can also work with three-dimensional letters. Encourage the child to discuss the differences among letters.

38. Cut apart cartoon strips and paste them on oak tag. Ask children to reassemble the cartoon in the correct order.

39. Give the child dotted forms to trace. Gradually reduce the number of dots so that there are only a few remaining. See if the child can remember how to make the letters or words. For example,

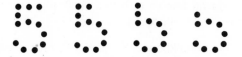

*40. Trace words and letters in any of the following media: finger paint, salt, sandpaper, felt, instant pudding, clay, or wet sand.

*41. Provide children with mixed-up words and ask them to arrange the letters correctly. For example, present *cat* as atc and *bag* as agb.

4. *Does the Child Recognize Sight Words?*

Informal Assessment Prepare a tape recording of the most common sight words. Have the child listen to the tape through earphones and follow a worksheet. The teacher's voice says, "Number 1 is *guess*, Number 2 is *could*," etc. To test a child, give him a word list without numbers and let him mark the worksheet as follows: "Put number 1 in front of *guess*; put number 2 in front of *could*;" etc. Check by using a key.

Instructional Activities ***42.** Write five sight words on the chalkboard. Read each one aloud and ask the children to close their eyes. Erase a word and ask, "What is missing?" Continue until all the words are erased. Next, ask the children to remember the five original words and write them again on the board. See who can read the entire list.

*43. Use the *Language Master* to teach new words or review those previously taught. Use the blank cards to program the most persistently miscalled words.

*44. Duplicate a sheet with groups of words that are similar in configuration. Direct the child to circle the word you read. For example,

1. <u>at</u>   is   it   in

2. see   saw   <u>sea</u>   sip

You may record the stimulus words if you want to use a tape recorder with this activity.

*45. Picture dictionaries can be helpful in learning words and associating meaning. Encourage children to make their own dictionaries with either magazine pictures or their own illustrations.

*46. In a group of assorted words written on tag board, write all difficult sight words in red to alert the child that he must recall the word by memory.

*47. With sight words on cards, a child can occasionally review words previously learned by placing the words he knows in a "Friends" pile and the troublesome words in an "Enemies" pile. Students may work in pairs.

*48. Draw a baseball diamond on the chalkboard. Place sight words printed on flash cards on the chalk ledge. Label the words "single," "double," "homerun," etc. Groups of children can play baseball by reading the words. This activity can also be adapted to football, fishing, mountain climbing, and so on.

*49. Tracing may be beneficial for children with poor visual memories. The child says the word as he traces it. Trace in the air, on the chalkboard, in salt trays, on large pieces of paper, etc.

*50. Pairs of words can be presented to children to facilitate memory. Examples include salt and pepper, bread and butter, black and white, hot and cold.

*51. Have the child match a stimulus word from a list of visually similar words, such as those illustrated in the following chart.

bed	bid	bad	bud	dab	bed
hop	hip	hop	bop	hup	dip
run	run	rat	run	sun	nun

This activity might be varied by calling out the stimulus word.

*52. *Word Bingo*, similar to *Letter Bingo* (see activity #11) may be played with small groups of children.

*53. Label objects around the room and periodically review these labels with the children. Mix the labels and have a child put them in the proper place.

*54. Some basic sight words are listed below (Ekwall, 1976).

PREPRIMER

a	do	here	look	put	two
and	down	him	make	run	water
are	eat	his	my	said	we
away	for	house	no	the	what
be	get	I	not	then	where
big	go	in	of	this	who
but	good	it	oh	three	will
can	has	know	one	to	you
come	have	like	play	too	your
did	her	little			

PRIMER

about	came	help	on	some	up
after	could	how	other	something	us
all	day	is	over	stop	very
am	find	jump	ran	take	want
an	fly	let	red	that	was
around	from	man	ride	them	way
as	funny	may	sat	there	went
back	give	me	saw	they	when
blue	green	mother	see	time	would
by	had	now	she	tree	yes
call	he	old	so		

FIRST READER

again	buy	girl	Mrs.	rabbit	think
any	children	got	much	read	thought
ask	cold	happy	must	shall	took
at	color	high	name	side	under
ate	cry	if	never	sleep	walk
ball	dog	into	new	soon	well
been	door	just	night	stand	were
before	far	laugh	or	tell	white
began	fast	light	out	than	why
better	father	long	party	thank	with
black	five	more	please	their	work
boy	four	morning	prĕtty	these	yellow
brown	fun	Mr.	pull		

READER 2

always	end	grow	live	place	ten
another	enough	hand	made	right	thing
because	even	hard	many	round	those
best	every	head	men	say	together
book	eye	hold	near	school	told
both	fall	home	next	should	until
box	first	hot	once	show	wait
bring	found	hurt	only	sit	warm
carry	friend	keep	open	six	which
clean	full	kind	out	start	while
cut	gave	last	own	still	wish
does	going	left	pick	sure	year
each					

READER 2

dear	most	present	sing	today	use
done	off	seem	small	try	wash
drink	people	seven	such	turn	write

READER 3

also	draw	goes	its	leave	upon
don't	eight	grand	king	myself	

5 Does the Child Recognize Prefixes, Suffixes, and Compound Words?

*Informal
Assessment*

Provide the child with a list of words and direct him to circle the root (graphemic base) in each word; for example, singing, jumps, ended. This activity may be separated for prefixes and suffixes.

*Instructional
Activities*

*55. Provide the child with a list of root words on oak tag strips and an envelope of endings that may be added to these root words. Ask the child to make as many words as he can.

*56. Give the child a series of sentences to which prefixes or suffixes must be added to complete certain words. Have the child complete each sentence. For example,

```
1.   Mary walk___ to the store each morning.

2.   She is ___sure of the correct street.

3.   They are play___ in the yard.

4.   He did not ___connect the refrigerator.
```

*57. For older children, give a root word and a meaning of a new word. Ask them to write the new word. An example is read—to read again (*reread*). The concentric circles described in activity #87 can be made for root words and suffixes. Have the child rotate the circle and say the root words that are made.

*58. Under two columns, list words that can be made into compound words. Leave a third column blank so that the child can complete the compound word.

```
Column A              Column B              Column C

base                  ball                  _____

cow                   boy                   _____

light                 house                 _____
```

*59. Activity #58 may be varied by leaving blank either Column A or Column B, in addition to Column C. Another variation could include placing a drawing in either of the first two columns.

```
Column A      Column B      Column C

base          🌙            _____

🐄            boy           _____

light         🏠            _____

_____      man           mailman
```

*60. You can use the words in the exercises above in random order. Ask the child to put together as many compound words as he can. For example,

```
ball, house, flash, boy, base, light, cow, boat
```

*61. Prepare a paragraph with missing parts of compound words. Ask the child to complete the missing parts. For example,

> John and Tom play base(ball) or (basket)ball every after(noon) on the (play)ground. (Some)times they also play (horse)shoes or play in the sand(box). In the winter, they build (snow)men and make snow(balls).

*62. Children can make their own compound words. Have them define each word they make.

AUDITORY SKILLS IN READING

Children with auditory skill deficiencies may have normal hearing acuity. However, they have difficulties in differentiating, synthesizing, and remembering the sounds of different letters and words. The child must learn to:

1. Discriminate among sounds,
2. Discriminate initial and final letter sounds,
3. Synthesize letter sounds into words,
4. Remember the sounds of letters and words.

Diagnostic questions, informal tests, and teaching suggestions for remediating auditory based reading problems are listed in this section.

HAS THE CHILD LEARNED THE AUDITORY SKILLS NECESSARY FOR READING?

Has the Child Mastered the Skills Prerequisite for Auditory Discrimination of Letter Sounds?

Informal Assessment

Read a word, such as *fat*. Ask the child to repeat the word. Then read a list of words, and have the child clap when he hears a word that rhymes with the stimulus word.

Instructional Activities

63. Select two different sounds, such as a bell and a drum. Stand behind the child and ring the bell. Ask the child to point to the object used to make the sound. Gradually increase the number of sounds that can be discriminated. Discriminations should also become finer as the child progresses.

64. With the aid of a tape recorder, ask the child to identify common sounds such as an airplane, a car, various animals, and household appliances. These sounds can gradually be changed to voices of familiar people.

65. In working with the sounds of letters, work initially with grossly different sounds, such as /m/ and /p/, /s/ and /b/, or /a/ and /v/. Gradually work into the finer discriminations such as /v/ and /f/ or /m/ and /n/.

66. Associate a sound with a picture or with a real object. The following pictures or items are often helpful to most children (Russell & Karp, 1938):

a—apple	j—jacks	s—sack
b—boat	k—kite	t—tail
c—cat	l—lamp	u—umbrella
d—duck	m—mouse	v—vest
e—egg	n—nest	w—wagon
f—fox	o—orange	x—xylophone
g—goat	p—pail	y—yard
h—house	q—queen	z—zebra
i—ice cream	r—rooster	

67. Write sounds on large pieces of paper and place them on the floor. As you say a word beginning (or ending) with a specific sound, have the child walk to the sound he has heard.

68. Give the child a box containing a number of different toy objects, such as boats, cars, plastic dishes, chalk, pencils, and erasers. Ask the child to select all the objects that begin with, for instance, the /p/ sound. You may have five or six boxes which emphasize different sounds.

69. In class, listen to commercial records which teach auditory awareness of sounds.

70. Provide the child with a number of different pictures. Direct him to match those pictures whose names rhyme. This activity may be varied by duplicating pictures for seatwork.

*71. Give the child a list of rhyming words and direct him to circle the parts of the words that are alike. This activity provides a check to see if the child is aware that many rhyming words have parts that are spelled similarly.

*72. Give children a list of words and ask them to circle all the words which rhyme with a given stimulus word. This activity may be varied by giving the child a list of words and instructing him to list a word which rhymes with the given word.

73. Read a sentence to the child with a word omitted. For example, "We play baseball with a ball and (bat)." Instruct the child to change the omitted word to one that rhymes with it. Acceptable responses for this example include *cat, mat, fat,* and *sat.*

Can the Child Discriminate Initial and Final Sounds?

Informal Assessment   Give the children two cards numbered one and two. As you say a word, instruct them to listen for a specific sound and indicate whether they heard it at the beginning or ending of the word by holding up card number one or card number two.

Instructional Activities   **74.** Say a word such as *sad* and require the child to provide a word which rhymes with it but has a different initial consonant.

75. Ask the children to say all the words they know that begin with a specific sound.

76. Make up nonsense sentences using the same letter at the beginning of each word. Examples could include "Bad Billy bit blueberries" or "Holy Harry has hot hands."

77. Provide children with a number of individual oak tag cards with one sound on each card. Instruct the child to listen carefully and hold up the letter he hears at the beginning (or end) of each word.

78. Instruct children to classify a number of pictures according to initial or final sounds. Appropriately labeled boxes are helpful for this activity. Have the children place pictures with the beginning /s/ sound in one box, the beginning /f/ sound in another box, etc.

*79. Give each child the same number of oak tag cards with words written on them. Ask for all the cards that begin with a certain sound, rhyme with a word, etc. For example, ask for all the cards that "end with the same sound as *bag*." Continue to ask questions until each child's pile of cards is depleted.

*80. Call out words which have the same blend in either the initial or final position in all the words. Let the child tell where he hears the blend. For example, you could use chip, chum, charge, search, patch, and march.

*81. Give the child the name of someone in the room. Let the child make up two descriptive words which have the same initial consonant sound. For example, prim, pretty Paula or skinny, silly Sam.

*82. Ask children to blend different consonants to a specific word family. For example, blend initial consonants to the *in* family (e.g., *pin, fin, tin*).

Can the Child Blend Letter Sounds into Words?

Informal Assessment   Ask the child to blend specific sounds to a given list of phonograms—for example, blending the /p/ sound to "at," "in," "it," "an," etc.

83. After children know specific sounds, give them three- to five-   *Instructional*
letter nonsense syllables. Ask them to blend the sounds. The   *Activities*
syllables can become progressively longer as the child improves in
this ability.

84. Provide the child with a picture of a specific object, such as a block. Below
the picture appears

_____ _____ o c k

Have the child supply the missing consonant blend, either by writing in the
missing part or saying it.

85. Have each child draw a word from a box containing words with blends.
The child must pronounce the word he chooses and give another word which
begins with the same blend.

86. Print words with blends on oak tag and cut the word after the blend. Mix up
a number of word parts, and have the child sort them correctly. Gradually
increase the number of words as the child succeeds with this task.

87. Make two concentric circles, one with blends and the other with phonograms. Have children rotate the circle and read the words. Circles for initial
consonants can also be made.

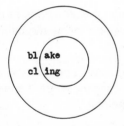

88. Give each child a large piece of paper with a blend written on it. Write a
phonogram on the chalkboard, and ask the children to make a word with their
blend and phonogram on the chalkboard.

***89.** Prepare a series of three stimulus words. Pronounce one of the words in
each series. Have the children listen and underline the word you pronounce
(Heilman, 1968). For example:

blue	black	<u>drum</u>	plain	dress
<u>blow</u>	<u>plank</u>	dear	<u>plant</u>	dire
brake	blank	drink	party	<u>drive</u>

Does the Child Remember Sounds, Including the Sounds of Letters and Words?

Informal   Present a series of verbal commands to the child. Instruct him to
Assessment   follow the sequence for the commands; for example, "John, throw
                this paper in the wastepaper basket, then pass out these books to
the boys, and then erase the chalkboard."

Instructional   **90.** Tap or clap out rhythm patterns and have the child repeat the
Activities   pattern.

91. Ask the child to repeat a sentence or phrase that you have said to him.

92. Present a series of movements to a small group of children and have them follow the sequence. For example, say "Jump, hop, clap, and skip."

93. Play a record of a story or tell a story to a small group of children. When you complete the story, have the children divide a paper into equal sections and draw the events of the story in sequence.

94. Instruct the child to close his eyes. While his eyes are closed, tap some object in the room or make another sound. When the child opens his eyes, ask him to identify the sound from among three that are presented. Include sounds such as crushing paper, knocking on the door, tapping on glass, whistling, animal sounds, and writing on the chalkboard.

95. Prepare treasure maps for each child. Give several instructions at one time (e.g., go up the green path by the white house and follow the circular drive). Children may compete to reach the treasure.

96. Ask children to trace and write letters or manipulate three-dimensional letters as they hear the name of a letter. Feeling and noting the way the speech organs perform in making different sounds is also helpful.

97. Give children a blank piece of paper. Direct the children to perform a variety of tasks. For example, say "Make a circle in the upper right-hand corner, draw a straight line in the middle of the paper, write your name on the line." This activity may be made more structured by preparing worksheets with various geometric designs and directing the children to perform specific tasks. For example, say "Write the first letter of the alphabet inside the square, and then color in the triangle with your red crayon." (The verbal directions for these activities may be put on a tape recorder.)

98. Help children play successive addition games, such as "I went to the zoo and saw a lion." The next child adds another animal. "I went to the zoo and saw a lion and a tiger." Continue adding animals with each successive child.

99. Take a walk with the children around the playground listening, watching, and observing. Once you are back in the classroom, have the children list by categories (e.g., animals, transportation) what they heard. This activity can also be used on field trips or when walking to and from school.

*100. Ask a child to describe another child in the room. Using only the pertinent characteristics, draw a picture of the child. After a number of these have been completed, ask individual children to identify and describe some of the pictures.

READING COMPREHENSION

Johnson and Myklebust (1967) indicate that the major problem of the child with reading difficulties is not in *understanding* what he reads, but in *processing* printed material. Consequently, once specific visual and auditory skill deficiencies have been corrected, teachers will often find corresponding improvement in reading comprehension. Teaching suggestions for remediating comprehension difficulties which persist when visual and auditory skills are adequate are listed below. Basic comprehension skills include:
1. Reading to get the main idea,
2. Remembering specific details,
3. Evaluating and making judgments.

DOES THE CHILD COMPREHEND WHAT HE READS?

/, *Does the Child Get the Main Ideas?*

Have children read untitled stories. When they complete each story, have them write an appropriate title.

Informal Assessment

101. A basic consideration in reading comprehension is to be sure the material is worth the effort the child will make to read it. In addition, the reading material should not be at a level that is too difficult for the child.

Instructional Activities

*102. Give the children a series of written true-false statements to answer. For example:

```
a.   Cats have three legs.

b.   A square has four sides.

c.   Triangles have five sides.
```

*103. Give the children a series of absurd short stories to read. Ask them to find the absurdity. For example:

> "The children put on their bathing suits.. They
> collected their shovels, pails, and snowballs to
> take to the ocean to swim."

*104. Have students read newspaper articles from which the headlines have been deleted. Then have them select the correct headline from a group arranged on your desk.

*105. After the children have read a story, print a list of phrases on the chalkboard. Some of the phrases should be related and others not related to the story. Ask the children to choose those that pertain to the reading selection.

*106. Point out devices used by authors to emphasize certain passages. Emphasize chapter titles, headings, subheadings, italics, indentions, etc.

*107. After reading a story, discuss it with the children, listing the main ideas in the story. Select children to illustrate specific story events with drawings. The story can be retold by rolling the drawings on a "TV" screen or overhead projector in sequence.

2. Does the Child Remember Specific Details?

*Informal
Assessment*

Following the reading of a story, ask the child a number of questions which require him to remember specific details. For example:

What grade did Ann fail?

Who gave Peter the black eye?

How much did the car cost?

*Instructional
Activities*

*108. After reading a story, ask the children to compose a telegram repeating the events of the story or of a certain part of the story. Limit the telegram to a specific number of words.

*109. After students have read a story, distribute a worksheet with three or four sentences that indicate a sequence of events pertaining to the story. Have the students arrange them in proper order.

*110. Ask children to read a stimulus sentence and four multiple-choice responses. Have them select the correct multiple-choice responses. To insure exacting reading, more than one response may be correct. For example,

> Mary and John are eight-year-old twins in the
> third grade at Smith School.
>
> a.   John is one year older than Mary.
>
> b.   John and Mary go to the same school.

   c.   John and Mary were probably born in the same
        year.

   d.   Mary and John do not have any other brothers
        and sisters.

*111. Encourage students to indicate exactly where in a particular story they first knew it was sad, funny, etc.

*112. Let one child take the role of a character in a story that the class has read. The rest of the class should try to guess the identity of the characters by considering clues given to them by the impersonator.

*113. Have children read a story on how to do some activity, e.g., building a kite, making soap, or baking a cake. Upon completion, ask them to perform the activity in sequence.

*114. Distribute specific instructions on paper slips. Ask children to carry out the instructions. For example, write "Put all the books in the library corner in order," or "Pass out a yellow piece of paper to each girl in the room."

3. Does the Child Evaluate What He Reads and Make Judgments?

Have students indicate whether a sentence is *fact* or *opinion,* and discuss reasons for particular responses. For example:

Informal Assessment

   1.   Virginia is the best state in the country for
        fishing.

   2.   She is 43 years old.

   3.   Jimmy Carter was elected President of the United
        States.

   4.   Pepperoni pizza is too spicy.

   5.   April is the fourth month.

*115. Tape record advertisements heard on radio and television, and have children discuss the merits of certain statements (Ekwall, 1977).

Instructional Activities

*116. Stop periodically while reading a story aloud, and ask children to predict outcomes.

*117. After reading a story, encourage children to discuss reasons why they liked or disliked certain characters in the story.

*118. Have students compare two editorials on the same subject (Lerner, 1976).

*119. Ask children to predict what a story will be about based upon chapter headings or illustrations.

*120. After reading a story on a controversial issue, discuss the pros and cons of the author's particular viewpoint.

READING PROGRAMS

A vast number of commercial materials are available for use with children experiencing specific reading difficulties. Many of these programs use developmental reading approaches which have been individually adapted for remedial instruction. In addition, a number of high interest, easy-to-read books have been successfully used with handicapped learners. Table 8-1 lists some of these high interest, easy-to-read books. Some of the more popular reading approaches for disabled children are also summarized in this section.

Table 8-1
High Interest, Easy-To-Read Books

titles	publisher
Basic Vocabulary Series	Garrard Publishing Co.
Break Through	Allyn & Bacon, Inc.
Cowboy Sam Series	Beckley-Cardy Co.
Deep Sea Adventure Series	Field Educational Publications
I Can Read Books	Harper & Row, Publishers
Jim Forest Series	Field Educational Publications
Little Wonder Books	Charles E. Merrill Publishing Co.
Morgan Bay Mysteries	Field Educational Publications
Readers Digest Skill Builders	Readers Digest Association
Scholastic Book Clubs	Scholastic Book Services
Walt Disney Story Books	The Macmillan Co.

Beginning to Read, Write, and Listen
(Rowland, 1971)

This is a multisensory program consisting of reading, spelling, handwriting, auditory skills, language activities, and art projects for children at the reading readiness level. Children are introduced to the alphabet by learning letter names, how to write the letters, what sounds the letters represent, and letter functions as they are blended into words. The letters are introduced in a carefully structured sequence by means of 24 different *letter books*. The workbooks include 3-D pop-outs for construction, sandpaper letters, *sniffies* to smell, and a writing slate. Cassettes and duplicating masters are also included with the program.

DISTAR Reading
(Engelmann & Bruner, 1969)

The *DISTAR Reading* system is a highly specific, beginning reading program intended for preschool and primary age children. The program teaches the child to decode various words through a series of highly structured and fast-paced drills which include symbol-action games, blending, and rhyming. Children are taught to blend by the *say-it-fast* procedure, and spelling words by sounds teaches the reverse process. A very precise teachers' manual, presentation books, and *take-home* worksheets comprise the major part of the program. A coordinated *DISTAR Library* provides the child with supplementary "book" reading.

Programmed Reading
(Buchanan, 1966)

The phonic-linguistics based series of reading workbooks is designed to teach reading skills through a concisely organized and sequential approach. The short learning units (or frames) require the child to be actively involved in the reading process by responding to each frame and immediately checking his response for correctness. The 21 books in the series may be used with elementary grade children and older remedial pupils. Students are encouraged to move through the workbooks at their own pace. A correlated set of readers is also available for the child to practice using the vocabulary introduced in the workbooks.

Reading Exercises
(Gates & Peardon, 1963)

These reading workbooks are intended for use with elementary grade students or older pupils with reading difficulties. The 13 books in the series are divided among five different levels which stress the ability to recall facts and details, understand the main idea, and follow directions. Stories in each of the workbooks are followed by questions to be answered by individual students. We have found the materials to be very appropriate for older pupils with rather involved reading problems.

Remedial Reading Drills
(Hegge, Kirk, & Kirk, 1955)

These reading drills were initially designed for use with mentally retarded children, but they have since been primarily used with reading disabled students. The program consists of lists of words emphasizing specific sounds and combinations of letters. It is intended that the child use various lists of words to learn to blend various sounds. A multisensory approach is suggested throughout the program. The use of the drills with reading disabled children helps to provide for constant practice with many sound-symbol relationships.

Specific Skill Series
(Boning, 1970)

> This program is designed to develop reading skills in following directions, using the context, getting the main idea, locating the answer, working with sounds, drawing conclusions, getting the facts, and detecting the sequence. The skills are developed through a series of progressively more difficult workbooks. The materials are appropriate for elementary age children and older students with specific reading handicaps. We believe the workbooks can serve as a very good supplement to on-going programs of instruction for both individuals and groups of children. Duplicating masters are also separately available for purchase.

ADDITIONAL READINGS

Arena, J. I. *Teaching educationally handicapped children*. San Rafael, Calif.: Academic Therapy Publications, 1967.

Bateman, B. (Ed.). *Learning disorders* (Vol. 4). Seattle: Special Child Publications, 1971.

Cartwright, C. A., & Cartwright, G. P. *Developing observation skills*. New York: McGraw-Hill, 1974.

Cohen, S. A. *Teach them all to read*. New York: Random House, 1969.

Duffy, G. G., & Sherman, G. B. *How to teach reading systematically*. New York: Harper & Row, 1973.

Durkin, D. *Teaching them to read* (2nd ed.). Boston: Allyn & Bacon, 1974.

Ekwall, E. E. *Diagnosis and remediation of the disabled reader*. Boston: Allyn & Bacon, 1976.

Ekwall, E. E. *Locating and correcting reading difficulties.* (2nd ed.). Columbus, Ohio: Charles E. Merrill, 1977.

Engelmann, S. *Preventing failure in the primary grades*. Chicago: Science Research Associates, 1969.

Gillespie, P. H., & Johnson, L. E. *Teaching reading to the mildly retarded child*. Columbus, Ohio: Charles E. Merrill, 1974.

Gilliland, H. *A practical guide to remedial reading*. Columbus, Ohio: Charles E. Merrill, 1974.

Gillingham, A., & Stillman, B. W. *Remedial training for children with specific disability in reading, spelling, and penmanship*. Cambridge, Mass.: Educators Publishing Service, 1960.

Goodman, K. S. Reading: A psycholinguistic guessing game. In H. Singer & R. Ruddell (Eds.), *Theoretical models and processes of reading*. Newark, Del.: International Reading Association, 1970. Pp. 259-272.

Goodman, Y. M., & Burke, C. I. *Reading miscue inventory: Manual procedure for diagnosis and remediation.* New York: Macmillan, 1972.

Guzak, F. J. *Diagnostic reading instruction in the elementary school.* New York: Harper & Row, 1972.

Hall, N. A. *A handbook of remedial reading techniques for the classroom teacher.* Stevensville, Mich: Educational Service, 1969.

Harris, A. *How to increase your reading ability* (5th ed.). New York: McKay, 1970.

Johnson, D. J., & Myklebust, H. R. *Learning disabilities: Educational principles and practices.* -New York: Grune & Stratton, 1967.

Kaluger, G., & Kolson, C. J. *Reading and learning disabilities* (2nd ed.). Columbus, Ohio: Charles E. Merrill, 1978.

Karlin, R. *Teaching elementary reading: Principles and strategies.* New York: Harcourt Brace Jovanovich, 1971.

Karnes, M. B. *Helping young children develop language skills.* Arlington, Va: The Council for Exceptional Children, 1968.

Lerner, J. W. *Children with learning disabilities* (2nd ed.). Boston: Houghton Mifflin, 1976.

Lowell, E. L., & Stoner, M. *Play it by ear.* Los Angeles: John Tracy Clinic, 1960.

Orton, J. L. *A guide for teaching phonics.* Cambridge, Mass.: Educators Publishing Service, 1964.

Platts, M. E., Marguerite, S. R., & Schumaker, E. *Suggested activities to motivate the teaching of the language arts.* Stevensville, Mich.: Educational Service, Inc., 1970.

Russell, D. H., & Karp, E. E. *Reading aids through the grades.* New York: Teachers College Press, 1938.

Smith, F. *Psycholinguistics and reading.* New York: Holt, Rinehart & Winston, 1973.

Spache, G. D. *The teaching of reading.* Bloomington, Ind.: Phi Delta Kappa, 1972.

Spache, G. D. *Diagnosing and correcting reading disabilities.* Boston: Allyn & Bacon, 1976.

Spache, G. D., & Spache, E. B. *Reading in the elementary school* (4th ed.). Boston: Allyn & Bacon, 1977.

Strang, R. *Diagnostic teaching of reading.* New York: McGraw-Hill, 1969.

Tinker, M. A., & McCullough, C. M. *Teaching elementary reading* (4th ed.). Englewood Cliffs, N.J.: Prentice-Hall, 1975.

Wallace, G., & Larsen, S. C. *The educational assessment of learning problems: Testing for teaching.* Boston: Allyn & Bacon, 1978.

Wallen, C. J. *Competency in teaching reading.* Chicago: Science Research Associates, 1972.

Wilson, R. M. *Diagnostic and remedial reading for classroom and clinic* (3rd ed.). Columbus, Ohio: Charles E. Merrill, 1977.

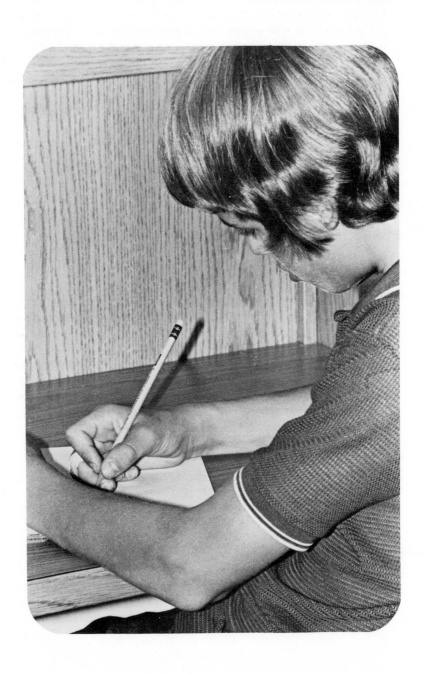

Written Language Problems

Written language is one of the highest forms of language and essentially the last to be learned (Johnson & Myklebust, 1967). Most people develop skills in listening, speaking, and reading before learning written language.

Many children with written language difficulties come to dislike the idea of written communication and either devise elaborate mental schemes to compensate for their deficits or simply avoid all written activities (Compton, 1965). To help a child overcome these difficulties, the teacher must be concerned with three specific questions:

1. What particular difficulties prevent the child from correctly manipulating the writting utensils to form letters?
2. What skill deficiencies interfere with producing the correct graphic form for each word?
3. What interferes with the child's ability to translate ideas into words and syntactic patterns?

ASSESSMENT

Teacher Observation

Direct observation of written language skills will give the teacher precise data on what a child can and cannot do. The teacher who closely observes the child during instruction will know the specific types of errors that he is making, and, therefore, have a basis for remediation. Copying exercises done at the chalkboard or at the pupil's desk, various types of dictation, and creative writing exercises are ideal for direct observation of handwriting, spelling, and written expression skills. The teacher should be particularly observant of:

1. Consistent difficulty in copying or revisualizing specific letters,
2. Patterns of linguistic errors in the spelling of specific words,
3. Misapplication of various spelling rules,
4. Pencil grasp and body posture problems,
5. Consistent syntactical or grammatical errors in the written expression of ideas,
6. Difficulties with the writing form (manuscript or cursive) being used.

Informal Assessment

Many skill deficiencies can be individually assessed through informal teacher-made tests. Analyzing errors on informal measures provides the teacher with pertinent diagnostic information that may be directly used in an instructional program. Examples of informal tests are provided in this chapter and in Otto, McMenemy, & Smith (1973) and Wallace and Larsen (1978).

Formal Tests

There are very few formal, standardized tests available to assess written language skills. Spelling and written expression subtests, which are part of larger achievement batteries, have not served adequately for diagnosis because of their emphasis on grade and age-level scores. Among the limited number of published tests in this area, we have chosen to review the more widely used tests.

Gates-Russell Spelling Diagnostic Test
(Gates & Russell, 1937)

This instrument appraises nine areas: (a) spelling words orally, (b) word pronunciation, (c) giving letters for sounds, (d) spelling one syllable, (e) spelling two syllables, (f) word reversals, (g) spelling attack, (h) auditory discrimination, and (i) the effectiveness of visual, auditory, kinesthetic, and combined methods of study. Grade scores are provided for each specific subtest. The test can be effectively used as an *initial* step in observing spelling difficulties (Wallace & Larsen, 1978).

Picture Story Language Test
(Myklebust, 1965)

This test is one of the few available published tests measuring a child's written expression. Following the presentation of a picture, the child is asked to write a story which is judged according to productivity, correctness, and meaning. The number of words, sentences, and words per sentence are computed for productivity, while word usage, word endings, and punctuation are judged for correctness. Story content is used for appraising the meaning scale. Scores for the test can be converted into age equivalents and percentiles. The test can also be utilized in informal assessment (Wallace & Larsen, 1978).

Spellmaster: Spelling, Testing, and Evaluation
(Cohen & Abrams, 1974)

This diagnostic spelling test measures three categories of words: (a) regular words with uniform phoneme-grapheme correspondences; (b) irregular words which do not follow basic phonological and morphological rules; and (c) homonyms which must be learned in conjunction with their meaning. A scope and sequence chart which includes the specific skills which are tested, and the grade level where each skill is usually taught, can help the teacher select the initial level for diagnostic testing Profile charts for individual students and classes are included, along with a very helpful chart correlating the phonetic and structural elements which are tested with a number of widely used spelling programs.

Test of Written Spelling
(Larsen & Hammill, 1976)

This test was specifically designed to pinpoint a child's current spelling level as well as to specify the basic types of words with which the pupil is having difficulty. The test involves administering a list of predictable and a list of unpredictable words. Raw scores are translated into a spelling age score, a spelling quotient, and a spelling grade equivalent. The test can be administered to small groups of children. It is an extensively normed test with consistently high reliability across grade levels. We believe this test is a valid measure of written spelling ability for children.

HANDWRITING SKILLS

Children who have handwriting problems basically have difficulties executing the motor patterns required for writing letters, words, or numbers. Basic handwriting skills include the following abilities:
1. Holding a writing utensil properly and performing various motor readiness activities (e.g., drawing lines and circles),
2. Properly using manuscript writing,
3. Properly using cursive writing,
4. For left-handed children, properly positioning the paper, hand, and posture.

DOES THE CHILD WRITE WITHOUT DIFFICULTY?

Has the Child Mastered the Skills Prerequisite for Writing?

Informal Assessment   Have the child perform body movements showing direction, such as *up* and *down, left* and *right, forward* and *back, out* and *in,* with gross body exercises. These activities should be done first without pencils, chalk, or other writing instruments.. For example, direct the child to:

"Raise your right hand *up* in the air."

"Make large circles with your writing hand *in front* of your body."

"Bring your arms *in* toward your body."

"Make long straight lines with your writing hand going from *top* to *bottom.*"

1. Use the chalkboard for some of the exercises listed above. For example, direct the child to:

Instructional Activities

"Make a long line from *left* to right."

"Draw a circle in *toward* your body."

"Make a line going from *bottom* to *top.*"

2. Some children must be taught how to hold the writing utensil. Practicing with a paint brush while painting may be helpful. McKenna (1970) also suggests the following finger exercises: finger-tapping on a desk, firmly and rhythmically; lifting and lowering designated fingers on command; sorting cards; and "playing the piano" on a desk, with hands arched properly and fingers pressing down firmly.

3. Some children may have difficulty remembering how to hold a pencil. Johnson and Myklebust (1967) suggest placing a piece of adhesive tape on the pencil, cutting a small notch in the wood, or painting the specific area where the fingers should be held.

4. Use geometric-figure templates for tracing with fingers, on the chalkboard, on paper, etc. Gradually encourage the child to make the figures freehand, using the template as an example. Templates may be made from oak tag, wood, plastic, foam rubber, and so on.

5. Use dot-to-dot figures on the chalkboard or on duplicating paper to teach a sequence of lines. Initially use circles and squares. Gradually the figures can include actual letters.

6. Children can trace figures and letters by placing tracing paper over the figure to be duplicated. During the beginning stages, you might need to tape or tack the tracing paper to the desk.

7. It is helpful for some children to reproduce figures with their fingers in wet sand, salt trays, pudding mixes, or finger paint.

8. Ask children to identify wooden figures or letter forms while their eyes are closed. If wooden forms are not available, letters can be drawn with the finger on the back of the child's hand or on his back. Children can work in pairs and tally points. Particularly difficult figures and letters can be stressed.

9. You can use games to have children draw the beginning strokes for most letters. Here are some examples:

Vertical lines
a. "Finish building the house."

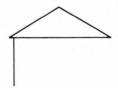

Sharp peaks
B. "Put a crown on the king's head."

Wavy lines
c. "Make some wiggly snakes."

Circles
d. "Finish the man's face and eyes."

Half-circles
e. "Put the handles on the other cups."

10. Gradually, children should be able to reproduce different shapes upon verbal direction of the teacher.

11. Many children must be taught the correct body posture and paper angle for good handwriting. A detailed description for teaching these skills is provided by Croutch (1970).

Does the Child Have Difficulty with Manuscript Writing?

Observe a child's daily written work and consider any deficits in letter forms, spacing, alignment, and size.

Informal Assessment

12. Use boxes to help teach correct forms for beginning letters. All of the basic vertical and horizontal letters may be taught with boxes, as shown below:

Instructional Activities

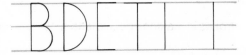

As the child progresses, the boxes should be gradually faded out.

13. Use masking tape as a tactile clue for margins and different letter placements. A section of masking tape along the left side of the paper provides the child with a clue for directionality. Smaller pieces of tape can be used for specific letter directions.

14. Arrow clues for specific letters can also be helpful; for example:

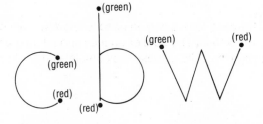

15. Some children are also aided by placing a little green dot at the starting position for the letter stroke, and a small red dot at the termination point for the letter:

16. The basic strokes comprising most letters can be taught sequentially. For example, the letter ⊤ can be taught as two separate strokes: | and —. Likewise, h is comprised of | and ∩. Eventually the basic strokes can be joined together.

17. Letters with easier strokes should be taught first. The following letters are considered the least difficult for children to learn: *c, i, l, o, t, v.*

18. A helpful device for some children is an individual alphabet taped to their desks. Dittoing the alphabet or parts of the alphabet at the top of a child's seatwork papers may also be helpful.

19. Clean, lined paper is necessary for children with aligning and spacing difficulties. Use color-coded paper or different colored ditto masters.

20. Capital letters should be introduced in familiar words, such as the child's name, his city, or the state in which he lives. The techniques used for teaching lowercase letters (boxes, color cues, masking tape) can be employed in teaching capital letter formation.

21. Teach children to "talk out" strokes in making specific letters; for example:

⌐ —short line down, back up, around, and down

W —slant down, slant up, slant down, slant up

i —short line, dot

† —tall line down, cross near top

22. For children with spacing difficulties, use plastic, wooden, felt, or oak tag letters. Instruct them to match the spacing in given words. Likewise, provide words with improper spacing, and instruct the children to space the letters properly.

Does the Child Have Difficulty with Cursive Writing?

Informal Assessment   Dot-to-dot or dash-to-dash letters can be used to informally assess for cursive writing readiness. The dots or dashes should be gradually faded out, allowing the child to make the complete letter. Judge the accuracy of the last letter.

Instructional Activities   ***23.** Cursive writing should not be taught to children who are still having difficulties with manuscript writing. In all likelihood, children with extreme difficulties with manuscript will also experience failure with cursive writing.

*24. Children who know the formation of manuscript letters can be shown the similarity to cursive writing by writing heavy cursive letters over the corresponding manuscript letter, like this:

This technique may be varied by using a different color pencil or a felt-tipped pen for the cursive letter.

*25. Many of the cursive strokes can be practiced through games like those listed in activity #9 above. Here are some examples:

Stringing the beads

Making waves

Making curly hair

Lassoing the horses

*26. Make any of the strokes above on ditto paper and have a child trace over them with his finger, pencil, crayon, etc. The commercially available *Trac-a-Bit* (Zaner-Bloser Co.) allows children to trace letters using an erasable grease pencil or crayon.

*27. Letters with similar movement patterns should be taught sequentially. The following four groups contain similar strokes:

a	c	d	g	o		
b	h	f	k	l	e	
i	j	p	r	s	t	u	w
m	n	v	x	y	z	

*28. In the beginning stages of cursive writing, above-the-line stops and below the line stops may be given as a cue for letter formation. The "stops" can consist of colored dots or short lines, or masking tape.

*29. For a child who has difficulty keeping his wrist on the desk in the proper position, a heavy (possibly weighted) bracelet or wristband will help keep the wrist in place.

*30. Cursive letters can also be broken into steps to analyze strokes and taught sequentially (see activity #16). For example, the letter *f* can be taught by slowly joining the following parts:

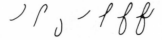

*31. Spacing difficulties in cursive writing can be helped by working with cursive letters cut from oak tag or wood. Children can match spacing in a number of given words, join letters to spell words given verbally by the teacher, etc.

*32. Verbal cues may be used in teaching cursive writing. If letters of similar strokes are learned in sequence, the child can easily see the verbal cues. The *a* strokes, for example, could be used in teaching the *g* strokes. "First come around like the *a*, then go up, ..."

Does the Left-Handed Child Position Paper, Head, and Body Correctly?

Informal Assessment   Observe whether the child uses the correct "bear-left" position, where the paper is positioned the opposite of the correct right-handed position with the arm kept parallel with the edge of the paper.

Instructional Activities   **33.** Taping the paper to the desk in the correct position serves as a reminder in the beginning stages of handwriting.

*34. The commercially available writing frame (a wire guide attached to the pencil) is an excellent device for teaching left-handers the correct hand position while writing. The frame can also be used for right-handers.

*35. The incorrect hooked-wrist position which many left-handers use may be helped by practice with paint brushes, chalk, crayons, magic markers, etc. Constant reinforcement of holding writing utensils properly will help many left-handed children to also hold pencils correctly.

*36. The left-hander's writing should be slightly sloped to the left, although the slope appears to be somewhat "backhand." Left-handed children should be given appropriate sloping examples to follow. Teachers can use left-handed teachers, older left-handed students, and left-handed children in the same classroom to help provide exemplary work and patterns. Of course, this suggestion is appropriate only if the other left-handers provide good models.

*37. Special equipment, such as left-handed scissors and left-handed desk-chairs, should be provided whenever possible.

*38. Trembly (1970) reported that a Southpaw Club was organized for left-handers in one school. Children in the group were able to pool their ideas and experiences. The boys in the club even organized a baseball team and challenged a group of right-handers.

*39. The Plunkett (1954) writing exercises are a commercial aid for left-handers. These materials offer a sequentially developed program of writing exercises.

SPELLING SKILLS

Spelling is believed to be a more difficult task than reading because, as Lerner (1976) points out, the opportunity to draw upon peripheral clues is greatly reduced. In reading, the child may use contextual, structural, or configuration clues. However, in spelling, the child must:
1. Remember the form of letters;
2. Remember the letter sequences and rules for particular words.

DOES THE CHILD SPELL ACCURATELY?

Does the Child Remember Letter Forms?

Provide children with a sheet of letters with similar configurations. Say a letter and direct the child to circle the correct one. As the child progresses, ask him to write the letter from dictation. Still later, ask the child to "write the letter that comes after *b* in the alphabet."

Informal Assessment

*40. Many of the activities suggested for the development of visual memory are also applicable here.

*41. Analyze the type of spelling errors that a child is making to distinguish the specific letter(s) that seem to be consistently troublesome. In addition, ask the child to write specific letters of the alphabet from dictation. Pronounce different letter sounds and ask the child to write the symbol which denotes that sound. This information may be used in formulating a remedial program.

*42 Ask the child to "write the letter that the word *ball* begins with" or "write the letter that *cup* ends with," etc.

*43. Ask children to complete missing words by filling in the omitted letter(s). For example, read "They like to (s)ing song(s). Mary (s)at on the (s)ixth chair. The dog(s) were very (s)ick." This activity may be varied by concentrating on specific letters in the initial, medial, or final positions.

*44. Provide the child with a word, such as *tablecloth*. Ask the student to write as many words as possible beginning with *t* or *l* (or any other letter), using only the letters in *tablecloth*. Children may compete to write the most words. Variations of this activity include letters in other positions or writing three-letter words only.

*45. The revisualization of specific letters may be strengthened by tracing the letter in various media, such as clay, salt, and sand. Providing tactile exercises such as sandpaper, felt, or wooden letters is also helpful.

*46. Ask the child to spell certain words, with the emphasis on specific letters, by providing him with letter cut-outs and letting him arrange the correct sequence of letters.

*47. Print difficult words on flash cards for periodic review by the child. Especially troublesome letters can be printed in red to mean caution. A child's attention is then concentrated on the difficult letter(s).

*48. Show a letter to the child for a short period of time, and have him circle the correct choice of four letters written on a worksheet. As the child improves with this activity, shorten the exposure time, expose multiple letters, gradually add words, or ask the child to write the letter(s) that were exposed. A tachistoscope is very useful here, but the letters or words may be presented on flash cards.

*49. Children can be asked to write letters that are verbally described by the teacher. For example, "Write the letter that looks like a wiggly snake (*s*)," or "write the letter that looks like a small circle (*o*)." Eventually, words can be spelled in this manner, and other children can be asked to describe the letters verbally.

*50. Give the child partially completed letters to complete. Omit additional parts of the letters progressively. For example, ask the child to complete the following:

*51. Assign memory clues for particularly troublesome letters. You should assign clues to a minimum number of letters, or the clues may be as difficult to remember as the letters. Associations provided by the child himself are much more effective than teacher-assigned clues. One child we know remembered the "i" by an upward-pointing arrow ↑ and the "a" by a circular arrow ↻.

*52. Just as you can trace letters on the back of the child's hand or his back, you can trace words. The child must keep the visual image of each letter in his memory until the word is completed. Then he writes the word on the chalkboard or on paper. Two- or three-letter words should be used for this activity at first.

*53. Cover up an entire word and gradually expose each succeeding letter until a child can guess the correct word. Letter clues such as "The next letter comes after *m* in the alphabet" can be supplied.

Does the Child Remember the Letter Sequences in Words?

Provide children with sets of four words and ask them to circle the correctly spelled version of the word. For example:

Informal Assessment

```
mega    gmae    game    gaem
talbe   table   taebl   tabel
bread   braed   brdae   bader
```

*54. Make crossword puzzles of particularly difficult words. The puzzles may be made by other children.

Instructional Activities

*55. Present configurations of specific words to the child, and ask him to match a given set of words with the configurations. For example, give these drawing and words to match.

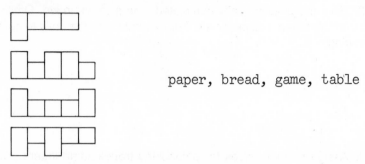

paper, bread, game, table

*56. As a child progresses with activity #55, ask him to identify similar configurations in words without being provided the visual forms. Present groups of four words and ask the child to circle the two words with a similar configuration. For example:

come   ball   park   talk

*57. Use the *Language Master* as a visual/auditory/kinesthetic reinforcement for the child. Whole words can be used, spelling the word letter-by-letter. The child can trace the word once it has been placed through the recorder.

*58. Assign children in the room different letters, blends, endings, etc. Call on a child to spell a word. The child must choose the easiest way to spell the word by selecting children who have the correct letters or groups of letters. For example, the word *jumping* can be more easily spelled by choosing a child with *-ing* than by choosing three separate children, one with *i*, one with *n*, and another with *g*. Encourage the children to look for the easiest way to spell a word (Arena, 1968).

*59. Individual alphabet charts on each child's desk can be a helpful revisualization device.

*60. Introduce a word family, such as *at*. Ask a child to list words in that family. This activity may be made more specific by directing children to add certain letters, blends, or endings and then pronounce the word.

*61. Write a difficult word on the chalkboard. Ask the children to study the word for a few seconds. Then erase the word, and ask them to write it from memory. Underline or circle difficult parts of the word as a memory device.

*62. Present a sentence composed of words with missing letters, words with mixed-up letters, and words portrayed by pictures. Ask them to complete the sentence. For example,

a.   The 🧍 wen(<u>t</u>) swimm(<u>i</u> <u>n</u> <u>g</u>) itwh   her
<u>   </u>(with)
(<u>M</u>)oth(<u>e</u> <u>r</u>) at the ceona.
(ocean)

b.   The 🕊 is fly(<u>i</u> <u>n</u> <u>g</u>) gihh in the (<u>s</u>)k(<u>y</u>).
(high)

*63. Make a spelling file box of difficult words. Have the child copy the words correctly on flash cards and periodically review them. Encourage the child to study his own flash cards, and write them from memory on the back of the card or on a piece of paper. Words may be deleted and others added as time progresses.

*64. Ask children to circle all the little words contained within a list of larger words. This activity often serves as a letter recall device for individual spelling of words. Some examples include *friend, follow, report, oral, hand,* and *easy.*

*65. Encourage associative relationships for word spelling. Some associations may be peculiar, but they serve as meaningful memory devices for individual children. Individual associations can often be the most effective method for revisualizing certain words.

*66. A self-discovery technique described by Wahl (1968) helps a child become aware of what he is doing wrong. You pronounce his misspelling the way he has written it and then respell the word correctly. Wahl cautions the teacher to select reasonably phonetic words to be used with this technique.

WRITTEN EXPRESSION

Some children have problems in properly translating thoughts into written communication. Adequate written expression is based upon:
1. Abundant oral expressive experiences,
2. Understanding and application of correct syntax, grammar, and usage patterns,
3. Ability or organize ideas into the appropriate communication form.

DOES THE CHILD HAVE DIFFICULTY EXPRESSING IDEAS IN WRITING?

Does the Child Have an Adequate Vocabulary?

Provide the child with a colorful and descriptive illustration or picture. Have the child tell a story about the picture (Zigmond, 1976).   *Informal Assessment*

*67. Give the children a word such as *run*, and ask them to list as many words as they can that are similar in meaning to *run* (e.g., *rush, scat, flashed, hurry, dash*). These words may be kept in a notebook to be used for reference when the children are writing stories.

*68. Play *word tennis* with teams of children. In this activity, two teams are chosen and the first person in one team says a word, such as *happy*. Synonyms are provided by successive team members, switching back and forth until one member can no longer think of a synonym. Variations in scoring include total points for each side for all synonyms and points against the team for running out of synonyms.

*69. Give the child a word with multiple meanings and ask him to write sentences using the different meanings. Upon completion, discuss the different meanings with the child. Examples of some appropriate words include *hit, run, show, bat, fan, fly, watch,* and *file.*

*70. Give children a list of meanings and a second list of words which must be matched with the meanings. To make the activity more challenging, choose unusual meanings of words. For example:

Word meanings	Words to choose from
a wispy puff of color in the sky	juice
mostly liquid, and sometimes good to drink	humid
sticky and moist	cloud

*71. Provide the child with a list of general categories and a large number of words which must be classified according to category. For example, categories such as *transporation, food,* and *music* may be used. Words to be classified would include *tugboat, drum, soup, rocket, feet, orchestra, sandwich,* and *singer.* The child should be able to make finer discriminations as he progresses. Eventually, supply only the categories and have the child provide the words under each category.

*72. Ask several questions to be answered by either selecting the correct word that fits the sentence or answering the question affirmatively or negatively. For example:

"Does the *spendthrift* or the *thrifty* man save his money?"

"Are the *jagged* rocks harder to climb than the *slick, rounded* rocks?

"Is the *senior* citizen an *oldster*?"

*73. Have children "invent" new words by joining together two familiar words. Definitions should be provided for the new words. For example, *squabbit* (cross between a squirrel and a rabbit) or *glup* (combination of a glass and a cup).

*74. Have the children find specific words in a story that answer questions asked by the teacher. For example, "Find the word in the third paragraph which describes the size of the town in which Tom lived," or "Find the expression on page 36 which tells you that Jane was very sad."

*75. Unusual or colorful words which children have read or heard (e.g., *argy-bargy*, a Scotch expression meaning argument or controversy) may be kept in a special notebook or placed on the bulletin board. Encourage the children to use these words in their written assignments.

*76. Provide children with input expriences such as field trips, reading stories, discussion periods, and oral-language activities. Many children will need a variety of experiences to stimulate ideas for written expression.

Does the Child Write with Correct Syntax, Grammar, and Usage?

Provide the child with sentences with grammar, usage, and/or syntax errors which he must correct. Initially, the exercises should concentrate on one type of error. Gradually, the sentences should progress to multiple types of errors. Sentence errors can be underlined during the beginning stages of this activity.   *Informal Assessment*

> Mary <u>have</u> two apples.
>
> John <u>in the morning</u> has breakfast.
>
> She <u>were</u> running down the path.
>
> Girls <u>plays</u> with dolls.

*77. Vary the informal assessment exercise by working on a specific skill, such as plurals, and leaving the emphasis word blank for the child to complete. Children may also be given a choice between two words for the correct answer. For example,   *Instructional Activities*

> Susan and Jane (play, plays) together each day.
>
> He (run, runs) to school.
>
> They (like, likes) to ride bikes.
>
> The children played many (game, games).

*78. Provide the child with a scrambled set of flash cards that matches a sentence that you verbalize. The child must place the words in the correct order to match your sentence. A tape recorder may be used for this activity.

*79. Provide children with a list of words for which they must furnish the past tense form. For example:

```
come (came)

go    (gone)

run  (ran)

see  (saw)
```

*80. Exercise #79 can be expanded into sentences where children are asked to provide the correct verb form.

```
He play with me yesterday.

After he jump, John hurt his finger.

Yesterday, Sally ride her horse.
```

*81. Write a *one-minute story* at the chalkboard by allowing each child in a group to write at the chalkboard for one minute. After one minute has elasped, the child must stop, and another child continues the story; finally, the last child writes a conclusion (Platts, Marguerite, & Shumaker, 1960).

*82. Provide the child with a story having incorrect syntax, grammar, and usage, and ask him to rewrite the story correctly.

*83. Have the child complete sentences with missing words, as:

```
She _____ two teeth missing.

Barbara thinks it is _____ hot.

Give me the _____ shoe.

To _____ he is talking?
```

Does the Child Have Difficulty Formulating Ideas in Writing?

*Informal
Assessment*

Give the child a list of words and ask him to write a short story using the words given. The story can be structured by providing a title.

*Instructional
Activities*

*84. Children experiencing difficulty in expressing their thoughts in writing will initially need very specific instructions, activities, and exercises. These children will respond to structured assignments that tell them exactly what to do. As the child progresses, the structure and specificity can gradually be decreased.

*85. Give each child an uncluttered picture of a specific object (or the actual object) and ask him to write its name. Gradually add descriptors until a sentence develops (e.g., <u>This</u> <u>is</u> <u>a</u> small, <u>red</u> <u>apple</u>). Some children may need experience in naming pictures before they progress to describing them.

*86. Give each child an action picture, such as a stock-car race. Instruct each child to write a one-sentence description of what is happening in the picture.

*87. Read an exciting story to the class, omitting the ending. Have the children finish the story by writing an ending to it.

*88. Have the child dictate a story on a specific topic using the tape recorder. Type the story on paper, leaving key words blank. Ask the child to read the story, completing the missing words. He can verify his choices by replaying the original tape.

*89. Provide the child with a number of different sentences. Ask him to rewrite each sentence, saying the same thing in a different way without changing the meaning of the sentence. Examples include:

```
The circus is an exciting place to visit.

It rained very hard last night.

She looked pretty in her new pink dress.
```

*90. Provide the child with a list of words and a paragraph with missing words. Ask the child to complete the paragraph using the list of words. For example:

```
      Today it (rained) all day.  We had to stay in the
(house) to (play).  The television was (broken), so
we listened to the (radio) awhile.  We also played
some (games) and painted some (pictures).  The best
part was when (mother) read us some (stories).

   stories    play     rained    pictures

   radio    broken    house    games  mother
```

*91. A daily diary may be kept by the class. Initially, let the class write the daily entry as a group. Eventually, permit individual children to write daily entries. Ultimately, each child in the class can keep his own diary.

*92. Ask the children to write a sentence summarizing a story that was read to them, a film that they viewed, a record that was played to them, or a story that they read. Gradually, increase the length of the summary or abstract.

WRITTEN LANGUAGE PROGRAMS

Very few commercial programs are available to help remediate the child with written language problems. Handwriting and spelling disorders are emphasized in the few programs which have been published, with very little attention given to remedial instruction in written expression. The following commercial programs illustrate the published materials in written language remediation.

A Spelling Workbook Series
(Plunkett & Peck, 1960; Plunkett, 1960; Plunkett, 1961)

The four workbooks which comprise this series are designed for corrective spelling teaching in the primary through secondary grades. The primary workbooks emphasize phonic elements of words in context, while the intermediate workbook is specifically designed for students with poor visual recall of letters and words. Spelling rules and generalizations are emphasized in the secondary-level workbook. The program provides a relatively large amount of kinesthetic reinforcement throughout the workbooks.

Handwriting with Write and See
(Skinner & Krakower, 1968)

The six books in this series are designed to teach manuscript and cursive writing to students who traditionally have had little interest in legible handwriting. The child progresses from very simple to more complex writing movements through the use of a fading technique to teach letter formation. The child writes with a special pen on specially prepared paper which turns a different color when incorrect letter formations are made. The program can be used with elementary school students. The individualized and self-pacing parts of the program make it ideally suited to the needs of children with handwriting difficulties.

Penskill
(Larson, 1962)

This program is designed to develop and improve cursive writing skills of students from fourth grade on. It emphasizes slant, size, spacing of letters and words, alignment, and shape. Practice in number formation is also included. No stylized form is advocated, and the ultimate goal of the program is a legible handwriting that suits each child. Although the program is not designed for children with writing problems, the programming allows the materials to be used individually with children encountering difficulties in this area. Special instructions are also included for the left-handed child.

Spelling
(Buchanan, 1967)

This programmed spelling series employs a linguistic progression of sound-symbol associations tightly controlled for consistency in phoneme-grapheme comparison. Words are taught as vocabulary items so that the student does not need advanced reading skills before beginning the program. The eight levels of the series are intended to be used during the first four elementary grades. The lesson format includes 30 minutes of a teacher-directed presentation and 30 minutes of individual workbook assignments. Audio tapes may also be purchased for individual presentation of the teacher-directed portion of the program.

ADDITIONAL READINGS

Arena, J. I. (Ed.). *Building spelling skills in dyslexic children.* San Rafael, Calif.: Academic Therapy Publications, 1968.

Arena, J. I. (Ed.). *Building handwriting skills in dyslexic children.* San Rafael, Calif.: Academic Therapy Publications, 1970.

Barbe, W. B. *Creative writing activities.* Columbus, Ohio: Highlights for Children, 1965.

Clark, M. M. *Left-handedness.* London: University of London Press, 1957.

DeHirsch, K., Jansky, J., & Langford, W. S. *Predicting language failure.* New York: Harper & Row, 1966.

Dolch, E. W. *Better spelling.* Champaign, Ill.: Garrard, 1960.

Fernald, G. M. *Remedial techniques in basic school subjects.* New York: McGraw-Hill, 1943.

Gillingham, A., & Stillman, B. *Remedial training for reading, spelling, and penmanship.* Cambridge, Mass.: Educators Publishing Service, 1965.

Glaus, M. *From thought to words.* Champaign, Ill.: National Council of Teachers of English, 1965.

Johnson, D. J., & Myklebust, H. R. *Learning disabilities: Educational principles and practices.* New York: Grune & Stratton, 1967.

Lerner, J. *Children with learning disabilities* (2nd ed.). Boston: Houghton Mifflin, 1976.

Otto, W., McMenemy, R. A., & Smith, R. J. *Corrective and remedial teaching* (2nd ed.). Boston: Houghton Mifflin, 1973.

Platts, M. E. *Anchor: A handbook of vocabulary discovery techniques for the classroom teacher.* Stevensville, Mich.: Educational Service, Inc., 1970.

Platts, M. E., Marguerite, S. R., & Shumaker, E. *Suggested activities to motivate the teaching of the language arts.* Stevensville, Mich.: Educational Service, 1970.

Spalding, R. B., & Spalding, W. T. *The writing road to reading.* New York: Morrow, 1957.

Wallace, G., & Larsen, S. C. *The educational assessment of learning problems: Testing for teaching.* Boston: Allyn & Bacon, 1978.

West, W. W. *Developing writing skills.* Englewood Cliffs, N.J.: Prentice-Hall, 1966.

Zigmond, N. *Teaching children with special needs.* Dubuque, Iowa: Gorsuch Scarisbrick Publishers, 1976.

Arithmetic Problems

The difficulties encountered by children with learning problems in arithmetic have not been as thoroughly studied or researched as other academic handicaps. In comparison to reading, for example, teachers will find fewer available tests, remedial programs, and instructional materials for helping children with arithmetic problems. It has been suggested that the widespread concern with making children literate, along with the feeling on the part of some teachers and parents that arithmetic is not as vital to academic success as other areas of the curriculum, may be partially responsible for this lack (Otto, McMenemy, & Smith, 1973). Nevertheless, it is important to note that arithmetic difficulties are often related to other academic problems. It is frequently necessary, therefore, to investigate the common characteristics of a child's learning problems for the purpose of parallel remediation. Difficulties in discrimination, memory, perception, comprehension, and handwriting can affect achievement in arithmetic as well as achievement in reading, written language, and other academic skills.

Spencer and Smith (1969) note that arithmetic skills are so complex in their interrelationships that children may have difficulty in achievement for a variety of reasons. However, three basic questions with which the classroom teacher must be concerned are:

1. What deficiencies in number readiness skills prevent the child from achieving in arithmetic?
2. What difficulties in computation skills and time and money concepts interfere with progress in arithmetic?
3. What specific skill difficulties prevent achievement in problem solving?

ASSESSMENT

Teacher Observation

The teacher should be very precise in pinpointing a child's arithmetic difficulties. Frequent observations of the child during written assignments, board work, and oral discussions will provide useful information for specifying particular problems and planning a remedial program. Spencer and Smith (1969) note that the chalkboard has the additional advantage of allowing a teacher to observe the work of several children simultaneously. Using a checklist during observation usually results in more precision, since the teacher can focus on the specific behaviors noted on the checklist. Checklists can be developed by teachers according to specific grade-level skills. Otto, McMenemy, and Smith (1973 and Wallace and Larsen (1978) provide diagnostic arithmetic checklists which can be used by classroom teachers.

One component of teacher observation might involve "interviewing" the child. In this approach, the child is usually asked to describe aloud the steps involved in solving a particular arithmetic problem. The child actually reworks the problem orally, while the teacher listens for misunderstandings and incorrect procedures.

Informal Assessment

Informal teacher-made measures of arithmetic ability are well-suited to the specificity of arithmetic difficulties. Various arithmetic skills may be evaluated by using items gathered from arithmetic workbooks. The items may be placed on cards for permanent use and administered to individual children. Separate tests should be developed for specific skills. Informal tests should be used to evaluate *one* particular task. The teacher will then be more aware of the exact difficulties the child is having. The use of informal arithmetic tests will help the teacher plan for individual needs within a class. A number of excellent suggestions for constructing informal tests are provided by Reisman (1978).

Formal Tests

Most group achievement tests include an arithmetic subtest as part of the complete battery. However, unless the test includes a profile analysis of specific arithmetic skills, the score will not be very helpful in planning an instructional program. Some of the more commonly used published tests are summarized in the following section.

Diagnostic Chart for Fundamental Processes in Arithmetic
(Buswell & John, 1925)

This instrument is intended to provide information concerning a child's specific errors in the addition, subtraction, multiplication, and division of whole numbers. Children complete a graded series of arithmetic examples arranged in order of increasing difficulty in each of the four fundamental processes. The child is asked to work each example aloud, while the administrator notes specific errors. The chart is not standardized, and the results are primarily aimed at helping classroom teachers assess the faulty arithmetic work habits of children in grades two and above. A manual of directions also provides a number of excellent remedial procedures for many arithmetic difficulties.

Diagnostic Tests and Self-Helps in Arithmetic
(Brueckner, 1955)

This complete series is comprised of four screening tests and 23 analytical tests and corrective exercises. The screening tests examine whole numbers, common fractions, decimals, and general arithmetic skills. The results of the screening tests show which of the 23 specific analytical tests should be administered. The self-help corrective exercises provide a basis for remediating any of the specific deficits noted on each of the analytical tests. These nonstandardized tests can be administered both individually and to groups of children. The tests enable teachers to pinpoint specific areas of difficulty, and the results provide a solid basis for implementing remedial teaching strategies.

Key Math Diagnostic Arithmetic Test
(Connolly, Nachtman, & Pritchett, 1971)

This is an individually adminstered diagnostic arithmetic test for children in preschool through grade six, with no upper limits for remedial use. Key Math is comprised of 14 subtests organized into the three areas of *content* (Numeration, Fractions, and Geometry/symbols), *operations* (Addition, Subtraction, Multiplication, Division, Mental Computation, and Numerical Reasoning), and *applications* (Word Problems, Missing Elements, Money, Measurement, and Time). The test requires very little reading or writing ability and may be administered in 20 to 30 minutes. Results include a grade equivalent score based on the total test performance, along with a diagnostic profile depicting the subject's relative performance in the 14 skill areas. A metric supplement is also available to assess a child's understanding of metric measurement.

Stanford Diagnostic Arithmetic Test
(Beatty, Madden, & Gardner, 1966)

This group-administered battery is available in two levels. Level I is intended for children in the latter part of second grade to the middle of grade four, while Level II may be used in the latter part of grade four to the middle of the eighth grade. Number-related skills dominate both levels of the test, with specific subtests measuring various aspects of computation, number facts, fractions, and decimals. Raw scores may be converted into stanines and grade level scores for most parts of the test. The test manual also provides many excellent suggestions for interpreting scores and planning remedial instruction.

ARITHMETIC READINESS SKILLS

Prior to performing adequately in basic computation, a child must be competent in a number of skills basic to understanding other arithmetic processes. The child must:
1. Be able to discriminate among different sizes, shapes, and quantities;
2. Understand one-to-one correspondence;
3. Be able to count meaningfully;
4. Be able to order number names and sets.

Diagnostic questions, informal tests, and teaching suggestions for remediating arithmetic problems are listed in the following section.

HAS THE CHILD MASTERED THE SKILLS PREREQUISITE FOR ARITHMETIC ACHIEVEMENT?

Does the Child Discriminate Different Sizes, Shapes, and Quantities?

Provide a worksheet with rows of three to four similar geometric designs and one different design (e.g., △ △ □ △ △).   *Informal Assessment* Ask the child to mark the different shape in each row. Size discrimination can be informally assessed by varying designs according to size (e.g., ▭ ▭ ▭ ▭ ▭) and directing the child to mark the smallest or largest design in each row. Varying quantities (e.g., [dots boxes]) in each row will serve as an informal assessment of quantity discrimination.

1. Cut different sized circles, squares, triangles, and rectangles   *Instructional Activities* from oak tag, felt, or wood. Have the child match the missing pieces to the correct spaces.

2. Provide children with different sized buttons, pencils, nails, or paper strips. Make sure that the objects are identical except in size. Ask the children to arrange the objects by size, beginning with the smallest and working toward the largest. Johnson and Myklebust (1967) suggest providing a key, such as a page of circles drawn in proper order, for children unable to arrange sizes by themselves.

3. Ask the child to find all the circular objects within the room. Contests can be held to see which child finds the greatest number of objects. Rectangular, triangular, and square shapes can be found also.

4. Provide the child with a number of different sized containers and lids. Instruct him to fit the lids to the containers. Stopwatches can be used to time individuals. Graphs can be kept to check progress.

5. Provide each child with a ball or a round object differing in size. Have the children line up according to the size of the ball they are holding from biggest to smallest ball. Direct the child with the smallest ball to sit down. Continue asking children to be seated, varying the directions from biggest to smallest, until all but one child is seated (Wagner, Hosier, & Gilloley, 1964).

6. Ask children to put together simple jigsaw puzzles of three to five pieces. More complex puzzles with additional pieces can eventually be used.

7. Matching index cards of various sizes to different sized envelopes provides experience in relating the size of an object to an area in which it is placed (Johnson & Myklebust, 1976).

8. Give the child a set of different sized cube blocks. Ask the child to find all the blocks that are the same size as one that you choose from the pile. Matching the cubes to an outline of paper is an extension of this activity that includes discrimination of size. The activity can be varied to teach shape discrimination by using blocks differing in form.

9. Provided the child with an assortment of different lengths of rope. Ask the child to select the rope that seems closest in size to a given object in a classroom (Behrmann & Millman, 1971).

10. Cut different shapes from felt and have children arrange them in order at the flannel board. The child is provided with the opportunity to feel and trace the outline of the shape.

Does the Child Understand One-to-one Correspondence?

Informal Assessment Place six chips or raisins in a row and ask a child to make another row with the same number of chips or raisins (Reisman, 1978); or ask a child to pass a paper to each boy (or girl) in the room.

Instructional Activities **11.** Provide the child with a pegboard design to duplicate. Give the child the exact number of pegs to arrange so his design will match the design that is provided.

12. Assign the child duties that require a one-to-one relationship, e.g., passing papers, pencils, or books to each child within a group or class.

13. Provide worksheets that require finishing incomplete pictures, for example, placing a tail on each dog or a roof on each house. Be sure that all pictures are missing the same part.

14. Ask the children to make a tally mark for each time a bell is rung, a note is played on the piano, hands are clapped, or a beat is heard on a drum.

15. Provide worksheets that require matching similar sets of objects on a page. The child draws lines connecting the boxes that contain the same number of objects. Eventually the child may be asked to match a numeral, such as 5, with a picture of five kites.

16. Smith (1974) suggests playing games of musical chairs, setting a table for the number of children in class or members of a family, or checking to see if enough glasses of milk are available for the class members as practical activities that enhance one-to-one correspondence.

17. "Prepare several pieces of flannel on which there are various numbers of buttons. Prepare a second set on which there are only button holes." Ask the child to match the pieces of flannel with the same number of buttons and holes (Johnson & Myklebust, 1967, p. 258).

18. Provide individual children with a stack of chips or toothpicks. Ask the child to match a given number that you draw at the chalkboard. Large groups of children can individually participate in this activity at their desks.

19. Discuss examples of one-to-one correspondence with the children. Ask them to provide suggestions. Examples include one person—one nose; one elephant—one trunk; one dog—one tail; one hand—one thumb.

20. Wagner et al. (1964) suggest asking children numerical questions and requiring them to provide an answer by showing the correct number of beads on a counting frame. Illustrations include:

"How many fingers on your hand?"

"How many windows in our room?"

"How many jars of paint on the easel?"

"How many children with glasses?"

"How many chairs in the front of the room?"

Does the Child Have Difficulty Counting?

Give a child a group of 20 to 30 toothpicks, bottle caps, or raisins to count aloud; or have the child count the beads on an abacus.

Informal Assessment

21. Have the child make a motor response as he counts. Counting pegs as they are placed in the pegboard or beads as they are put on a string will often help the child who skips numbers while counting.

Instructional Activities

22. Let the child use an abacus. The abacus provides the child with a device to manipulate and a visual image as he is counting.

23. Have the child establish the counting principle through motor activities such as clapping four times, jumping two times, or tapping on the table three times (Lerner, 1976).

24. Spitzer (1961) recommends asking one child to count the number of children in the room during morning attendance or counting aloud rather slowly and deliberately to "see how long it takes" the children to get ready for recess.

25. Provide worksheets with a certain quantity of objects (e.g., balls, lollipops, houses). Below each group write the numbers from 1 to 5 or 1 to 10. Ask the children to circle the correct number for each group. More than one group of objects may appear on each worksheet.

26. Write the numbers from 1 to 20 on a worksheet. Include one number twice. Ask the child to circle all the numbers from 1 to 20 and find the extra number. Various adaptations include writing more than one number twice and extending the sequence beyond 20 (Platts, 1964).

27. Bereiter and Engelmann (1966) describe a program for teaching children to count aloud. The detailed description of their program lists basic operational skills required for this fundamental skill.

28. "Prepare a series of cards with directions for bead stringing. The number on the card indicates the number of beads to be strung for that color. At the beginning level, use actual color cues" (Wedemeyer & Cejka, 1970, p. 99).

29. Have the child close his eyes and listen to the beats of a drum as he concentrates on counting. Eventually, ask him to make a mark on paper for each sound he hears (Johnson & Myklebust, 1967).

*30. Dot-to-dot puzzles where the dots are numbered in sequence can be followed to complete a picture. The sequence of numbers can be gradually increased, and pictures may become more detailed.

*31. Number lines permanently attached to the top of each child's desk provide a constant point of reference. Longer number lines extending to larger numbers can be placed at the top of the chalkboard or on the floor. Here is a shorter number line:

```
0   1   2   3   4   5   6   7   8   9   10
```

*32. Provide worksheets with blank spaces before or after a number. Ask the child to fill in the missing numbers. For example:

_____ 7   _____ 13   19 _____

Eventually the child can be instructed to fill in the missing numbers in a series. For example:

23, __, __, 26, 27, __, 29, __, __, 32

Does the Child Understand Groups or Sets?

Prepare a series of cards showing various groupings of symbols for numbers (e.g., 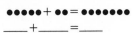). Have the child organize the cards in piles according to number.

33. Make children aware of groups by pointing out that similar things form a group. Show pictures or point out groups of animals, fruit, people, etc. Younger children can be permitted to cut and paste pictures from magazines and group them according to similarities.

34. As the child progresses in his grouping ability, ask him to group objects according to more precise criteria involving combinations of color, size, shape, quantity, etc.

35. Provide a variety of simple pictures or drawing which vary in the number of objects shown. Ask the child to match pictures according to the number of objects they contain.

36. Ask children to arrange pegs or blocks in various groupings. Instruct the child to arrange six blocks in three groups of two, for example, or twelve blocks into four groups of three. Eventually, ask the child to arrange as many groupings as possible for a certain number.

37. Prepare a series of cards which show groupings of symbols for numbers. Ask the child to organize the cards in piles according to number. All the groupings that add up to eight would be placed in one pile, nine in another, etc. For instance, groupings of five could include:

38. Provide simple addition and subtraction statements, such as 5+2, and ask the child to draw a number in each group. You might also provided groupings and ask the child to write the appropriate numerical statement. For example,

●●●●● + ●● = ●●●●●●●
____ + ____ = ____

39. Johnson and Myklebust (1967) recommend cutting strips of paper into pieces 1-inch wide, varying in length from 1 to 10 inches. Ask the child which strip is the longest, the shortest, etc. Demonstrate the many ways the strips can be grouped to make a length that is equal to a longer strip.

40. Use egg cartons to demonstrate how groups are made up of individual "members." Cut the cartons into sections and place them together to show how a group might be visualized.

*41. Cuisenaire Rods are excellent for grouping work. The rods may be grouped according to size or classified according to color.

*42. Platts (1964) suggests preparing a worksheet similar to the example below. Ask the children to draw circles to group the dots according to directions.

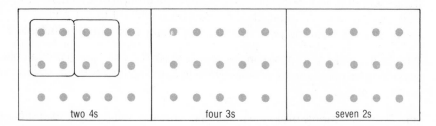

| two 4s | four 3s | seven 2s |

COMPUTATION SKILLS AND TIME AND MONEY CONCEPTS

Most problems in arithmetic are due to deficiencies in basic computation skills. Adequate computation and conceptual skills which are fundamental to successful arithmetic achievement include:
1. An understanding of place value;
2. The ability to add, subtract, multiply, and divide;
3. An understanding of fractions;
4. The ability to tell time;
5. A knowledge of monetary values.

Diagnostic questions, informal tests, and teaching suggestions for remediating computation difficulties are listed in the following section.

HAS THE CHILD MASTERED BASIC COMPUTATION SKILLS AND TIME AND MONEY CONCEPTS?

Does the Child Understand Place Value?

*Informal
Assessment*   Prepare a worksheet with three columns. The right column should be labeled "ones," the middle column "tens," and the left column "hundreds." Provide children with numbers such as 130, 28, 497, 5, 17. Instruct them to place the numbers in the correct column on the paper.

45. Cut 30 squares of tagboard and number each card, starting *Instructional* from 0 to 9, making three cards for each number. Write "ones" *Activities* under each number in one set, "tens" under each number in the second set, and "hundreds" under each number in the third set. Distribute one card to each child in the room. Call out particular numbers, such as 238, and have those children holding the cards needed to form that number come to the front of the room and arrange themselves in the proper order to form that number (Platts, 1964).

46. Prepare a series of cards similar to the example below and ask the child to figure out the number on the front of the card. The back of each card can correctly identify the number.

Front   Back

Tens	Ones
///	/////

35

47. The abacus is an excellent aid in seeing that position determines the numerical value of symbols. Children can represent numbers by moving the appropriate numbers of beads for numbers called by the teacher.

48. Smith (1974) suggests using a "place-value box" as part of the instruction in simple addition and subtraction. A small box with three equal-size compartments labeled "ones," "tens," and "hundreds" from right to left is used for inserting sticks, such as tongue depressors. Children add to or remove sticks from the groups located in various compartments as they add or subtract.

49. Prepare a set of cards numbered from 0 to 9. Screw three cup hooks into a board and write the words "hundreds," "tens," and "ones" over the hooks. Call out a number and have the child place the cards on the correct hook corresponding to the place value (Wedemeyer & Cejka, 1970).

50. The teacher or a child makes a statement such as "I am thinking of a number that is two tens and four ones." Children are asked to write the number on the chalkboard or on a worksheet. Eventually the hundreds place may be added (Wagner et al., 1964).

*51. Ask the child questions such as, "What place does the 5 represent in 352?" or "Can you write a numeral with a 7 in the hundreds place?"

*52. Sticks or papers tied together and placed as "ones" or "tens" demonstrate the idea of number bases. For example, 37 would be represented by three bundles of "tens" sticks on the left with seven "ones" sticks on the right. Children can practice with popsicle sticks in making bundles representing different numbers.

*53. The "ones" and "tens" blocks of the Cuisenaire Rods can also be used to demonstrate the collective value of ten "ones" equalling one "ten." Various numbers may be represented by organizing the blocks similarly to the popsicle sticks mentioned in activity #52. To represent *place* value, the blocks must be properly arranged *spatially* (i.e., ones to the right of tens, etc.).

Does the Child Have Difficulty with the Fundamental Operations of Addition, Subtraction, Multiplication, and Division?

Informal   Teacher-made tests in any of the basic computation processes
Assessment   should include a broad sample of skills in each. Tasks should be
                  sequenced from relatively basic to more difficult examples. Here is
an informal subtraction test.

skill to be assessed	examples of problems				
Number facts up to 10	8 − 5	9 − 2	7 − 4	8 − 6	6 − 4
Number facts above 10	11 − 8	17 − 9	17 − 8	13 − 7	12 − 4
No borrowing	38 − 5	79 − 8	57 − 3	68 − 8	95 − 3
With borrowing	40 − 7	63 − 9	56 − 7	70 − 4	21 − 6
Two numbers no borrowing	57 −37	68 −45	87 −24	88 −30	59 −36
Two numbers with borrowing	51 −18	72 −38	81 −29	73 −24	46 −28

Source: From "Arithmetic Skills" by E. F. Spencer and R. M. Smith. In R. M. Smith (Ed.), Teacher diagnosis of educational difficulties. Columbus, Ohio; Charles E. Merrill, 1969, p. 165. Copyright 1969 by Bell & Howell Company. Reprinted by permission.

Instructional   **54.** Use your fingers to make various addition and subtraction
Activities   combinations. Hold up a certain number of fingers and add or
                  subtract other fingers.

55. Provide the child with many concrete experiences in learning to add or subtract. Use sticks, paper clips, buttons, raisins, etc. The objects can be used to form groupings for the more difficult combinations.

56. Give the child auditory clues by clapping out the addition or subtraction combinations. The teacher can initiate the clapping, and gradually the child can do his own clapping. Adaptions include foot tapping, jumping, or hand tapping on the desk.

57. Prepare worksheets that illustrate number problems. Use dots, circles, lines, and so on for the groupings. Have the child fill in the correct numerals. For example:

●●●● + ●● = ●●●●●●
____ + ____ = ____

58. Wagner et al. (1964) suggest using an "addition ferris wheel" to reinforce addition facts. Draw a large circle with numbers written around it on the chalkboard. Place one number in the middle of the circle and ask children to see how quickly they can go around the "ferris wheel" by adding the middle number on the outside of the circle. This activity can easily be adapted to basic subtraction, multiplication, and division facts.

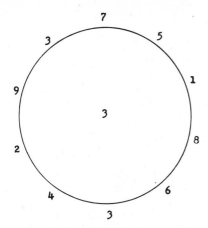

59. Provide children with a card having a number from 1 to 20 written on it. Call out various combinations, such as 7 + 5 or 2 × 4. The child with the correct answer holds up his card. Higher combinations can gradually be added to the cards. Eventually children may be given more than one card to hold.

*60. Flash cards of basic combinations in addition, subtraction, multiplication, and division can be used for developing quicker recognition of the combinations. Children can work individually, in pairs, or in groups, either writing or calling out the answers.

*61. The tachistoscope can be used to measure the recognition rate of number facts. Lerner and Vaver (1970) suggest placing number facts on transparencies, cutting them into strips, and inserting them in a filmstrip projector. The projector can then be used as a tachistoscope by exposing the facts for the desired length of time.

62. Children's games, as illustrated below, can be adapted to practicing number combinations by using addition, subtraction, multiplication, or division facts.

Hop scotch

$\begin{array}{r} 7 \\ -2 \end{array}$	$\begin{array}{r} 8 \\ -3 \end{array}$	$\begin{array}{r} 4 \\ -2 \end{array}$
$\begin{array}{r} 9 \\ -5 \end{array}$	$\begin{array}{r} 6 \\ -1 \end{array}$	$\begin{array}{r} 5 \\ -3 \end{array}$
$\begin{array}{r} 8 \\ -6 \end{array}$	$\begin{array}{r} 1 \\ -0 \end{array}$	$\begin{array}{r} 7 \\ -5 \end{array}$

Climbing the ladder

8 x 5
7 x 3
2 x 4
6 x 1
5 x 5
3 x 7

Tic-tac-toe

7 + 5	9 + 4	5 + 3
8 + 3	4 + 8	3 + 7
2 + 1	5 + 6	7 + 2

*63. Have children use dice to practice addition, subtraction, and multiplication facts. Children may write or call out the various answers. Points can be accumulated for each successful answer. Children may continue throwing the dice until they respond incorrectly.

*64. Prepare approximately 40 cards with numbers between 1 and 10 written on each card. Place the cards face down, and have the child turn up two cards.

Direct the child to add, subtract, or multiply the two cards (Wedemeyer & Cejka, 1970).

*65. Prepare number-sentence worksheets, leaving different frames blank. Ask children to supply the missing number. For example:

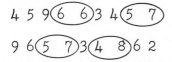

$$6 + \square \ = 13$$

$$\square \ \text{x} \ 7 = 56$$

$$7 - \square \ = 2$$

*66. Prepare a worksheet with several rows of figures. Ask the children to circle any two numbers in the sequence that add up to a specific number, such as 12 (Platts, 1964).

$$4 \ 5 \ 9 \ \boxed{6 \quad 6} 3 \ 4 \boxed{5 \quad 7}$$

$$9 \ 6 \boxed{5 \quad 7} 3 \boxed{4 \quad 8} 6 \ 2$$

*67. Play *Bingo* with small groups of children. Numbers appear in each of the spaces on the card. The teacher reads different combinations, such as $5 + 6$, $7 - 3$, 6×2. Spaces are covered if the child has the appropriate answer on his card.

*68. The number line is effective for demonstrating the fundamental operations. The example $3 + 5$ is taught by starting at three and jumping five places to eight.

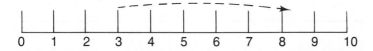

*69. Record number combinations with answers on a tape recorder. Ask children to write or say the answer before they hear it on the tape. This activity can be individually or group administered.

*70. Provide children with a variety of long-division problems. Ask them to find just the *first* number in the quotient. They can also be provided with the first number and asked to show that it is correct.

71. Prepare a worksheet with columns of boxes. Write a number in the bottom box of each column, as illustrated below. Ask the children to fill in each box with a different combination that adds up to the number at the bottom. Subtraction facts can also be used for this activity.

72. Spitzer (1961) suggests providing a variety of orally presented division questions such as:

"12 can be divided into how many 4s?"

"24 divided by 6 in how many?"

"How many 2s equal 12?"

73. Duplicate or have each child make a multiplication chart. Explain its usage and encourage the children to use it freely.

1	2	3	4	5	6	7	8	9	10
2	4	6	8	10	12	14	16	18	20
3	6	9	12	15	18	21	24	27	30
4	8	12	16	20	24	28	32	36	40
5	10	15	20	25	30	35	40	45	50
6	12	18	24	30	36	42	48	54	60
7	14	21	28	35	42	49	56	63	70
8	16	24	32	40	48	56	64	72	80
9	18	27	36	45	54	63	72	81	90
10	20	30	40	50	60	70	80	90	100

74. Prepare a division worksheet where the numbers are illustrated. Have the child fill in the correct numerical statement. For example:

$$\_\_\_ \div \_\_\_ = \_\_\_$$

75. Platts (1964) suggests providing children with "preceding-fact" clues for specific combinations. For example, if $3+7=10$, then what is $3+8$? This activity can also be adapted for subtraction, multiplication, or division facts.

Does the Child Understand Fractions?

Younger children may be informally evaluated by asking them to color in fractional components of various geometric shapes:

Informal Assessment

color 1/2 ◯   color 1/4 ▭

color 1/3 ▭   color 2/5 ▭

Informal survey tests for fractions should include a sample of skills in each computational area:

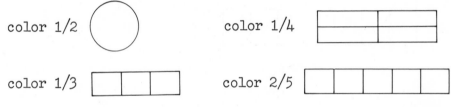

76. Initiate fraction instruction with halves, followed by quarters and eighths. Provide children with familiar pictures that are cut in half. Ask the child to put the halves together. This procedure can also be used with foods, such as fruits, sandwiches, and cookies.

Instructional Activities

77. The importance of parts to a whole can be visually illustrated by providing pictures with obvious parts missing. Have them find the missing part (Behrmann & Millman, 1971).

78. Flannel board fractional cut-outs and paper pie plates that are divided into different colored fractional parts are materials children can manipulate to better their understanding of fractions.

79. Prepare a worksheet with a different number of circles in each box on the page. Ask the child to split each circle in the first box into halves, each circle in the second box into thirds, etc. Younger children enjoy coloring parts of the circle.

80. Smith (1974) suggests using charts similar to those below to illustrate the relationships of fractional parts to a whole.

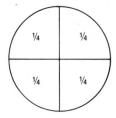

81. Provide children with a worksheet in which circles or squares are already divided and shaded. Provide a box in which the child is to write the appropriate fraction for the shaded part (Engelmann, 1969). For example:

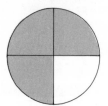 

82. Gradually introduce assignments where children are working with fractions without visual clues. Have children work with fractional quantities, choosing the largest and smallest quantity from a given list of fractions.

*83. Prepare a worksheet comprised of a number of equivalent fractions and ask the child to circle the two equivalent fractions in each line. For example:

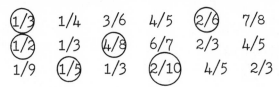

*84. Use fraction number lines to introduce children to whether a fraction is equal to one whole, is greater than one whole, or is less than one whole. Counting forwards and backwards on the number line may also be helpful.

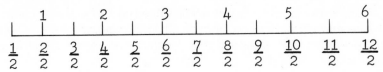

*85. Use the measurements in simple recipes to reinforce fractional components. Have children do the measuring for the baking of cookies, pancakes, or cakes.

Does the Child Have Difficulty Telling Time?

Prepare a worksheet with a number of clock faces. Instruct the child to draw in the hands of the clock at certain times. The times may be called aloud by the teacher or written under the faces.

Informal Assessment

86. Provide children with real clocks or teacher-made (or pupil-made) clocks to teach time telling. Clocks may be inexpensively made by attaching cardboard hands to a paper plate. Teaching clocks may also be commercially purchased through most school supply companies.

Instructional Activities

87. Use individual clocks for group activities. Ask the children a variety of time-related questions and have them set their individual clocks. For example:

The time school begins.

The time we eat lunch at school.

The time school ends for the day.

The time you go to bed.

88. Lerner (1976) suggests the following sequence for teaching time:
   a. The hour,
   b. The half-hour,
   c. The quarter-hour,
   d. Five-minute intervals,
   e. Before and after the hour,
   f. Minute intervals,
   g. Seconds.

89. The fractions on the clock may be taught by having a child stand with his hands pointed straight up. He can represent various times as he lowers his hands. The teacher can call out the times as the children move their hands accordingly (Behrmann & Millman, 1971).

*90. Prepare a series of cards with a time written on the front of the card and a clock face showing that time on the back. Children may use the cards individually by setting their own clocks and checking their work against the backs of the cards (Platts, 1964).

*91. Ask children to perform activities where they can be timed.

"How long will it take Margaret to take these papers to the office?"

"Let's see how long it will take us to clean up our desks."

"We may all go outside for 5 minutes."

"We have 3 minutes to finish the arithmetic paper."

"How long did it take you to read this story?"

*92. Provide the children with TV, plane, or train schedules, and ask them questions based upon the schedules. Relate the schedules to the clock and have them find the time on the clock.

*93. Have each child make up an individual time schedule or log of his day. Include activities such as the time for getting up, catching the bus, going to recess, eating lunch, going home, playing, and going to bed.

*94. Show children pictures (e.g., getting out of bed; eating lunch) and ask them to set their clocks at the times indicated by the pictures. Individual differences must be taken into account.

*95. Hofmeister (1968) has developed a highly structured program to teach time telling. The program gradually introduces time-telling skills sequentially.

Does the Child Understand Monetary Values?

Informal   Prepare a worksheet with coin denominations in separate boxes.
Assessment   Instruct the children to draw a line connecting the boxes that equal
               the same amount of money. For example, five pennies would equal
one nickel and two dimes and one nickel would equal one quarter.

96. Provide real money whenever possible to teach money values. When real money is not available, authentic-looking rubber stamp reproductions of actual U.S. coins may be purchased.

97. Platts (1964) suggests preparing a worksheet with problems similar to those below and asking children to choose the greater amount and find the sum.

```
Quarter + nickel + dime OR quarter + quarter

Dollar OR nickel + three quarters

Seven dimes OR three quarters

Quarter + dime + half dollar OR three quarters

Dime + dime + dime + nickel + quarter OR half dollar
+ nickel
```

98. Show children combinations of coins and ask them to total the amounts. Actual coins pasted to cards should be used when possible. Otherwise, the reproduction (see activity #96) may be stamped on the cards.

99. Set up a grocery store in the classroom with empty boxes and cans of food. Price each item and allow children to be the store-keeper, cashier, and shoppers using real or play money to conduct business. Adaptations of this activity include holding several items before the entire class and asking them to add the total cost.

100. Paste objects (food, toys, and clothes) on cards and label each object with a price. Flash the cards to an individual child and ask him to write down the change he would receive from a certain amount of money.

*101. Give children a certain amount of money and ask them to purchase as many different items as possible with the available money. The child who is able to buy the greatest number of different items without exceeding his supply of money wins the game.

*102. Arrange with the cafeteria manager to have certain children act as the cashier for specified periods of time. Let other children collect and total milk or bus money in school.

*103. Provide actual or play restaurant menus. Ask the children to order a meal and total the cost. More advanced students should add tax and tip.

*104. Give children newspaper grocery advertisements, if you are unable to set up a school store. Ask children to do the "weekly shopping" for their parents and total the cost of the groceries (Platts, 1964).

*105. If a token reinforcement system is being used in the classroom, there are many opportunities to teach monetary concepts based on the exchange of tokens for reinforcers (see chapter 2). Play currency may be made by the teacher and used as tokens. A currency-based token economy teaches many arithmetic skills directly, including monetary value.

PROBLEM-SOLVING SKILLS

Some children with arithmetic difficulties are unable to operationalize number skills in story problems due to specific problem-solving deficiencies. Adequate problem-solving skills in artihmetic are based upon the child's:
1. Ability to understand the language of arithmetic,
2. Reasoning and analysis skills in reading story problems.

Diagnostic question, informal tests, and teaching suggestions for remediating problem-solving difficulties are listed in the following section.

HAS THE CHILD DEVELOPED PROBLEM-SOLVING SKILLS?

Does the Child Understand Arithmetic Terms and Signs?

*Informal
Assessment*

Prepare a worksheet where the operation signs are missing. Ask the child to fill them in. For example:

$$6 \underline{\hphantom{+}} 3 = 3$$

$$1 \underline{\hphantom{+}} 2 = 3$$

$$2 \underline{\hphantom{+}} 4 = 6$$

$$1 + 1 \underline{\hphantom{+}} 2$$

$$7 \underline{\hphantom{+}} 5 = 2$$

*Instructional
Activities*

106. The terms *longer* and *shorter* may be better understood if the teacher draws lines of various lengths on the board and asks the child to make them longer or shorter. Children may also sort various objects, such as sticks, in piles of longer or shorter (Wagner et al., 1964).

107. The number lines may be used to develop vocabulary such as *before, after, between, larger than, smaller than,* and *the same as.* Children may refer to the number line in answering questions such as:

What number comes just *before* 7? _____

What number comes just *after* 13? _____

What number comes *between* 6 and 8? _____

108. Auditory stimulation may be used to develop the concepts of *more* and *less* by clapping the number of letter in each child's name. Ask the child if T-i-m has *more* claps than C-h-r-i-s; or M-i-s-s-y has *less* claps than J-i-m (Behrmann & Millman, 1971).

109. Provide children with different colored beads on a string and ask them specific questions such as:

"Are there *more* blue beads than red beads?"

"Are there *fewer* yellow beads than black beads?"

"Which color has the *same* number of beads as red?"

110. Prepare a worksheet similar to the example below for use with a number line.

(Check the correct answer)				
	Larger than	Smaller than	the Same as	
Is 2 + 2				3 + 1
Is 5 + 1				3 + 3
Is 17				71
Is 3 + 1				1 + 3
Is 6 + 2				4 + 5

111. Give children a set of cards numbered from 1 to 10. Instruct the child to turn up one card, and ask him if the number comes *before* or *after* a number that you choose at random. *More* or *less* and *smaller than* or *larger than* can also be used for this activity.

112. Give children practice in reading arithmetic problems without working them. Have the children read "2+2=4" or "5−3=2" with the emphasis on the operation signs (Johnson & Myklebust, 1967).

*113. Print operation signs on flash cards. The children can practice with the cards—similar to sight word flash cards—every day. Kinesthetic clues can be added by cutting the signs out of sandpaper and pasting them on the cards.

*114. Provide color cues for operation signs to call attention to the sign. Circles or boxes drawn around the signs may also enable a child to attend more closely to the sign.

Does the Child Have Difficulty Analyzing Story Problems?

Informal Assessment   Present story problems orally and direct the child to solve the problem without using pencil or paper. Children are required to listen closely to the presentation. Children who successfully arrive at the answer can explain the process they used.

Instructional Activities   ***115.** Have the children read story problems and decide on the mathematical operation required to work the problem, without actually doing the computation. Encourage them to discuss why a specific mathematical operation is required for a particular problem.

*116. Discuss *clue words* in story problems that indicate mathematical operations. Make children more aware of these key words by underlining or circling them on seatwork papers. The clue words in the examples below are in boxes.

> Michael had 9 marbles. He (lost) 3 of them in the park. How many does he have (left) ?

> Mother baked 2 pies yesterday (and) 1 pie today. How many pies did Mother bake (altogether) ?

*117. Ask children to write a number sentence after having read a story problem. This process helps a child to see the numerical relationships prior to working out the answer. A number sentence follows the story problem below.

> Richard has 7 cents. He owes Jackie 3 cents. How much will Richard have left after he pays Jackie?

$$7 - 3 = \rule{2cm}{0.4pt}$$

*118. Provide story problems that require a one-step process. The length of the sentences should be short, and only essential vocabulary should be included during beginning instruction in problem solving.

*119. Johnson and Myklebust (1967) suggest using sentences that emphasize "logic and rational thought" rather than rote memorization (p. 270). Practice sentences of this nature might include answering the following as true or false.

"John, who is 38 inches tall, is shorter than Bill, who is 3 feet tall."

"I will have to wait for 14 more days if my cousin will be visiting me in 2 weeks."

"There are spaces for one dozen, or 14, more cars."

*120. Visually represent the numerical amounts that are presented in the story problem. For examples, problems involving money can be visualized by actually providing the child with the appropriate amount of real or play money.

*121. Spitzer (1961) suggests using analogous problems with easier numbers to solve more difficult story problems. Numbers that may be computed more easily often simplify the solution to a more complicated problem.

*122. Permit children to make up their own story problems. Other children in the class might be required to solve the problems, or children can also provide answers to their own problems. Direct the children to write problems involving specific operations, such as addition and subtraction.

*123. Orally analyze the steps that are required to solve a particular problem. Spitzer (1961) lists the following procedures to be used in problem analysis. He recommends using only one or two steps with any one problem.

> (1) What is given,
> (2) What is asked,
> (3) What operation or operations to use,
> (4) An estimate of the answer,
> (5) The solution, and
> (6) A check of the answer. (p. 256)

*124. Diagram or illustrate the story problems on the chalkboard for the child Discuss each part of the illustration. Allow children to illustrate selected story problems.

ARITHMETIC PROGRAMS

Manipulative materials, repetition, and *color* are emphasized in many arithmetic programs used with children experiencing learning problems (Wallace & McLoughlin, 1975). Some representative commercial arithmetic programs are described in this section.

Cuisenaire Rods
(Davidson, 1969)

The Cuisenaire Rods are a set of over 200 color-coded rods which were primarily designed to teach understanding of the basic structure of mathematics. The rods vary in length, and each rod is systematically associated with a different number. The rods are commonly used in the primary grades for all basic arithmetic processes, and with older children experiencing severe arithmetic difficulties. In using the rods, the emphasis is on meaning and discovery. The combined visual, tactile, and auditory modes certainly make the rods very appropriate as a supplementary aid for children with learning handicaps.

DISTAR Arithmetic
(Engelmann & Carnine, 1969)

> This is a highly directive beginning arithmetic program with carefully structured lessons intended for small groups of children. The ordered sequence of steps is designed to develop understanding of basic arithmetic skills through active participation by the child. The program includes counting, algebra, addition and subtraction, story problems, and counting by various numbers. Immediate feedback and repetition are an integral part of the program. The materials are primarily designed for primary age children, although the program can be easily adapted for older children. The teachers' manual is highly specific and very well-organized.

Merrill Mathematics Skilltapes
(Sganga, 1969)

> A series of 40 audio cassette tapes and accompanying student workbooks comprise this basic arithmetic program. Skills are presented in a logical and sequential order with the following topics included: counting; addition, subtraction, multiplication, and division of whole numbers; fractions; and decimals. Each of the 40 lessons includes separate cassettes with 15 to 18 minutes playing time on each side of the cassette. The tapes can serve as a very important addition to any basic arithmetic program for many children with learning problems.

Programmed Math Series One
(Sullivan Associates, 1968)

> This is a series of eight programmed texts originally designed for individualized instruction with educationally handicapped children. Although computation skills are emphasized throughout the program, the workbooks also include work extending from number formation through operations with mixed numerals and measurement. A placement test is included with the series, along with progress tests and eight problem books. The immediate feedback nature of the program seems ideally suited to the needs of the handicapped learner. In addition, the student workbooks do not require any reading ability.

Structured Arithmetic
(Stern, Stern, & Gould, 1952)

> This is a complete mathematics program intended for use with children in kindergarten through third grade. The materials can be easily adapted for older students with arithmetic difficulties. The program includes a number of manipulatable materials, including number markers, unit box with unit blocks, pattern board, and groups of cubes. The student is expected to gain insight

into number relationships and basic arithmetic operations by experimenting with the materials. Roman numerals, fractions, measurement, and monetary values are also included. The well-organized teachers' manual provides a number of excellent suggestions for individualizing, enrichment, and assessment.

ADDITIONAL READINGS

Arena, J. (Ed.). *Teaching educationally handicapped children.* San Rafael, Calif.: Academic Therapy Publications, 1967.

Behrmann, P., & Millman, J. *How many spoons make a family?* San Rafael, Calif.: Academic Therapy Publications, 1971.

Bereiter, C. *Arithmetic and mathematics.* San Rafael, Calif: Dimensions Publishing Co., 1968.

Bereiter, C., & Engelmann, S. *Teaching disadvantaged children in the pre-school.* Englewood Cliff, N.J.: Prentice-Hall, 1966.

Dutton, W. H., & Adams, L. J. *Arithmetic for teachers.* Englewood, Cliffs, N.J.: Prentice-Hall, Inc., 1961.

Feingold, A. *Teaching arithmetic to slow learners and retarded.* New York: John Day, 1965.

Lerner, J. *Children with learning disabilities* (2nd ed.). Boston: Houghton Mifflin, 1976.

Otto, W., McMenemy, R. A., & Smith, R. J. *Corrective and remedial teaching* (2nd ed.). Boston: Houghton Mifflin, 1973.

Platts, M. E. *Plus.* Stevensville, Mich.: Educational Service, 1964

Reisman, F. K. *A guide to the diagnostic teaching of arithmetic* (2nd ed.). Columbus, Ohio: Charles E. Merrill, 1978.

Sharp, F. A. *These kids don't count.* San Rafael, Calif.: Academic Therapy Publications, 1971.

Spitzer, H. F. *The teaching of arithmetic.* Boston: Houghton Mifflin, 1961.

Swenson, E. J. *Teaching arithmetic to children.* New York: Macmillan, 1964.

Wagner, G., Hosier, M., & Gilloley, L. *Arithmetic games and activities.* Darien, Conn.: Teachers Publishing Corp., 1964.

Wallace, G., & Larsen, S. C. *The educational assessment of learning problems: Testing for teaching.* Boston: Allyn & Bacon, 1978.

Wedemeyer, A., & Cejka, J. *Creative ideas for teaching exceptional children.* Denver: Love, 1970.

Visual-Motor Problems

Barsch (1965, 1967, 1968), Delacato (1959, 1966), Getman (1965), and Kephart (1963, 1967, 1968, 1971) each proposed a theory relating academic problems to perceptual–motor deficiencies. These theories and models had wide impact and appeal to people in many different disciplines. However, during the last few years, increased attention has been given to the efficacy of visual-motor assessment and remediation. As a result of many recent studies and research, there is very little support for the use of perceptually based tests or training programs with children with academic learning problems (Hammill & Wiederholt, 1973; Hammill & Larsen, 1974; Larsen, Parker, & Sowell, 1976).

We have devoted a chapter to this topic because of the widespread use in the schools of training procedures for visual-motor problems. The instructional activities outlined here are primarily intended to be implemented at the pre-school level. The activities are *not* recommended as an alternative to academic skills instruction. The two basic questions of particular concern in this chapter are:
1. In what motor skills is the child deficient?
2. Which visual-perceptual skills are causing the child difficulty?

ASSESSMENT

Teacher Observation

The alert classroom teacher will be able to use observational methods expertly as an important source of diagnostic information. Chaney and Kephart (1968) advise the teacher to "look for a pattern of difficulties and try to relate that which is observed to the overall problem" (p. 42). More specifically, Smith (1969) suggests the following as important considerations:

(1) how the child holds his pencil and the manner in which he draws and writes;
(2) how well he can copy and trace;
(3) the technique which he uses to form numerals and letters;
(4) whether a consistent pattern of reversals is evidenced;
(5) how well he organizes materials for play and work;
(6) how well he can move about the room without bumping into or tipping over objects;
(7) how well he can identify and separate foreground objects from the background;
(8) the degree to which discrimination among sizes, shapes, and colors is a problem;
(9) how well the child can accomplish a task that requires a certain sequence of activities; and
(10) whether objects in space appear confusing to him. (p. 62)

Detailed observation checklists for use in the regular classroom have also been developed by Chaney and Kephart (1968).

Informal Assessment

Many of the suggestions listed under specific headings later in this chapter can be used as informal procedures to evaluate particular visual-motor skills. The child's performance is a measure of skill development within each area. Careful and precise use of informal tests provides the teacher with exacting information which can be used in planning an instructional program.

Formal Tests

There are a number of published tests available for assessing visual-motor skills. Although some of the tests require specialized training for proper administration, classroom teachers should become familiar with these tests since the results, in most cases, are directly applicable to classroom instruction. Some of the more widely used formal tests are reviewed below.

Developmental Test of Visual-Motor Integration
(Berry & Buktenica, 1967)

Twenty-four geometric figures arranged in order of increasing difficulty comprise this test of visual-motor coordination. Children are required to copy figures from a presented model. The test is designed for preschool and primary age children but may be administered to older children. Raw scores can be interpreted in terms of age. The ease of administration and scoring make the test useful for both screening and appraising specific problems among individual children.

Bender Visual-Motor Gestalt Test
(Bender, 1938)

The *Bender* is a widely used test of visual perceptual abilities which has also been used to measure maturational level, brain injury, emotional adjustment, and intelligence. The test consists of nine graphic forms that the student is asked to reproduce on a plain sheet of white paper. Drawings are judged according to a number of categories, including rotation, distortion of shape, perseverations, and failure to integrate parts of a figure. Forms for children from 4 through 11 years old have been developed. An alternative scoring procedure has also been developed by Kippitz (1964).

Bruininks-Oseretsky Test of Motor Proficiency
(Bruininks, 1977)

This test is the most recent modification of an assessment device designed to estimate a child's gross and fine motor ability. The Bruininks revision includes normative information for children 4 to 18 years of age. Subtests include Running Speed and Agility, Balance, Bilateral Coordination, Strength, Upper Limb Coordination, Response Speed, Visual-Motor Control, and Upper Limb Speed and Dexterity. The test must be individually administered, and results are provided as age equivalents and percentiles for each child's general motor ability.

Marianne Frostig Developmental Test of Visual Perception
(Frostig, Lefever, & Whittlesey, 1964)

This measure attempts to assess five operationally defined visual perceptual skills: eye-motor coordination, figure-ground discrimination, form constancy, position in space, and spatial relationships. The test is suitable for group or individual administration, and normative data are available for children between the ages of 4 and 8 years. Raw scores can be converted into scaled scores, perceptual ages, and an overall perceptual quotient. The test has been recommended as a screening tool for young children with visual perceptual problems.

Motor-Free Visual Perceptual Test
(Colarusso & Hammill, 1972)

This is an individually administered, multiple-choice test of visual perception. The subject is merely required to *point* to one of four alternatives, thus avoiding any need for fine motor skills. The 36-item test is divided into five subtests: Spatial Relationships, Visual Discrimination, Figure-Ground, Visual Closure, and Visual Memory. The test takes approximately 10 minutes to administer and yields a perceptual age (PA) and a perceptual quotient (PQ). The measure is a highly reliable and quick screening tool which can be used for both diagnosis and research.

Purdue Perceptual-Motor Survey
(Roach & Kephart, 1966)

This informal instrument was designed to measure the perceptual-motor abilities of children in the early grades. The survey is composed of 22 scorable items divided into 11 specific subtests. Basically, the major sections of the test include balance and posture, body image and differentiation of body parts, perceptual-motor matching, ocular control, and form perception. The survey is relatively easy to administer and few specialized materials are required.

GENERAL MOVEMENT PATTERNS

The child with deficient motor skills may appear clumsy and awkward in basic movement patterns. Overcoming motor problems involves developing:

1. Adequate gross motor skills,
2. The ability to maintain balance and move rhythmically,
3. Body image and body awareness,
4. Lateral consistency in body orientation,
5. Directional orientation,
6. Adequate fine motor skills.

Diagnostic questions, informal tests, and teaching suggestions for remediating general movement difficulties are listed in this section.

HAS THE CHILD MASTERED ADEQUATE MOVEMENT PATTERNS?

Does the Child Have Difficulty with Gross Motor Movements?

Use *Simon Says* to assess movement skills such as running, hopping, jumping, walking, and throwing.

Informal Assessment

1. Have children practice walking movements, including walking freely forward, backward, sideward, zigzag, on tiptoes, on heels, with legs stiff, and on a straight line.

Instructional Activities

*2. Have the child practice running movements, including running in place, around and between objects, in slow motion, and following another child. Also, have the child run and stop on signal or change directions on signal.

*3. Have the child practice jumping, hopping, and leaping across lines, forward, for height, for distance, with partners, over hurdles, and as quietly as possible.

*4. Teach the child to skip as high off the ground as possible, in narrow areas, backwards, in a square or circle, and while clapping hands.

*5. Have the child work on throwing and catching a ball by throwing the ball back and forth with a partner using a push pass. Later, add the over-the-head toss and the underhand toss. Have the child bounce the ball before he throws it or try to throw the ball into a basket.

*6. Provide the child with a number of tires to jump in and out of, to leap over, to run around, to walk on the rim, or to be used in an obstacle course.

*7. Many of the balance beam suggestions discussed in activity #20 may be used to develop gross motor skills.

*8. Have the child practice motor movements on the trampoline or skateboard. These activities should be closely supervised and kept simple until the child becomes more skillful in gross motor movements.

*9. Use "training" steps so the child can practice going up and down steps. Hackett and Jensen (1966) suggest making steps 1 foot deep and 10 feet wide. They also provide additional suggestions for constructing training steps.

10. The AAHPER Youth Fitness Test (President's Council on Physical Fitness, 1967) can be used as a guide to developing overall gross motor movements. The test includes the following seven skills:

    a. *Pull-up:* for judging arm and shoulder girdle strength.
    b. *Sit-up:* for judging efficiency of abdominal and hip flexor muscles.
    c. *Shuttle run:* for judging speed and change of direction.
    d. *Standing broad jump:* for judging explosive muscle power of leg extensors.
    e. *Fifty yard dash:* for judging speed.
    f. *Softball throw for distance:* for judging skill and coordination.
    g. *Six hundred yard run-walk:* for judging cardiovascular efficiency.

Does the Child Have Difficulty with Balance and Rhythm?

Informal Assessment   Prepare an obstacle course composed of chairs, tables, tires, balance beams, and hoops. Have the child move through the course in different positions, including crawling, walking, running, hopping, and jumping.

Instructional Activities   ***11.** Use rhythm records to teach children to walk, run, hop, and skip to the beat of the music. Also, use rhythm band instruments to teach different beats.

*12. Use the trampoline to develop balance. Have the child learn to sit and bounce on his seat before bouncing on his feet. Gradually, have the child bounce straight by bending his knees and thrusting against the bed with his feet. Be sure to have adequate protection on all four sides of the trampoline. Allow only one child on the trampoline at a time.

*13. Have the child learn to jump rope in rhythm while listening to a record or according to a particular beat or chant sung by the children. Use different types of rope turning (e.g. *cradle*, in which the rope is swung back and forth as a pendulum; *back turns*, in which the rope is moved away from the jumper at the bottom of the turn).

*14. Teach the child some of the following stunts.

Raggedy Ann. Walk like a rag doll with very relaxed head, body, and arms.

Elevator. Stoop slowly to a three-quarter squat position. Keep body and head erect throughout, with the arms remaining at the sides.

Bear Walk. Assume an all-fours position. Walk forward slowly, rolling from side to side, moving right arm and leg, then left arm and leg.

Leg Roll. Lie flat on back, arms extended over head, legs straight, feet together. Slowly roll over and over on mat without using arms or elbows to propel body.

Heel-toe Walk. Walk forward, touching heel to toe on each step. Gradually build up speed with practice.

*15. Teach the child to bounce a ball to a rhythmic beat. Bouncing is taught first with two hands and then with one. Walking while bouncing should also be practiced, along with bouncing a ball to a partner.

*16. Use hopping on one foot, hopping on two feet, and skipping in a variety of patterns. Alternate hops forward, backward, and sideward. Hop twice on the right foot, twice on the left, etc.; hop twice on the right foot, once on the left, etc.; and skip twice, hop once, etc.

*17. Valett (1967) suggests setting the metronome at a slow speed or using bongo drums, alternating simple beats, to teach children to walk rhythmically.

*18. Have relays where the children line up in a row, and at the signal the first child raises the ball over his head and passes it to the player behind him. Each player repeats the action until the last person in line receives the ball. He runs with the ball to the front of the line and begins the overhead passing. This continues until the first player heads the line again.

*19. Teach the child to use rhythm in hitting ping-pong or tennis balls. Gradually encourage the children to use the skills in actually playing these games.

*20. Have the child walk on a balance beam. Chaney & Kephart (1968) list 69 variations for balance-beam walking, including walking forward with hands on hips, walking the beam sideward with eyes closed, and walking backward with an eraser balanced on top of the head. They suggest a standard beam size of 2 in x 4 in x 10 ft, with supports which prevent the board from tipping over. As children improve in balancing skills, the width of the beam should be narrowed.

Does the Child Have Difficulty with Body Image and Awareness?

Touch different parts of your body and have the children imitate you. Have the children call out the names of body parts as they touch them. Include identification of the head, shoulders, ankles, hips, elbows, back, and wrists.

Informal Assessment

21. Assume different poses involving the entire body and have the children imitate the position. Slowly change positions and gradually speed up the tempo. Children can also take turns in assuming different poses.

22. Have children lie on the floor with their eyes closed. Ask them to slowly raise different parts of their bodies off the floor.

23. Chaney & Kephart (1968) suggest sticking small pieces of gummed paper on various body parts and having the child locate and remove them, or hiding parts of the body with a towel or sand and having the child uncover them.

24. Play *Hoky Poky* with the children. Have them stand in a circle and give the following directions:
  "Put your left arm in."
  "Take your left arm out."
  "Put your left arm in and shake it all about."
  "Put your right foot in."
  "Take your right foot out."
  "Put your right foot in and shake it all about."

25. Lerner (1976) suggests having children pantomime actions of bus drivers driving a bus, policemen directing traffic, etc., or having the child look at pictures of people and tell whether the person is happy, sad, etc.

26. Have children draw around parts of themselves (e.g., fingers or foot) or trace an outline around another child. Ask them to draw in body and facial parts.

*27. Provide puzzles of people or animals to put together. Initially have the child replace just certain body parts; eventually permit him to work on the entire puzzle.

*28. Have the child step, walk, or run in empty space. Gradually have the child control his movement by jumping or stepping into hoops on the ground (Hackett & Jensen, 1966).

*29. Play *Simon Says*. Have the children follow different commands such as "Simon says, touch your knee" or "Simon says, close your eyes and touch your ears." Allow a child to be the leader of this game.

*30. Have the children lie flat on their backs on the floor with arms at their sides and feet together. Ask them to play *Angels-in-the-Snow* by moving their feet apart as far as possible with knees stiff. Have them bring their feet together by clicking their heels. The arms are similarly moved. Kephart (1971) further explains a number of variations of this activity.

*31. Provide clay to model human figures. Clay modeling can be done initially as a group exercise.

*32. Prepare pictures of humans with different body parts missing. Ask the child to tell what is missing or have him draw in the missing part.

Does the Child Have Difficulty with Laterality (complete motor awareness of the two sides of the body)?

Observe the child using climbing apparatus on which he can coordinate the use of both hands and legs. Have him climb ladders, jungle gyms, hand bars, etc. *Informal Assessment*

*33. Have the child use the balance beam as suggested by Chaney and Kephart (1968). Use a variety of activities in working with the balance beam, including moving forward, backward, and sideward. *Instructional Activities*

*34 Have the child practice throwing, catching, and kicking by playing games with large balls. Kickball and soccer are particularly good games for developing these skills.

*35. Play darts, archery, and target shooting to develop eye dominance. Encourage the child to sight the target with his dominant eye (Valett, 1967).

*36. The trampoline teaching suggestions described in activity #12 help to develop total body control and balance.

*37 Have the child do a variety of head, shoulder, trunk, arm, and leg differentiation exercises. Benyon (1969) lists a number of suggestions for each of these areas.

*38. Have the child practice creeping by extending the arm and leg in various combinations. Creep on the floor, up and down stairs, around and over objects, and through tunnels.

*39. Abernethy, Cowley, Gillard, and Whiteside (1970) present a wide range of suitable activities for laterality difficulties. They include individual, partner, and group activities to be used with or without equipment.

*40. Draw footprints on the floor and have the child place his feet on the prints and follow them. Gradually reduce the space left between footprints.

Does the Child Have Difficulty with Directionality (right-left, up-down, forward-backward, etc.)?

Call out commands to the child. For example: *Informal Assessment*

"Stand *by* the door."

"Crawl *through* the hoop."

"Walk to the *right* side of Jeff's desk."

41. Put a mark (e.g., removable paint or masking tape) on the hand or foot of the side to be taught. Give directions or play *Simon Says*, directing the child to raise certain body parts involving right and left, up and down, front and back, etc.

42. Prepare a worksheet of sample pictures with instructions to follow. For example:

```
Put a line under the house.

Put an X on the apple.

Put a circle around the boy.
```

43. Have the children sort and identify right and left boots, shoes, gloves, hand outlines, etc. (Valett, 1967).

44. Have two children face each other with one calling out directions such as "Clap left hands" or "Touch fingers." The other child follows the directions (Wedemeyer & Cejka, 1970).

45. Provide on the child himself a cue for right–left such as a ring on the left hand or watch on the right arm (Johnson & Myklebust, 1967). Freckles or other marks on the hands can also serve as right-left reminders.

46. Construct a large map of a town on paper. Have the child guide toy cars on the roads, verbalizing turns and directions. Give the child some specific directions to follow on the map. Have him guide the car to the final destination using the directions given.

47. Provide a pegboard and a number of different pegs. Direct the child in placing the pegs in the pegboard by providing specific directions. For example:

"Put the green peg *over* the blue peg."

"Put the red peg to the *left* of the brown peg."

"Put the orange peg *under* the yellow peg."

48. Play games in which the child closes or covers his eyes. Make various sounds in different parts of the room and ask the child to identify the direction of the sound.

49. Valett (1967) suggests teaching map directions by marking the sides of the room "North," "South," "East," and "West." Play games where children place themselves according to map directions, such as "Rose, go to the north of John" or "Gertrude, stand to the west of Vin."

50. Prepare a scrapbook of pictures that illustrate position words such as *in, out, above, below, under, on, up,* and *down*. Ask the children to find pictures in magazines that illustrate these words.

51. Use red and green margin markers to emphasize left–right progression, or use masking tape to provide a tactile clue for letter placement in writing exercises.

*52. The obstacle course described earlier can be used to develop understanding of position words such as *under, over, in,* and *out.*

*53. Prepare a series of maze puzzles. Ask the child to verbalize the directions that he takes with his pencil.

Does the Child Have Difficulty with Fine Motor Movements?

Provide children with zippers to zip, buckles to buckle, locks to open with keys, snaps to fasten, shoes to lace, boots to tie and untie, and buttons to button and undo. — *Informal Assessment*

54. Have the child weave boot laces or yarn through picture lacing boards. Lerner (1976) suggests making the lacing boards from a cardboard punched with holes or a pegboard with a design or picture painted on it. — *Instructional Activities*

55. Ask the child to sort beads according to size, color, or shape. Provide a pattern to duplicate with beads, or ask the child to create his own pattern.

56. Provide model clay to manipulate. Ask the child to mould particular objects (e.g., balls or fruits) or have the child create his own figures.

57. Have the child fold a paper following a step-by-step procedure after observing the teacher. Start with simple patterns and repeat the folding procedures several times. Children can eventually be asked to fold patterns from memory.

58. Ask the child to duplicate a design or picture with some specific pasting material (e.g., paper, felt, macaroni, or toothpicks).

59. Wedemeyer & Cejka (1970) suggest fastening a large button at the center of a cardboard square and stapling loops of narrow elastic around the edge of the board. Direct the child to stretch and fasten each loop around the button.

60. Provide a small wooden ladder and ask the child to "climb up" and "climb down" the ladder with one finger. The child can also "walk" the ladder while it is in a horizontal position, "stepping" from one rung to the next (Murphy, 1971).

61. Manipulating tools or kitchen utensils provides excellent fine motor practice. Screw drivers, hammers, wrenches, egg beaters, spoons, and cutlery can be used in a variety of situations.

62. Have the child play games such as *Pick-up Sticks* or *Jacks*, both of which require finger dexterity.

63. Encourage the child to make letters in the air during the beginning stages of writing. The child should begin with movements which gradually become finer.

64. Have the child practice strokes at the chalkboard. Make lines, triangles, squares, etc. In making circles, have the child practice with one hand and two hands, both clockwise and counterclockwise (Kephart, 1971).

*65. Play card games with the child where the child must manipulate a number of cards at one time, deal cards, and shuffle the deck.

*66. Have the child throw, catch, bounce, and roll various objects such as balls or balloons. Provide targets such as boxes and cans.

VISUAL-PERCEPTUAL SKILLS

The teaching activities listed in the following section are primarily intended for use with preschool and kindergarten children. The activities should be used where improvement in visual-perceptual skills is the goal, and never as a replacement for academic skill instruction.

Competency in visual perception includes:
1. Discriminate the constancy of form,
2. Perceive objects in foreground and background and meaningfully separate them,
3. Perceive different parts of an object in relation to the observer,
4. Coordinate vision with movements of the body.

Diagnostic questions, informal tests, and teaching suggestions for remediating visual-perceptual skills are listed in this section.

DOES THE CHILD HAVE ADEQUATE VISUAL PERCEPTION?

Does the Child Have Difficulty Discriminating the Constancy of Form?

Informal Assessment

Have the child sort objects according to shape. Beads, blocks, and paper shapes can be used.

Instructional Activities

67. Have the child trace templates at the chalkboard. Eventually have him trace smaller templates at his desk. Use circle, square, triangle, rectangle, and diamond templates. Gradually lead the child to trace the form from memory.

68. Have children match manipulatable shapes (made of wood, plastic, tag board, etc.) to similar shapes on a paper. Use blocks which directly match the block designs on paper.

69. Provide a bag full of different sized wooden shapes. Have the child *feel* and *describe* one shape in the bag.

70. Arrange four checker patterns, three identical and one slightly different. Have the child pick out the different pattern and explain the difference. This activity may also be used with dominoes, blocks, sticks, pegs, etc. (Valett, 1967).

71. Play the game *Twenty Questions,* using shapes within the room. Have one child choose an object in the room, and let other children ask questions about the shape.

72. Have children toss bean bags to holes of particular shapes. Before each toss, instruct the child to "toss the bean bag to the square holes" or "toss the bean bag to the round holes."

73. Present a series of identical designs, numbers, or letters with one smaller or larger than the others. Have the child choose the one that is different (Valett, 1967).

74. Older children can match letters presented in manuscript, cursive, and typed forms. Also, ask children to identify letters or numbers presented in a variety of positions.

75. Have children match lowerand uppercase letters. This activity can be varied by having children find and cut out as many A's, m's, etc., as they can find in magazines.

76. Behrmann (1970) suggests using a worksheet similar to the example below. The children circle the word that is the same as the word at the top of the column.

clock	floor	lead
cling	flute	leaf
click	flour	lead
clock	flood	leak
clear	float	lean
clean	floor	leap

Does the Child Have Difficulty Perceiving Objects in Foreground and Background and Separating Them?

Informal Assessment

Provide the child with a picture and ask him to point to various objects. For example:

"Point to the *smallest* child."

"Point to the *upstairs* window in the house."

"Point to the girl's *earrings*."

Instructional Activities

77. Keep the child's desk and work area as free as possible of visual stimuli. Portable study carrels often provide an effective noncluttered environment.

78. Have the child sort objects according to size, color, texture, or shape. Gradually build up the number of objects to be sorted.

79. Play games such as *Hide the Thimble* and *Huckle Buckle Beanstalk*. These group activities help a child to focus attention on a single object.

80. Place a series of red and white X's on the floor. Play a record and have the children march around, stepping only on the red X's (Compton, 1965).

81. Have children play games to discriminate objects in a room. Ask the child to find the square objects, the wooden objects, the objects larger than a chair, etc.

82. Prepare pictures with "hidden" figures. Ask the child to find all the shoes, pencils, or cups in the picture.

83. Behrmann (1970) suggests having a child stand in front of the room and letting the other children study him for a short period of time. Have the child leave the room and change something (e.g., remove a belt, change bracelets to another hand). On his return to the room, let the other children try to determine what is different.

84. Draw overlapping figures and designs for the child to visually differentiate (Valett, 1967). Acetate overlays can be placed over pictures, and the child can locate specific objects with a grease pencil or his finger.

85. Underline sentences to be copied from the board with colored chalk, and place a crayon line of corresponding color on the paper (Compton, 1965).

86. Older children can be asked to find a certain sequence of letters in a word, a sequence of sentences in a paragraph, or a name in a telephone directory.

Does the Child Have Difficulty with Spatial Perception?

Have the child stand, sit, or lie *on, in, under, in front of, behind,* and *beside* various objects. Have the child verbalize these positions as he performs the action.

87. Draw lines on the floor to represent a road. Ask the child to walk across it, along it, beside it, down the middle, etc.

88. Use toy garages, houses, farms, and so on to have the child manipulate objects upon command. For example, ask the child to:

"Put the car *in* the garage."

"Put the doll *into* the bed."

"Place the truck at the *back* of the house."

89. Provide the child with a block design with blocks in specific patterns. Have the child duplicate the design exactly.

90. Instruct the child in building simple projects using Lincoln Logs, Tinker Toys, and erector sets. Have him build various models using model-building kits.

91. Present various geometric forms (e.g., cones, cubes, cylinders, and pyramids). Have the child feel and build spontaneous structures using the forms (Valett, 1967).

92. Present a design made of checkers on one half of a checkerboard. Have the child duplicate the design on the other half of the board.

93. Give the child dot-to-dot puzzles to complete. The puzzles should become increasingly more difficult. Have the children develop their own dot-to-dot puzzles for other children to complete.

94. Provide scrambled sets of words and sentences to unscramble. Also, give the child a list of words all spelled correctly except one. Ask the child to circle the misspelled word.

95. Have the child build words by using link or anagram letters, or cut flash strip sentences into separate words and have the child rebuild the sentence (Compton, 1965). Children may also print words by using a rubber stamp.

96. Have children locate specific positions on maps and globes. Give each child a road map and ask them to draw a line from one city to another using the shortest route possible.

Does the Child Appropriately Coordinate Eye Movements with Hand Movements?

Informal Assessment   Have the child copy various designs from the chalkboard. Gradually increase the complexity of the design. This activity may be varied by having the child copy a design from a card at his desk.

Instructional Activities   **97.** Have the child participate in physical activities such as bean bag games, ball throwing, and rolling a hoop.

98. Give the child simple dot-to-dot puzzles to complete. Initially dots may be connected at the chalkboard. Later dot-to-dot worksheets may be assigned as seatwork.

99. Practice writing vertical, horizontal, diagonal, and curved lines at the chalkboard, at the painting easel, on writing paper, and in the air. These strokes can also be practiced in sand, finger paint, or clay.

100. Give the child pictures, stencils, and templates to trace. Ask the child to color and cut the traced copy.

101. Ask the child to clip clothespins onto a line or box. Keep a graph showing the child's progress over a period of time.

102. Provide activities that involve cutting with scissors. Simple straight lines should be cut first, followed by slanted and curved lines. Double-handed scissors may be needed for the child with severe difficulties in this area.

103. Provide the child with a hammer to pound pegs into holes, nails into boards, or nails into various designs.

104. Give the child a needle to thread or have him sew with yarn to complete various designs. Small weaving looms can be used to make pot holders, etc.

105. Have the child play dominoes, darts, marbles, or checkers to develop eye–hand coordination.

106. Direct the child to use tongs or tweezers to pick up a series of objects (beads, pencils, etc.) and place them in a small-necked bottle or a box with a small hole at the top (Wedemeyer & Cejka, 1970).

107. Have the child play *Jacks*. Start with a larger ball and work initially with only one jack. Gradually, increase the number of jacks and reduce the size of the ball.

108. Many of the teaching suggestions for fine motor skills can be used for developing eye-hand coordination because of the close association between these two skills.

109. Suspend a ball from the ceiling with elastic. Have the child swing the ball to a specified target within the room.

VISUAL-MOTOR PROGRAMS

The vast majority of research studies do not support the use of visual-motor programs for training perceptual deficits. Programs designed to remediate perceptual deficits have been demonstrated to be nonproductive for most children (Wallace & Larsen, 1978). Our descriptions in the following section should not be considered an endorsement of these programs. We have merely attempted to summarize some of the programs which continue to be widely used in many schools.

Dubnoff School Program 1–Level 2
(Dubnoff, Chambers, & Schaeffer, 1969)

This program is most applicable to children 5 to 8 years of age. Various spatial and directional skills are developed through a series of exercises which include motor coordination, visual discrimination, directionality, sequencing, and laterality. The components of the program are designed to allow for individual self-pacing and self-checking. The authors feel that the complete training program could be used as readiness training, or as a remedial technique for children with specific visual-perceptual problems.

The Frostig Program for the Development of Visual Perception
(Frostig & Horne, 1964, 1968)

This program was designed to correspond to the test of visual perception developed by the same author. The program consists of worksheets divided into sections for the following visual perception skills: eye-motor coordination, figure-ground discrimination, form constancy, position in space, and spatial relationships. The program is primarily intended for children in kindergarten and first grade, or older children who may profit from the training exercises. Research results indicate that this program does not affect the reading ability of children, and provides very limited value in improving perception (Wiederholt & Hammill, 1971; Hammill & Wiederholt, 1972).

Fairbanks-Robinson Program, Level 1 and Level 2
(Fairbanks & Robinson, 1967)

The two levels of this program are designed to develop a number of visual perceptual skills, including figure-ground discrimination, spatial orientation, form recognition and discrimination, visual sequencing, eye-hand coordination, and manipulative dexterity. The kits contain skill development worksheets, tactile materials, games, and puzzles. The well-organized teachers' manual sequences each section from simple to more complex skills and from gross motor to more intricate fine motor skills. No special teacher training is required.

Ruth Cheves Program I
(Cheves, 1972)

This is a six-part program, with the first three sections designed to develop the concepts of shape, same or different, position, spatial organization, and sequence. The program is intended for kindergarten and primary grade children. It uses a game and puzzle format. Activities are sequentially structured from easy to more complex. The materials are highly attractive, yet simple in design. The ultimate importance of the teacher is emphasized throughout the program.

ADDITIONAL READINGS

Abernethy, K., Cowley, J., Gillard, H., & Whiteside, J. *Jumping up and down.* San Rafael, Calif.: Academic Therapy Publications, 1970.

Arena, J. I. (Ed.). *Teaching through sensory-motor experiences.* San Rafael, Calif.: Academic Therapy Publications, 1969.

Barsch, R. H. *A movigenic curriculum.* Madison, Wisc.: Department of Public Instruction, Bureau for the Handicapped, 1965.

Barsch, R. H. *Achieving perceptual-motor efficiency* (Vol. 1). Seattle: Special Child Publications, 1967.

Barsch, R. H. *Enriching perception and cognition* (Vol. 2). Seattle: Special Child Publications, 1970.

Buktenica, N. A. *Visual learning.* San Rafael, Calif.: Dimensions, 1968.

Chaney, C. M., & Kephart, N. C. *Motoric aids to perceptual training.* Columbus, Ohio: Charles E. Merrill, 1968.

Cohen, S. A. Studies in visual perception and reading in disadvantaged children. *Journal of Learning Disabilities,* 1969, *2,* 498-507.

Cratty, B. J. *Learning and playing.* Freeport, N.Y.: Educational Activities, n.d.

Cratty, B. J. *Developmental sequences of perceptual-motor tasks.* Freeport, N.Y.: Educational Activities, 1967.

Delacato, C. H. *The treatment and prevention of reading problems.* Springfield, Ill.: Charles C Thomas, 1959.

Delacato, C. H. *Neurological organization and reading.* Springfield, Ill.: Charles C Thomas, 1966.

Getman, G. N. The visumotor complex in the acquisition of learning skills. In J. Hellmuth (Ed.), *Learning disorders* (Vol. 1). Seattle: Special Child Publications, 1965. Pp. 49-76.

Getman, G. N., Kane, E. R., & McKee, G. W. *Developing learning readiness programs.* Manchester, Mo.: McGraw-Hill, 1968.

Hackett, L. C., & Jensen, R. C. *A guide to movement exploration.* Palo Alto, Calif.: Peek Publications, 1966.

Hallahan, D. P., & Cruickshank, W. M. *Psychoeducational foundations of learning disabilities.* Englewood Cliffs, N.J.: Prentice-Hall, 1973.

Hammill, D. D., & Larsen, S. C. The relationship of selected auditory perceptual skills and reading ability. *Journal of Learning Disabilities,* 1974, *1*, 429-436.

Hammill, D. D., & Wiederholt, J. L. *The resource room: Rationale and implementation.* Philadelphia: JSE Press, 1972.

Hammill, D. D., & Wiederholt, J. L. Review of the Frostig Visual Perception Test and the related training program. In L. Mann & D. Sabatino (Eds.), *The first review of special education* (Vol. 1). Philadelphia: Grune & Stratton, 1973. Pp. 33-48.

Kephart, N. C. *The brain-injured child in the classroom.* Chicago: National Society for Crippled Children and Adults, 1963.

Kephart, N. C. Perceptual-motor aspects of learning disabilities. In E. Frierson & W. Barbe (Eds.), *Educating children with learning disabilities.* New York: Appleton-Century-Crofts, 1967. Pp. 405-413.

Kephart, N. C. *Learning disability: An educational adventure.* West Lafayette, Ind.: Kappa Delta Pi Press, 1968.

Kephart, N. C. *The slow learner in the classroom* (2nd ed.). Columbus, Ohio: Charles E. Merrill, 1971.

Kirshner, A. J. *Training that makes sense.* San Rafael, Calif.: Academic Therapy Publications, 1972.

Larsen, S. C., Parker, R., & Sowell, V. *The effectiveness of the MWM program in developing language abilities.* Unpublished manuscript, The University of Texas at Austin, 1976.

Lerner, J. *Children with learning disabilities* (2nd ed.). Boston: Houghton Mifflin, 1976.

Magdol, M. S. *Perceptual training in the kindergarten.* San Rafael, Calif.: Academic Therapy Publications, 1971.

Murphy, P. *A special way for the special child in the regular classroom.* San Rafael, Calif.: Academic Therapy Publications, 1971.

Myers, P. I., & Hammill, D. D. *Methods for learning disordered* (2nd ed.). New York: Wiley, 1976.

Neilson, N. P. *Physical education for elementary schools.* New York: Ronald Press, 1956.

Schurr, E. *Movement experiences for children.* New York: Appleton-Century-Crofts, 1967.

Valett, R. E. *The remediation of learning disabilities.* Palo Alto, Calif.: Fearon Publishers, 1967.

Van Witsen, B. *Perceptual training activities handbook.* New York: Columbia University Press, 1967.

Wallace, G., & Larsen, S. C. *The educational assessment of learning problems: Testing for teaching.* Boston: Allyn & Bacon, 1978.

Wedemeyer, A., & Cejka, J. *Creative ideas for teaching exceptional children.* Denver: Love, 1970.

Wiederholt, J. L., & Hammill, D. D. Use of the Frostig-Horne perception program in the urban school. *Psychology in the Schools,* 1971, *8*, 268-274.

REFERENCES

Abernethy, K., Cowley, J., Gillard, H., & Whiteside, J. *Jumping up and down.* San Rafael, Calif.: Academic Therapy Publications, 1970.

Adamson, G., & Van Etten, C. Prescribing via analysis and retrieval of instructional materials in the Educational Modulation Center. *Exceptional Children,* 1970, *36,* 531-533.

Allen, K. E., Hart, B. M., Buell, J. S., Harris, F. R., & Wolf, M. M. Effects of social reinforcement on isolate behavior of a nursery school child. *Child Development,* 1964, *35,* 511-518.

Anderson, S. B., Bogatz, G. A., Draper, T. W., Jungeblut, A., Sidwell, G., Ward, W. C., & Yates, A. *CIRCUS.* Princeton, N.J.: Educational Testing Service, 1974.

Arena, J. I. (Ed.) *Building spelling skills in dyslexic children.* San Rafael, Calif.: Academic Therapy Publications, 1968.

Bandura, A. *Principles of behavior modification.* New York: Holt, Rinehart & Winston, 1969.

Barber, R. M., & Kagey, J. R. Modification of school attendance for an elementary population. *Journal of Applied Behavior Analysis,* 1977, *10,* 41-48.

Barsch, R. H. *A movigenic curriculum.* Madison, Wisc.: Department of Public Instruction, Bureau for the Handicapped, 1965.

Barsch, R. H. *Achieving perceptual-motor efficiency* (Vol. 1). Seattle: Special Child Publications, 1967.

Barsch, R. H. *Enriching perception and cognition* (Vol. 2). Seattle: Special Child Publications, 1968.

Beatty, L. S., Madden R., & Gardner, E. F. *Stanford Diagnostic Arithmetic Test* (Level 1 and Level II). New York: Harcourt, Brace, Jovanovich, 1966.

Becker, W. C., Engelmann, S., & Thomas, D. R. *Teaching: A course in applied psychology.* Chicago: Science Research Associates, 1971.

Becker, W. C., Thomas, D. R., & Carnine, D. *Reducing behavior problems: An operant conditioning guide for teachers.* Urbana, Ill.: ERIC Clearinghouse on Early Childhood Education, 1969.

Behrmann, P. *Activities for developing visual-perception.* San Rafael, Calif.: Academic Therapy Publications, 1970.

Behrmann, P., & Millman, J. *How many spoonfuls make a family?* San Rafael, Calif.: Academic Therapy Publications, 1971.

Bender, L. *Visual-Motor Gestalt Test and its clinical use.* New York: American Ortho-psychiatric Association, 1938.

Benyon, S. D. *Laterality and directionality.* In J. Arena (Ed.), *Teaching through sensory-motor experiences.* San Rafael, Calif.: Academic Therapy Publications, 1969.

Bereiter, C., & Englemann, S. *Teaching disadvantaged children in the preschool.* Englewood Cliffs, N.J.: Prentice-Hall, 1966.

Berkowitz, P. H., & Rothman, E. P. *The disturbed child.* New York: New York University Press, 1960.

Berman, M. L. Instructions and behavior change: A taxonomy. *Exceptional Children,* 1973, *39,* 644-650.

Berry, K. E., Buktenica, N. A. *Developmental Test of Visual-Motor Integration.* Chicago: Follett, 1967.

Bettelheim, B. Listening to children. In P. A. Gallagher & L. L. Edwards (Eds.), *Educating the emotionally disturbed: Theory to practice.* Lawrence, Kan: University of Kansas, 1970.

Birnbrauer, J. S., Burchard, J. D., & Burchard, S. N. Wanted: Behavior analysis. In R. H. Bradfield (Ed.), *Behavior modification: The human effort.* San Rafael, Calif.: Dimensions, 1970.

Blessing, K. (Ed.). *The role of the resource consultant in special education.* Washington, D. C.: Council for Exceptional Children, 1969.

Boehm, A. E. *Boehm Test of Basic Concepts.* New York: The Psychological Corporation, 1971.

Boning, R. A. *Specific skill series.* Rockville Centre, N.Y.: Barnell Loft, 1970.

Bornstein, P. H., & Quevillon, R. P. The effects of a self-instructional package on overactive preschool boys. *Journal of Applied Behavior Analysis,* 1976, *9,* 179-188.

Botel, M. *Botel Reading Inventory.* Chicago: Follett, 1966.

Bower, E. M. *Early identification of emotionally handicapped children in school* (2nd ed.). Springfield, Ill.: Charles C Thomas, 1969.

Bower, E. M., & Lambert, N. M. *A process for in-school screening of children with emotional handicaps.* Princeton, N.J.: Educational Testing Service, 1962.

Broden, M., Hall, R. V., & Mitts, B. The effect of self-recording on the classroom behavior of two eighth-grade students. *Journal of Applied Behavior Analysis,* 1971, *4,* 191-199.

Brown, P., & Elliott, R. Control of aggression in a nursery school class. *Journal of Experimental Child Psychology,* 1965, *2,* 103-107.

Brueckner, L. J. *Diagnostic tests and self-helps in arithmetic.* Monterey, Calif.: CTB/McGraw-Hill, 1955.

Bruininks, R. H. *Bruininks-Oseretsky Test of Motor Proficiency.* Circle Pines, Minn.: American Guidance Service, 1977.

Bryan, R. *When children speak.* San Rafael, Calif.: Academic Therapy Publications, 1971.

Buchanan, C. D. *Programmed reading.* New York: McGraw-Hill, 1966.

Buchanan, C. D. *Spelling*. Palo Alto, Calif.: Behavioral Research Laboratories, 1967.

Bush, W. J., & Giles, M. T. *Aids to psycholinguistic teaching* (2nd ed.). Columbus, Ohio: Charles E. Merrill, 1977.

Buswell, G. T., & John, L. *Diagnostic chart for fundamental processes in arithmetic*. Indianapolis: Bobbs-Merrill, 1925.

Caldwell, B. M. *Preschool Inventory* (rev. ed.). Princeton, N.J.: Educational Testing Service, 1967.

Cartwright, C. A., & Cartwright, G. P. *Developing observational skills*. New York: McGraw-Hill, 1974.

Chaney, C. M., & Kephart, N. C. *Motoric aids to perceptual training*. Columbus, Ohio: Charles E. Merrill, 1968.

Charles, C. M. *Individualizing instruction*. St. Louis, Mo.: Mosby, 1976.

Cheves, R. *Ruth Cheves Program I*. Boston: Teaching Resources, 1972.

Cheyney, A. B. *Teaching culturally disadvantaged in the elementary school*. Columbus, Ohio: Charles E. Merrill, 1967.

Cohen, C. R., & Abrams, R. M. *Spellmaster: Spelling, Testing, and Evaluation*. Exeter, N. H.: Learnco, Inc., 1974.

Colarusso, R., & Hammill, D. D. *The Motor-Free Test of Visual Perception*. San Rafael, Calif.: Academic Therapy Publications, 1972.

Compton, C. Teaching in the classroom. Mimeographed lecture, San Francisco: Summer, 1965.

Connolly, A. J., Nachtman, W., & Pritchett, E. M. *Key Math Diagnostic Arithmetic Test*. Circle Pines, Minn.: American Guidance Service, 1971.

Cooper, J. O. *Measurement and analysis of behavioral techniques*. Columbus, Ohio: Charles E. Merrill, 1975.

Cooper, J. O., Payne, J. S., & Edwards, C. Food for thought: An objective approach to changing children's food preferences. *Teaching Exceptional Children,* 1971, *3,* 73-76.

Copeland, R. E., Brown, R. E., & Hall, R. V. The effects of principal-implemented techniques on the behavior of pupils. *Journal of Applied Behavior Analysis,* 1974, *7,* 77-86.

Crabtree, M. *The Houston Test for Language Development*. Houston: Houston Press, 1963.

Cravioto, J., & DeLicardie, E. R. Environmental and learning deprivation in children with learning disabilities. In W. M. Cruickshank & D. P. Hallahan (Eds.), *Perceptual and learning disabilities in children. Vol. 2: Research and theory*. Syracuse, N.Y.: Syracuse University Press, 1975.

Croutch, B. Handwriting and correct posture. In J. I. Arena (Ed.), *Building handwriting skills in dyslexic children*. San Rafael, Calif.: Academic Therapy Publications, 1970.

Cruickshank, W. M. Special education, the community and constitutional issues. In D. L. Walker & D. P. Howard (Eds.), *Special education: Instrument of change in education for the 70's*. Charlottesville, Va.: Department of Special Education, University of Virginia, 1972.

Cruickshank, W. M., Bentzen, F. A., Ratzeburg, F. H., & Tannhauser, M. T. *A teaching method for brain-injured and hyperactive children*. Syracuse, N.Y.: Syracuse University Press, 1961.

Cullinan, D., Kauffman, J. M., & LaFleur, N. K. Modeling: Research with implications for special education. *Journal of Special Education,* 1975, *9,* 209-221.

Davidson, J. *Using the Cuisenaire Rods.* New Rochelle, N.Y.: Cuisenaire Company, 1969.

Deitz, S. M. An analysis of programming DRL schedules in educational settings. *Behavior Research and Therapy,* 1977, *15,* 103-111.

Deitz, S. M., & Repp, A. C. Decreasing classroom misbehavior through the use of DRL schedules of reinforcement. *Journal of Applied Behavior Analysis,* 1973, *6,* 457-463.

Delacato, C. H. *The treatment and prevention of reading problems.* Springfield, Ill.: Charles C Thomas, 1959.

Delacato, C. H. *Neurological organization and reading.* Springfield, Ill.: Charles C Thomas, 1966.

Dinkmeyer, D. *Developing Understanding of Self and Others.* Circle Pines, Minn.: American Guidance Service, 1970, 1973.

Drabman, R. S., & Lahey, B. B. Feedback in classroom behavior modification: Effects on the target and her classmates. *Journal of Applied Behavior Analysis,* 1974, *7,* 591-598.

Dubnoff, B., Chambers, I., & Schaeffer, F. *Dubnoff school program 1—Level 2.* Boston: Teaching Resources, 1969.

Dumas, M. *Questions for determining remedial strategies.* Unpublished manuscript, University of Virginia, 1972.

Dunn, L. M. *Peabody Picture Vocabulary Test.* Minneapolis: American Guidance Service, 1965.

Dunn, L. M. Special education for the mildly retarded—Is much of it justifiable? *Exceptional Children,* 1968, *35,* 5-22.

Dunn, L. M., Horton, R., & Smith, J. *Peabody Language Development Kit: Level P.* Circle Pines, Minn.: American Guidance Service, 1968.

Dunn, L. M., & Smith, J. (Eds.). *Peabody Language Development Kit: Level 1.* Circle Pines, Minn.: American Guidance Service, 1965.

Dunn, L. M., & Smith, J. (Eds.). *Peabody Language Development Kit: Level 2.* Circle Pines, Minn.: American Guidance Service, 1966.

Dunn, L. M., & Smith J. (Eds.). *Peabody Language Development Kit: Level 3.* Circle Pines, Minn.: American Guidance Service, 1967.

Dupont, H., Gardner, O. S., & Brody, D. S. *Toward affective development: A program to stimulate psychological and affective development.* Circle Pines, Minn.: American Guidance Service, 1974.

Durrell, D. D. *Durrell analysis of reading difficulty.* New York: Harcourt, Brace, Jovanovich, 1955.

Eaton, M., & Lovitt, T. C. Achievement tests vs. direct and daily measurement. In G. Semb (Ed.), *Behavior analysis and education*. Lawrence, Kan.: Department of Human Development, University of Kansas, 1972.

Eisenson, J. *Aphasia in children*. New York: Harper & Row, 1972.

Ekwall, E. E. *Diagnosis and remediation of the disabled reader*. Boston: Allyn & Bacon, 1976.

Ekwall, E. E. *Locating and correcting reading difficulties* (2nd ed.). Columbus, Ohio: Charles E. Merrill, 1977.

Engelmann, S. *Preventing failure in the primary grades*. Chicago: Science Research Associates, 1969.

Engelmann, S., & Bruner, E. C. *DISTAR Reading*. Chicago: Science Research Associates, 1969.

Engelmann, S., & Carnine, D. *DISTAR Arithmetic*. Chicago: Science Research Associates, 1969.

Engelmann, S., Osborn, J., & Engelmann, T. *DISTAR Language 1*. Chicago: Science Research Associates, 1969.

Ensminger E. E. A proposed model for selecting, modifying, or developing instructional materials for handicapped children. *Focus on Exceptional Children, 1970, 1,* 1-9.

Fagen, S. A., Long, N. J., & Stevens, D. J. *Teaching children self-control: Preventing emotional and learning problems in the elementary school*. Columbus, Ohio: Charles E. Merrill, 1975.

Fairbanks, J., & Robinson, J. *Fairbanks–Robinson program, Level 1 and Level 2*. Boston: Teaching Resources, 1967.

Foxx, R. M., & Azrin, N. H. Restitution: A method of eliminating aggressive-disruptive behavior of retarded and brain damaged patients. *Behavior Research and Therapy, 1972, 10,* 15-27.

Frankenburg, W. Increasing the lead time for the preschool age handicapped child. In M. Karnes (Ed.), *Not all little wagons are red*. Arlington, Va.: Council for Exceptional Children, 1973.

Freud, A. The relation between psychoanalysis and pedagogy. In N. J. Long, W. C. Morse, & R. G. Newman (Eds.), *Conflict in the classroom*. Belmont, Calif.: Wadsworth, 1965.

Freud, S. *On aphasia*. New York: International Universities Press, 1953.

Frostig, M., & Horne, D. *The Frostig Program for the Development of Visual Perception*. Chicago: Follett, 1964.

Frostig, M., & Horne, D. *The Frostig Program for the Development of Visual Perception: Teacher's guide*. Chicago: Follett, 1968.

Frostig, M., Lefever, W., & Whittlesey, J. R. *Marianne Frostig Developmental Test of Visual Perception*. Palo Alto, Calif.: Consulting Psychologists Press, 1964.

Gallagher, P. A. *Positive classroom performance: Techniques for changing behavior*. Denver: Love, 1971.

Garber, H., & Heber, R. *The Milwaukee project: Early intervention as a technique to prevent mental retardation*. Technical paper, The University of Connecticut, 1973.

Gast, D. L., & Nelson, C. M. Time out in the classroom: Implications for special education. *Exceptional Children, 1977, 43,* 461-464.

Gast, D. L., & Nelson, C. M. Legal and ethical considerations for the use of time-out in special education settings. *Journal of Special Education,* in press.

Gates, A. I., & McKillop, A. S. *Gates-McKillop Reading Diagnostic Tests*. New York: Bureau of Publications, Teachers College, Columbia University, 1962.

Gates, A., & Peardon, C. C. *Reading exercises*. New York: Teachers College Press, 1963.

Gates, A., & Russell, D. *Gates-Russell Spelling Diagnostic Test*. New York: Teachers College, Columbia University, 1937.

Gelfand, D. M., & Hartman, D. P. *Child behavior: Analysis and therapy*. New York: Pergamon, 1975.

Getman, G. N. The visumotor complex in the acquisition of learning skills. In J. Hellmuth (Ed.), *Learning disorders* (Vol. 1.). Seattle: Special Child Publications, 1965.

Gilliland, H. *A practical guide to remedial reading*. Columbus, Ohio: Charles E. Merrill, 1974.

Glazzard, M. The effectiveness of three kindergarten predictors for first-grade achievement. *Journal of Learning Disabilities,* 1977, *10,* 95-99.

Goldman, R., & Lynch, M. E. *Goldman-Lynch Sounds and Symbols Development Kit*. Circle Pines, Minn.: American Guidance Service, 1971.

Goldstein, H. *The social learning curriculum*. Columbus, Ohio: Charles E. Merrill, 1975.

Goldstein, H., Moss, J. W., & Jordan, L. J. *The efficacy of special class training on the development of mentally retarded children* (U.S. Office of Education Cooperative Research Program, Project 619, summary report). University of Illinois, 1965.

Goldstein, K. *Language and language distrubances*. New York: Grune & Stratton, 1948.

Greenwood, C. R., Hops, H., Delquadri, J., & Guild, J. Group contingencies for group consequences in classroom management: A further analysis. *Journal of Applied Behavior Analysis,* 1974, *7,* 413-425.

Grieger, T., Kauffman, J. M., & Grieger, R. M. Effects of peer reporting on cooperative play and aggression of kindergarten children. *Journal of School Psychology,* 1976, *14,* 307-313.

Hackett, L. C., & Jensen, R. C. *A guide to movement exploration*. Palo Alto, Calif.: Peek Publications, 1966.

Hainsworth, P. K., & Siqueland, M. L. *Early identification of children with learning disabilities: The Meeting Street School Screening Test*. Providence, R.I.: Crippled Children and Adults of Rhode Island, Inc., 1969.

Hall, R. V. *Managing behavior*. Lawrence, Kan.: H. & H. Enterprises, 1971.

Hall, R. V., Axelrod, S., Foundopoulos, M., Shellman, J., Campbell, R. A., & Cranston, S. S. The effective use of punishment to modify behavior in the classroom. *Educational Technology,* 1971, *11,* (4), 24-26.

Hall, R. V., Cristler, C., Cranston, S., & Tucker, B. Teachers and parents as researchers using multiple baseline designs. *Journal of Applied Behavior Analysis,* 1970, *3,* 247-255.

Hall, R. V., Fox, R., Willard, D., Goldsmith, L., Emerson, M., Owen, M., Davis, F., & Porcia, E. The teacher as observer and experimenter in the modification of disrupting and talking-out behavior. *Journal of Applied Behavior Analysis,* 1971, *4,* 141-149.

Hallahan, D. P., & Kauffman, J. M. *Introduction to learning disabilities: A psycho-behavioral approach.* Englewood Cliffs, N. J.: Prentice-Hall, 1976.

Hallahan, D. P., & Kauffman, J. M. *Exceptional children: An introduction to special education.* Englewood Cliffs, N.J.: Prentice-Hall, 1978.

Hammill, D. D. Evaluating children for instructional purposes. *Academic Therapy,* 1971, *6,* 341-353.

Hammill, D. D., & Bartel, N. *Teaching children with learning and behavior problems* (2nd ed.). Boston: Allyn & Bacon, 1978.

Hammill, D. D., & Larsen, S. C. The relationship of selected auditory perceptual skills and reading ability. *Journal of Learning Disabilities,* 1974, *1,* 429-436.

Hammill, D. D., & Wiederholt, J. L. *The resource room: Rationale and implementation.* Philadelphia: JSE Press, 1972.

Hammill, D. D., & Wiederholt, J. L. Review of the Frostig Visual Perception Test and the related training program. In L. Mann & D. Sabatino (Eds.), *The first review of special education* (Vol. 1). Philadelphia: Grune & Stratton, 1973.

Haring, N. G., Hayden, A. H., & Allen, K. E. Intervention in early childhood. *Educational Technology,* 1971, *11,* (2), 52-61.

Haring, N. G., & Phillips, E. L. *Educating emotionally disturbed children.* New York: McGraw-Hill, 1962.

Haring, N. G., & Phillips, E. L. *Analysis and modification of classroom behavior.* Englewood Cliffs, N.J.: Prentice-Hall, 1972.

Haring, N. G., & Schiefelbusch, R. L. (Eds.). *Teaching special children.* New York: McGraw-Hill, 1976.

Haring, N. G., & Whelan, R. J. Experimental methods in education and management. In N. J. Long, W. C. Morse, & R. G. Newman (Eds.), *Conflict in the classroom.* Belmont, Calif.: Wadsworth, 1965.

Hawthorne, L. W., & Larsen, S. C. The predictive validity and reliability of the Basic School Skills Inventory. *Journal of Learning Disabilities,* 1977, *10,* 44-50.

Hayden, A. Perspectives of early childhood education in special education. In N. Haring (Ed.), *Behavior of exceptional children: An introduction to special education.* Columbus, Ohio: Charles E. Merrill, 1974.

Hegge, T. G, Kirk, S. A., & Kirk, W. D. *Remedial reading drills.* Ann Arbor, Mich.: George Wahr, 1940.

Heilman, A. W. *Phonics in proper perspective.* Columbus, Ohio: Charles E. Merrill, 1968.

Heilman, A. W. *Principles and practices of teaching reading* (4th ed.). Columbus, Ohio: Charles E. Merrill, 1977.

Helwig, J. J, Johns, J. C., Norman, J. E., & Cooper, J. O. The measurement of manuscript letter strokes. *Journal of Applied Behavior Analysis,* 1976, *9,* 231-236

Hersen, M., & Barlow, D. H. *Single case experimental designs: Strategies for studying behavior change.* New York: Pergamon, 1976.

Hewett, F. M. *The emotionally disturbed child in the classroom.* Boston: Allyn & Bacon, 1968.

Hobbs, N. (Ed.). *Issues in the classification of children* (Vols. 1& 2). San Francisco: Jassey-Bass, 1975.

Hofmeister, A. *Programmed time telling*. Eugene, Ore.: Regional Special Education Instructional Materials Center, University of Oregon, 1968.

Homme, L. E. *How to use contingency contracting in the classroom*. Champaign, Ill.: Research Press, 1969.

Hopkins, B. L., Schutte, R. C., & Garton, K. L. The effects of access to a playroom on the rate and quality of printing and writing of first and second grade students. *Journal of Applied Behavior Analysis*, 1971, *4*, 77-87.

Johnson, D. J., & Myklebust, H. R. *Learning disabilities: Educational principles and practices*. New York: Grune & Strutton, 1967.

Jordan, T. E., & DeCharms, R. The achievement motive in normal and mentally retarded children. *American Journal of Mental Deficiency*, 1959, *64*, 457-466.

Kaluger, G., & Kolson, C. J. *Reading and learning disabilities* (2nd ed.). Columbus, Ohio: Charles E. Merrill, 1978.

Karlin, R. *Teaching elementary reading: Principles and strategies*. New York: Harcourt, Brace, Jovanovich, 1971.

Karnes, M. B. *Helping young children develop language skills*. Arlington, Va.: Council for Exceptional Children, 1968.

Kauffman, J. M. Behavior modification. In W. M. Cruickshank & D. P. Hallahan (Eds.), *Perceptual and learning disabilities in children. Vol. 2: Research and theory*. Syracuse, N.Y.: Syracuse University Press, 1975.

Kauffman, J. M. Nineteenth century views of children's behavior disorders: Historical contributions and continuing issues. *Journal of Special Education*, 1976, *10*, 335-349.

Kauffman, J. M. *Characteristics of children's behavior disorders*. Columbus, Ohio: Charles E. Merrill, 1977.

Kauffman, J. M., Cullinan, D., Scranton, T. R., & Wallace, G. An inexpensive device for programming ratio reinforcements. *Psychological Record*, 1972, *22*, 543-544.

Kauffman, J. M, & Hallahan, D. P. Control of rough physical behavior using novel contingencies and directive teaching. *Perceptual and Motor Skills*, 1973, *36*, 1225, 1226.

Kauffman, J. M., & Hallahan, D. P. The medical model and the science of special education. *Exceptional Children*, 1974, *41*, 97-102.

Kauffman, J. M., & Hallahan, D. P. Evaluation of teaching performance. In W. M. Cruickshank & D. P. Hallahan (Eds.), *Perceptual and learning disabilities in children: Vol. 1: Psychoeducational practices*. Syracuse, N.Y.: Syracuse University Press, 1975.

Kauffman, J. M., & Scranton, T. R. Parent control of thumbsucking in the home. *Child Study Journal*, 1974, *4*, 1-10.

Kauffman, J. M., & Vicente, A. R. Bringing in the sheaves: Observations on harvesting behavorial change in the field. *Journal of School Psychology* 1972, *10*, 263-268.

Kazdin, A. E. *Behavior modification in applied settings*. Homewood, Ill.: Dorsey, 1975.

Kazdin, A. E., & Bootzin, R. R. The token economy: An evaluative review. *Journal of Applied Behavior Analysis*, 1972, *5*, 343-372.

Keogh, B. K., & Becker, L. D. Early detection of learning problems: Questions, cautions, and guidelines. *Exceptional Children*, 1973, *40*, 5-11.

Kephart, N. C. *The brain-injured child in the classroom*. Chicago: National Society for Crippled Children and Adults, 1963.

Kephart, N. C. Perceptual-motor aspects of learning disabilities. In E. Frierson & W. Barbe (Eds.), *Educating children with learning disabilities*. New York: Appleton-Century-Crofts, 1967.

Kephart, N. C. *Learning disability: An educational adventure*. West Lafayette, Ind.: Kappa Delta Pi Press, 1968.

Kephart, N. C. *The slow learner in the classroom* (2nd ed.). Columbus, Ohio: Charles E. Merrill, 1971.

Kern, W. H., & Pfaeffle, H. A comparison of social adjustment of mentally retarded children in various educational settings. *American Journal of Mental Deficiency*, 1962, *67*, 407-413.

Kirby, F. D., & Toler, H. C. Modification of preschool isolate behavior: A case study. *Journal of Applied Behavior Analysis*, 1970, *3*, 309-314.

Kirk, S. A. *Educating exceptional children* (2nd ed.). Boston: Houghton Mifflin, 1972.

Kirk, S. A., McCarthy, J. J., & Kirk, W. D. *Illinois Test of Psycholinguistic Abilities* (rev. ed.). Urbana: University of Illinois Press, 1968.

Knapczyk, D. R., & Livingston, G. The effects of prompting question-asking upon on-task behavior and reading comprehension. *Journal of Applied Behavior Analysis*, 1974, *7*, 115-121.

Knapp, T. The Premack Principle in human experimental and applied settings. *Behaviour Research and Therapy*, 1976, *14*, 133-147.

Knight, M. F., & McKenzie, H. S. Elimination of bedtime thumbsucking in home settings through contingent reading. *Journal of Applied Behavior Analysis*, 1974, *7*, 33-38.

Koppitz, E. M. *The Bender Gestalt test for children*. New York: Grune & Stratton, 1964.

Koupernik, C., MacKeith, R., & Francis-Williams, J. Neurological correlates of motor and perceptual development. In W. M. Cruickshank & D. P. Hallahan (Eds.). *Perceptual and learning disabilities in children. Vol. 2: Research and theory*. Syracuse, N.Y.: Syracuse University Press, 1975.

Krumboltz, J. D., & Krumboltz, H. B. *Changing children's behavior*. Englewood Cliffs, N.J.: Prentice-Hall, 1972.

Kuypers, D. S., Becker, W. C, & O'Leary, K. D. How to make a token system fail. *Exceptional Children*, 1968, *35*, 101-109.

Lahey, B. B., Busemeyer, M. K., O'Hara, C., & Beggs, V. E. Treatment of severe perceptual-motor disorders in children diagnosed as learning disabled. *Behavior Modification*, 1977, *1*, 123-140.

Lahey, B. B., McNees, M. P., & Brown C. C. Modification of deficits in reading for comprehension. *Journal of Applied Behavior Analysis*, 1973, *6*, 475-480.

Lahey, B. B, McNees, M. P., & McNees, M. C. Control of an obscene "verbal tiz" through timeout in an elementary school classroom. *Journal of Applied Behavior Analysis*, 1973, *6*, 101-104.

Landsman, M., & Dillard, H. *Evanston Early Identification Scale* (field research ed.). Chicago: Follett, 1967.

Lane, H. *The wild boy of Aveyron*. Cambridge, Mass.: Harvard University Press, 1976.

Larsen, S. C, & Hammill, D. D. *The Test of Written Spelling*. Austin, Tex.: Empiric Press, 1976.

Larsen, S. C., Parker, R., & Sowell, V. *The effectiveness of the MWM program in developing language abilities*. Unpublished manuscript, The University of Texas at Austin, 1976.

Larson, R. G. *Penskill*. Chicago: Science Research Associates, 1962.

Lazarus, P. W. The medium is not the method. *Academic Therapy*, 1971, *6*, 229-232.

Lee, L. *Northwestern Syntax Screening Test*. Evanston, Ill.: Northwestern University, 1969.

Leitenberg, H. (Ed.). *Handbook of behavior modification and behavior therapy*. Englewood Cliffs, N.J.: Prentice-Hall, 1976.

Lerner, J. W. *Children with learning disabilities* (2nd ed.). Boston: Houghton Mifflin, 1976.

Lerner, J. W., & Vaver, G. Filmstrips in learning. *Academic Therapy*, 1970, *5*, 320-324.

Long, J. D., & Williams, R. L. The comparative effectiveness of group and individually contingent free time with inner-city junior high school students. *Journal of Applied Behavior Analysis*, 1973, *6*, 465-474.

Lovitt, T. C. Assessment of children with learning disabilities. *Exceptional Children*, 1967, *34*, 233-239.

Lovitt, T. C. Behavior modification: The current scene. *Exceptional Children*, 1970, *37*, 85-91.

Lovitt, T. C. *In spite of my resistance*. Columbus, Ohio: Charles E. Merrill, 1977.

Lovitt, T. C. & Curtiss, K. A. Effects of manipulating an antecedent event on mathematics response rate. *Journal of Applied Behavior Analysis*, 1968, *1*, 329-333.

Lovitt, T. C., & Esveldt, K. A. The relative effects on math performance of single- versus multiple-ratio schedules: A case study. *Journal of Applied Behavior Analysis*, 1970, *3*, 261-270.

Lovitt, T. C., & Smith, J. O. Effects of instructions on an individual's verbal behavior. *Exceptional Children*, 1972, *38*, 685-693.

MacDonald, W. S., Gallimore, R., & MacDonald, G. Contingency counselling by school personnel: An economical method of intervention. *Journal of Applied Behavior Analysis*, 1970, *3*, 175-182.

MacMillan, D. L., & Becker, L. D. Mainstreaming the mildly handicapped learner. In R. D. Kneedler & S. G. Tarver (Eds.), *Changing perspectives in special education*. Columbus, Ohio: Charles E. Merrill, 1977.

MacMillan, D. L., Forness, S. R., & Trumbull, B. M. The role of punishment in the classroom. *Exceptional Children*, 1973, *40*, 85-96.

MacPherson, E. M., Candee, B. L., & Hohman, R. J. A comparison of three methods for eliminating disruptive lunchroom behavior. *Journal of Applied Behavior Analysis*, 1974, *7*, 287-297.

Madsen, C. H., Becker, W. C., & Thomas, D. R. Rules, praise, and ignoring: Elements of elementary classroom control. *Journal of Applied Behavior Analysis*, 1968, *1*, 139-150.

Madsen, C. H., & Madsen, C. K. *Teaching/discipline*. Boston: Allyn & Bacon, 1970; 2nd ed., 1974.

Madsen, C. H., Madsen, C. K., & Thompson, F. Increasing rural Head Start children's consumption of middle-class meals. *Journal of Applied Behavior Analysis,* 1974, 7, 257-262.

Madsen, C. K., & Madsen, C. H. *Parents/children/discipline.* Boston: Allyn & Bacon, 1972.

Mager, R. F. *Preparing instructional objectives.* Palo Alto, Calif.: Fearon, 1962.

Magliocca, L. A., Rinaldi, R. T., Crew, J. L., & Kunzelmann, H. P. Early identification of handicapped children through a frequency sampling technique. *Exceptional Children,* 1977, *43,* 414-420.

Mahoney, M. J. *Cognition and behavior modification.* Cambridge, Mass.: Ballinger, 1974.

Martin, B. Parent-child relations. In F. D. Horowitz (Ed.), *Review of child development research* (Vol. 4). Chicago: University of Chicago Press, 1975.

McGee, C. S., Kauffman, J. M., & Nussen, J. L. Peers as therapeutic change agents: Reinforcement intervention paradigms. *Reviews of Educatonal Research,* in press.

McKenna, A. R. Some notes on the teaching of handwriting. In J. I. Arena (Ed.), *Building handwriting skills in dyslexic children.*San Rafael, Calif.: Academic Therapy Publications, 1970.

McKenzie, H. S., Egner, A., Knight, M., Perelman, P., Schneider, B., & Garvin, J. Training consulting teachers to assist elementary teachers in the management and education of handicapped children.*Exceptional Children,* 1970,*37,* 137-143.

Mecham, M., Jex, J. L., & Jones, J. D. *Utah Test of Language Development.* Salt Lake City: Communication Research Associates, 1967.

Meichenbaum, D., & Goodman, J. Training impulsive children to talk to themselves: A means of developing self-control. *Journal of Abnormal Psychology,* 1971,*77,* 115-126.

Meyen, E. L. *Developing units of instruction: For the mentally retarded and other children with learning problems.* Dubuque, Iowa: Wm. C. Brown, 1972.

Minskoff, E., Wiseman, D., & Minskoff, G. *The MWM Program for Developing Language Abilities.* Ridgefield, N.J.: Educational Performance Associates, 1973.

Murphy, P. *A special way for the special child in the regular classroom.* San Rafael, Calif.: Academic Therapy Publications, 1971.

Myers, G. C. Creative thinking activities. In *Highlights handbook.* Columbus, Ohio: Highlights for Children, 1965.

Myers, P. I., & Hammill, D. D. *Methods for learning disorders* (2nd ed.). New York: Wiley, 1976.

Myklebust, H. R. *Auditory disorders in children: A manual for differential diagnosis.* New York: Grune & Stratton, 1954.

Myklebust, H. R. *Picture Story Language Test: The development and disorders of written language* (Vol. 1). New York: Grune & Stratton, 1965.

Nay, W. R., Schulman, J. A., Bailey, K. G., & Huntsinger, G. M. Territory and classroom management: An exploratory case study. *Behavior Therapy,* 1976, *7,* 240-246.

Nazzaro, J. Head Start for the handicapped—What has been accomplished? *Exceptional Children,* 1974, *21,* 103-108.

Newcomer, P. L., & Hammill, D. D. *The Test of Language Development*. Austin, Texas: Empiric Press, 1977.

Novack, H. S., Bonaventura, E. F., & Merenda, P. F. *Rhode Island Pupil Identification Scale*. Author, 1972.

O'Leary, K. D., & Drabman, R. Token reinforcement programs in the classroom: A review. *Psychological Bulletin,* 1971, *75,* 379-398.

O'Leary, K. D., & O'Leary, S. G. (Eds.). *Classroom management: The successful use of behavior modification*. New York: Pergamon, 1972.

O'Leary, S. G., & O'Leary, K. D. Behavior modification in the school. In H. Leitenberg (Ed.), *Handbook of behavior modification and behavior therapy*. Englewood Cliffs, N.J.: Prentice-Hall, 1976.

Osborn, J. *Teaching a teaching language to disadvantaged children*. Mimeographed paper, University of Illinois, 1968.

Otto, W., McMenemy, R. A., & Smith, R. J. *Corrective and remedial teaching*. Boston: Houghton Mifflin, 1973.

Pate, J. E., & Webb, W. W. *First Grade Screening Test*. Circle Pines, Minn.: American Guidance Service, 1969.

Payne, J. S., Finegold, I., & Cooper, J. O. Transportation for the betterment of children. Paper presented at Conference on the Education of Mentally Retarded Persons, St. Louis, September 1971.

Payne, J. S., Polloway, E. A., Kauffman, J. M., & Scranton, T. R. *Living in the classroom: The currency-based token economy*. New York: Human Sciences Press, 1975.

Phillips, E. L. Problems in educating emotionally disturbed children. In N. G. Haring & R. L. Schiefelbusch (Eds.), *Methods in special education*. New York: McGraw-Hill, 1967.

Piaget, J. *The origins of intelligence in children*. New York: International Universities Press, 1952.

Pinkston, E. M., Reese, N. M., LeBlanc, J. M., & Baer, D. M. Independent control of a preschool child's aggression and peer interaction by contingent teacher attention. *Journal of Applied Behavior Analysis,* 1973, *6,* 115-124.

Platts, M. E. *Plus*. Stevensville, Mich.: Educational Service, 1964.

Platts, M. E. *Anchor: A handbook of vocabulary discovery techniques for the classroom teacher*. Stevensville, Mich.: Educational Service, 1970.

Platts, M. E., Marguerite, S. R., & Shumaker, E. *Suggested activities to motivate the teaching of the language arts*. Stevensville, Mich.: Educational Service, 1960.

Plunkett, M. *A writing manual for teaching the left-handed*. Cambridge, Mass.: Educators Publishing Service, 1954.

Plunkett, M. *A spelling workbook for corrective drill for elementary grades*. Cambridge, Mass.: Educators Publishing Service, 1960.

Plunkett, M. *A spelling workbook emphasizing rules and generalizations for corrective drill*. Cambridge, Mass.: Educators Publishing Service, 1961.

Plunkett, M., & Peck, C. *A spelling workbook for early primary and corrective work*. Cambridge, Mass.: Educators Publishing Service, 1960.

Premack, D. Toward empirical behavior laws: I. Positive reinforcement. *Psychological Review,* 1959, *66,* 219-233.

President's Council on Physical Fitness. *AAHPER youth fitness test manual.* Washington, D. C.: President's Council on Physical Fitness, 1967.

Quay, H. C. Patterns of aggression, withdrawal, and immaturity. In H. C. Quay & J. S. Werry (Eds.), *Psychopathological disorders of childhood.* New York: Wiley, 1972.

Rainwater, N., & Ayllon, T. Increasing academic performance by using a timer as antecedent stimulus: A study of four cases. *Behavior Therapy,* 1977, *7,* 672-677.

Reisman, F. K. *A guide to the diagnostic teaching of arithmetic* (2nd ed.). Columbus, Ohio: Charles E. Merrill, 1978.

Risely, T. R., & Baer, D. M. Operant behavior modification: The deliberate development of behavior. In B. M. Caldwell & H. N. Ricciuti (Eds.), *Review of child development research* (Vol. 3). Chicago: University of Chicago Press, 1973.

Roach, C., & Kephart, N. *The Purdue Perceptual-Motor Survey.* Columbus, Ohio: Charles E. Merrill, 1966.

Robins, L. N., West, P., & Herjaniz, B. Arrests and deliquency in two generations: A study of urban families and their children. *Journal of Child Psychology and Psychiatry,* 1975, *16,* 125-140.

Ross, S. L., DeYoung, H. G., & Cohen, J. S. Confrontation: Special eduation placement and the law. *Exceptional Children,* 1971, *38,* 5-12.

Rowland P. T. *Beginning to read, write, and listen.* Boston: Boston Educational Research Co., 1971.

Russell, D. H., & Karp, E. E. *Reading aids through the grades.* New York: Teachers College Press, 1938.

Salzberg, B. H., Wheeler, A. J., Devar, L. T., & Hopkins, B. L. The effect of intermittent feedback and intermittent contingent access to play on printing of kindergarten children. *Journal of Applied Behavior Analysis,* 1971, *4,* 163-171.

Sameroff, A. J., & Chandler, M. J. Reproductive risk and the continuum of caretaking casuality. In F. D. Horowitz (Ed.), *Review of child development research* (Vol. 4). Chicago: University of Chicago Press, 1975.

Scarr-Salapatek, S. Genetics and the development of intelligence. In F. D. Horowitz (Ed.), *Review of child development research* (Vol. 4). Chicago: University of Chicago Press, 1975.

Sganga, F. T. *Merrill mathematics skilltapes.* Columbus, Ohio: Charles E. Merrill, 1969.

Sherman, J. A., & Bushell, D. Behavior modification as an educational technique. In F. D. Horowitz (Ed.), *Review of child development research* (Vol. 4). Chicago: University of Chicago Press, 1975,

Silvaroli, N. J. *Classroom reading inventory* (2nd ed.). Dubuque, Iowa: Wm. C. Brown, 1973.

Simon, K. A., & Grant, W. V. (Eds.). *Digest of educational statistics.* Washington, D. C.: U. S. Office of Education, 1968.

Skiba, E. A., Pettigrew, L. E., & Alden, S. A. A behavioral approach to the control of thumbsucking in the classroom. *Journal of Applied Behavior Analysis,* 1971, *4,* 121-125.

Skinner, B. F. *Science and human behavior.* New York: Free Press, 1953.

Skinner, B. F. *Verbal behavior.* New York: Appleton-Century-Crofts, 1957.

Skinner, B. F. *Beyond freedom and dignity.* New York: Knopf, 1971.

Skinner, B. F., & Krakower, S. A. *Handwriting with write and see.* Chicago: Lyons and Carnahan, 1968.

Smith, D. D., & Lovitt, T. C. The use of modeling techniques to influence the acquisition of computational arithmetic skills in learning disabled children. In E. Ramp & G. Semb (Eds.), *Behavior analysis: Areas of research and application.* Englewood Cliffs, N.J.: Prentice-Hall, 1975.

Smith, J. A. *Creative teaching of the language arts in the elementary school.* Boston: Allyn & Bacon, 1967.

Smith, R. M. (Ed.). *Teacher diagnosis of educational difficulties.* Columbus, Ohio: Charles E. Merrill, 1969.

Smith, R. M. *Clinical teaching: Methods of instruction for the retarded.* New York: McGraw-Hill, 1974.

Smith, R. M., & Neisworth, J. T. Fundamentals of informal educational assessment. In R. M. Smith (Ed.), *Teacher diagnosis of educational difficulties.* Columbus, Ohio: Charles E. Merrill, 1969.

Spache, G. D. *Diagnostic Reading Scales.* Monterey, Calif.: Del Monte Research Park, California Test Bureau, 1963.

Spache, G. D. *Diagnosing and correcting reading disabilities.* Boston: Allyn & Bacon, 1976.

Spencer, E. F., & Smith, R. M. Arithmetic skills. In R. M. Smith (Ed.), *Teacher diagnosis of educational difficulties.* Columbus, Ohio: Charles E. Merrill, 1969.

Spitzer, H. F. *The teaching of arithmetic* (3rd ed.). Boston: Houghton Mifflin, 1961.

Spradlin, J. Procedures for evaluating processes associated with receptive and expressive language. In R. Schiefelbusch, R. Copeland, & J. O. Smith (Eds.), *Language and mental retardation.* New York: Holt, Rinehart & Winston, 1967.

Stainback, W., Payne, J. S., Stainback S., & Payne, R. A. *Establishing a token economy in the classroom.* Columbus, Ohio: Charles E. Merrill, 1973.

Stanton, J. E., & Cassidy, V. M. Effectiveness of special classes for educable mentally retarded. *Mental Retardation,* 1964, *2,* 8-13.

Stephens, T. *Implementing behavioral approaches in elementary and secondary schools.* Columbus, Ohio: Charles E. Merrill, 1975.

Stern, C., Stern, M., & Gould, T. *Structured arithmetic.* Boston: Houghton Mifflin, 1952.

Strain, P.S., & Wiegerink, R. The effects of sociodramatic activities on social interaction among behaviorally disordered preschool children. *Journal of Special Education,* 1976, *10,* 71-75.

Strang, R. *Diagnostic teaching of reading* (2nd ed.). New York: McGraw-Hill, 1969.

Sullivan Associates. *Programmed Math Series One.* Palo Alto, Calif.: Behavioral Research Laboratories, 1967.

Sulzbacher, S. I., & Houser, J. E. A tactic to eliminate disruptive behaviors in the classroom: Group contingent consequences. *American Journal of Mental Deficiency,* 1968, *73,* 88-90.

Tharp, R. G., & Wetzel, R. J. *Behavior modification in the natural environment.* New York: Academic Press, 1969.

Trembly, D. Should your child write with the left hand? In J. I. Arena (Ed.), *Building handwriting skills in dyslexic children.* San Rafael, Calif.: Academic Therapy Publications, 1970.

Valett, R. E. *The remediation of learning disabilities.* Palo Alto, Calif.: Fearon, 1967.

Van Houten, R., Hill, S., & Parsons, M. An analysis of a performance feedback system: The effects of timing and feedback, public posting, and praise upon academic performance and peer interaction. *Journal of Applied Behavior Analysis,* 1975, *8,* 449-457.

Van Houten, R., Morrison, E., Jarvis, R., & McDonald, M. The effects of explicit timing and feedback on compositional response rate in elementary school children. *Journal of Applied Behavior Analysis,* 1974, *7,* 547-555.

Wagner, G., Hosier, M., & Blackman, M. *Listening games: Building listening skills with instructional games.* New York: Teachers Publishing, 1970.

Wagner, G., Hosier, M., & Gilloley, L. *Arithmetic games and activities.* Darien, Conn.: Teachers Publishing Corp., 1964.

Wahl, J. Two approaches to spelling problems: Self-discovery and phonics. In J. Arena (Ed.), *Building spelling skills in dyslexic children.* San Rafael, Calif.: Academic Therapy Publications, 1968.

Wahler, R. G. Setting generality: Some specific and general effects of child behavior therapy. *Journal of Applied Behavior Analysis,* 1969, *2,* 239-246.

Walker, H. M. Empirical assessment of deviant behavior in children. *Psychology in the Schools,* 1969, *6,* 93-97.

Wallace, G., & Larsen, S. C. *The educational assessment of learning problems: Testing for teaching.* Boston: Allyn & Bacon, 1978.

Wallace, G., & McLoughlin, J. A. *Learning disabilities: Concepts and characteristics.* Columbus, Ohio: Charles E. Merrill, 1975.

Wallen, C. J. *Competency in teaching reading.* Chicago: Science Research Associates, 1972.

Wedemeyer, A., & Cejka, J. *Creative ideas for teaching exceptional children.* Denver: Love, 1970.

Weinthaler, J., & Rotberg, J. M. The systematic selection of instructional materials based on an inventory of learning abilities and skills. *Exceptional Children,* 1970, *36,* 615-619.

Wiederholt, J. L. A review of the Illinois Test of Psycholinguistic Abilities. In O. K. Buros (Ed.), *Eighth mental measurement yearbook.* Highland Park, N.J.: The Gryphon Press, 1978.

Wiederholt, J. L., & Hammill, D. D. Use of the Frostig-Horne perception program in the urban school. *Psychology in the Schools,* 1971, *8,* 268-274.

Woodcock, R. W. *Woodcock Reading Mastery Tests.* Circle Pines, Minn.: American Guidance Service, 1974.

Woolbright, W. J. Test results and what they mean. *Academic Therapy,* 1971, *6,* 429-431.

Worell, J., & Nelson, C. M. *Managing instructional problems: A case study workbook.* New York: McGraw-Hill, 1974.

Wulbert, M., & Dries, R. The relative efficacy of methylphenidate (Ritalin) and behavior-modification techniques in the treatment of a hyperactive child. *Journal of Applied Behavior Analysis,* 1977, *10,* 21-31.

Zigmond, N. *Teaching children with special needs.* Dubuque, Iowa: Gorsuch Scarisbrick Publishers, 1976.

Zigmond, N. K., & Cicci, R. *Auditory learning.* San Rafael, Calif.: Dimensions, 1968.

Zimmerman, I. L., Steiner, V. G., & Evatt, R. L. *Preschool language manual.* Columbus, Ohio: Charles E. Merrill, 1969.

THE AUTHORS

Gerald Wallace is an Associate Professor and Coordinator of Graduate Programs in Learning Disabilities at the University of Virginia. A graduate of Central Connecticut College, he received his master's from the University of Arizona and a doctoral degree from the University of Oregon. Dr. Wallace taught learning disabled children in Palo Alto, California. His wife, Marti, is a graduate student in psychiatric nursing. They are the parents of Christopher, 10, and T.J., who is 8.

James M. Kauffman is an Associate Professor and Chairperson of the Department of Special Education at the University of Virginia. After receiving his undergraduate degree from Goshen College, he taught emotionally disturbed children at the Menninger's Clinic in Topeka, Kansas. Dr. Kauffman's advanced degrees were received from Washburn University and the University of Kansas. His wife, Myrna, is a registered nurse. Their children are Tim, 12, and Missy, who is 9.

SUBJECT INDEX

NAME INDEX